Kenji Sonishi's
Neko Ramen
ネコラーメン

...roducing

Taisho

Tanaka-san

Mii-chan

Shige-chan

The Critic

Ramen like you've never experienced before!

Hey! Order Up!

Neko Ramen Volume 1
Created by Kenji Sonishi

Translation - Kristy Harmon
English Adaptation - Emily Gordon and Kumail Nanjiani
Retouch and Lettering - Star Print Brokers
Production Artist - Rui Kyo
Graphic Designer - Chelsea Windlinger

Editor - Cindy Suzuki
Print Production Manager - Lucas Rivera
Managing Editor - Vy Nguyen
Marketing Manager - Kasia Piekarz
Senior Designer - Louis Csontos
Art Director - Al-Insan Lashley
Director of Sales and Manufacturing - Allyson De Simone
Associate Publisher - Marco F. Pavia
President and C.O.O. - John Parker
C.E.O. and Chief Creative Officer - Stu Levy

A **TOKYOPOP** Manga

TOKYOPOP and ⬤ are trademarks or registered trademarks of TOKYOPOP Inc.

TOKYOPOP Inc.
5900 Wilshire Blvd. Suite 2000
Los Angeles, CA 90036

E-mail: info@TOKYOPOP.com
Come visit us online at www.TOKYOPOP.com

ISBN: 978-1-4278-1779-2

First TOKYOPOP printing: June 2010
10 9 8 7 6 5 4 3 2 1
Printed in the USA

NEKO RAMEN NEKO RAMEN NEKO RAMEN NEKO RAMEN NEKO

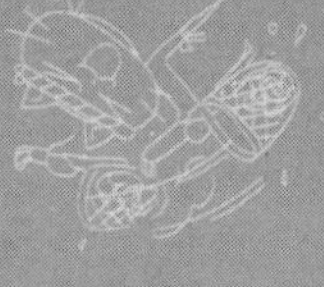

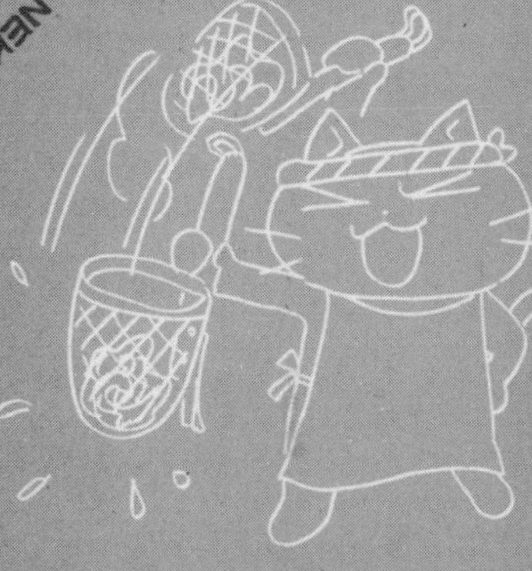

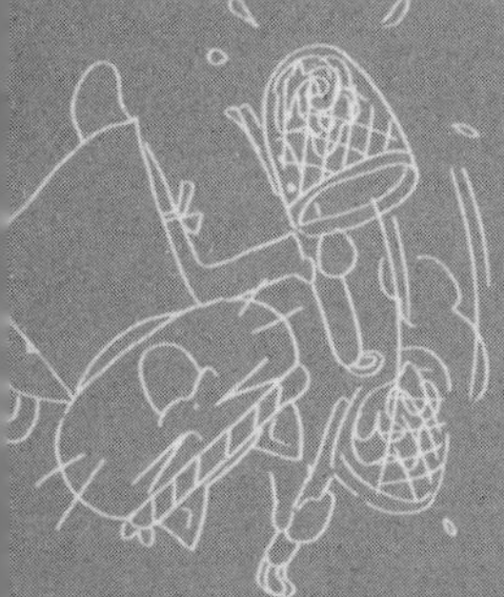

猫ラーメン

そにしけんじ

1

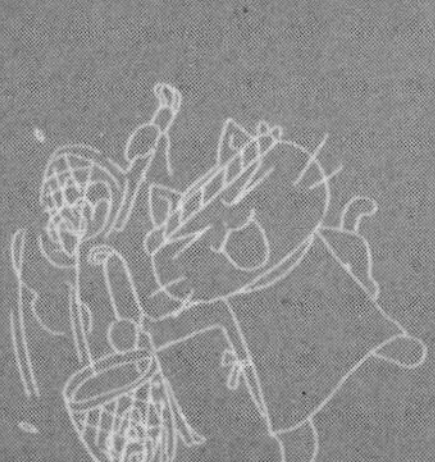

CONTENTS

Passion

Salt
Miso
SLIDE
ラ
WELCOME.
TURNS
HOLD, IT!
LEAVING BE-CAUSE I'M A CAT?!
I'VE GOT MORE THAN ENOUGH RAMEN PASSION TO MAKE UP FOR MY APPEAR-ANCE!
SLAM
EAT FIRST, THEN JUDGE!!!
......
... IT'S AWFUL ...
THAT'S WHAT I WAS AFRAID OF...
WHAT DO YOU THINK'S THE PROB-LEM?

Flip pages to see a small animation!

Taisho's Morning Routine

猫ラーメン

Chapter 1

Goals

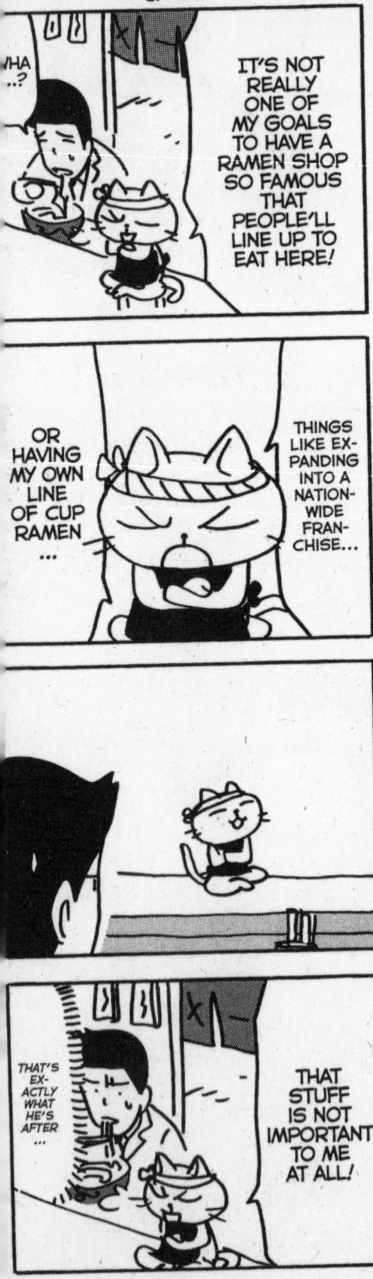
HA
..?
IT'S NOT REALLY ONE OF MY GOALS TO HAVE A RAMEN SHOP SO FAMOUS THAT PEOPLE'LL LINE UP TO EAT HERE!
THINGS LIKE EX-PANDING INTO A NATION-WIDE FRAN-CHISE...
OR HAVING MY OWN LINE OF CUP RAMEN ...
THAT STUFF IS NOT IMPORTANT TO ME AT ALL!
THAT'S EX-ACTLY WHAT HE'S AFTER ...

The Problem

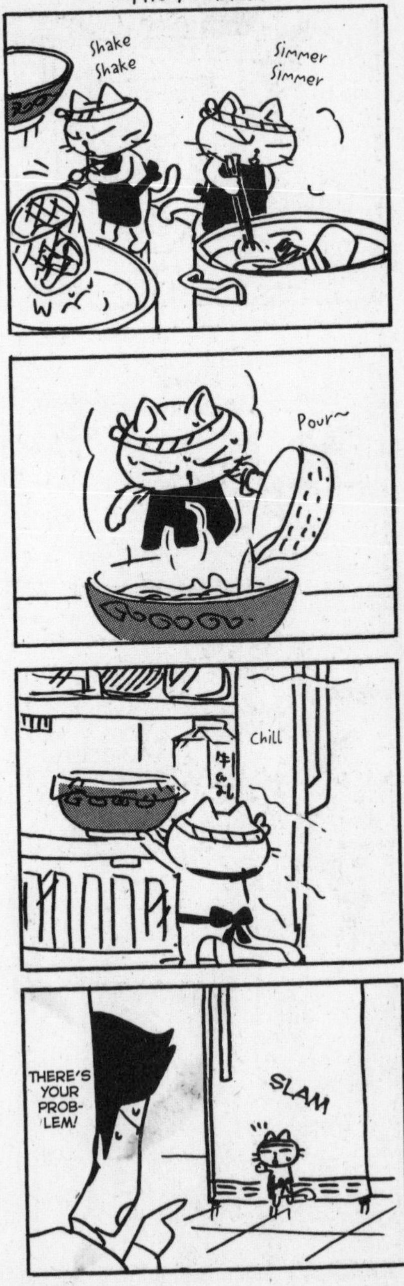
Shake Shake
Simmer Simmer
Pour~
Chill
THERE'S YOUR PROB-LEM!
SLAM

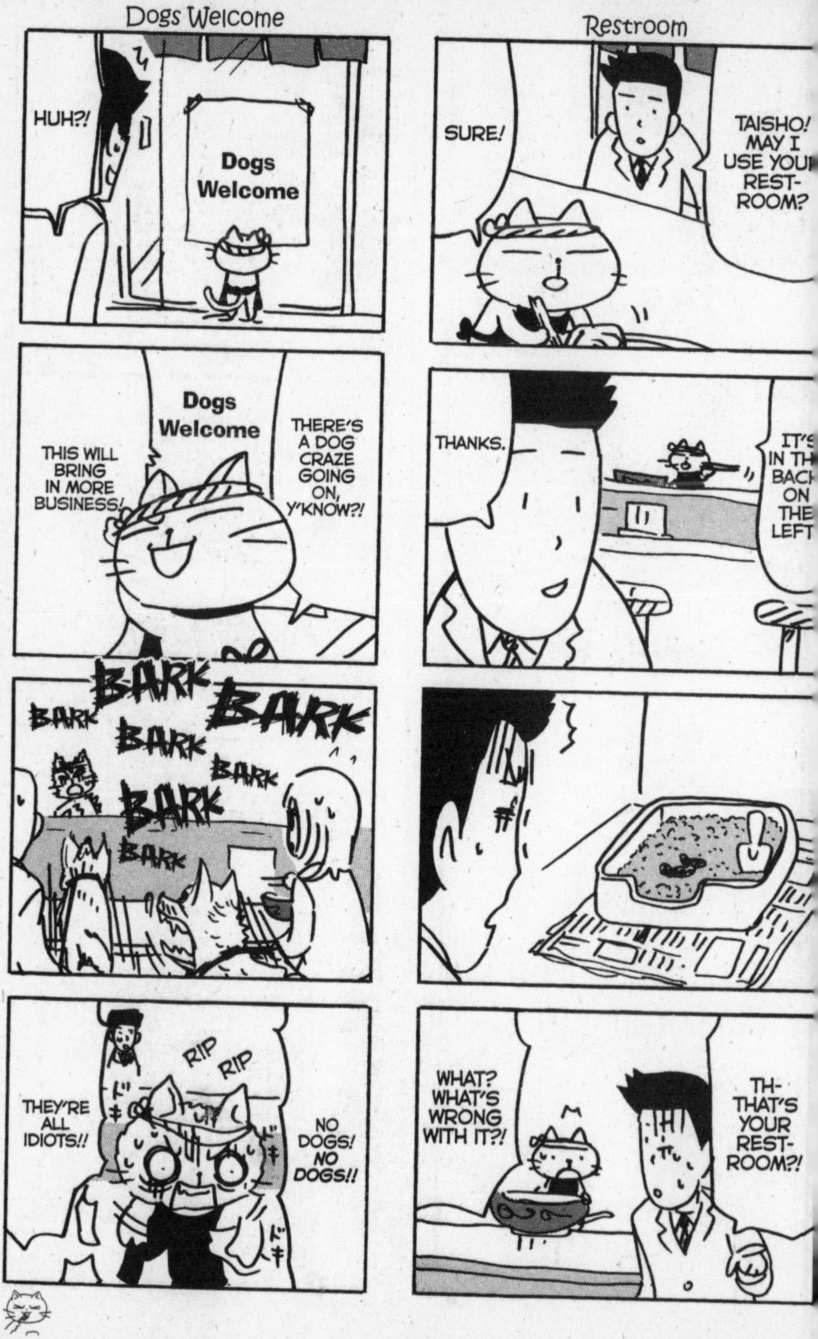

Restroom
TAISHO! MAY I USE YOUR REST-ROOM?
SURE!
IT'S IN THE BACK ON THE LEFT
THANKS.
TH-THAT'S YOUR REST-ROOM?!
WHAT? WHAT'S WRONG WITH IT?!
Dogs Welcome
Dogs Welcome
HUH?!
THERE'S A DOG CRAZE GOING ON, Y'KNOW?!
Dogs Welcome
THIS WILL BRING IN MORE BUSINESS!
BARK
BARK
BARK
BARK
BARK
BARK
BARK
RIP
RIP
NO DOGS! NO DOGS!!
THEY'RE ALL IDIOTS!!

Mii-chan

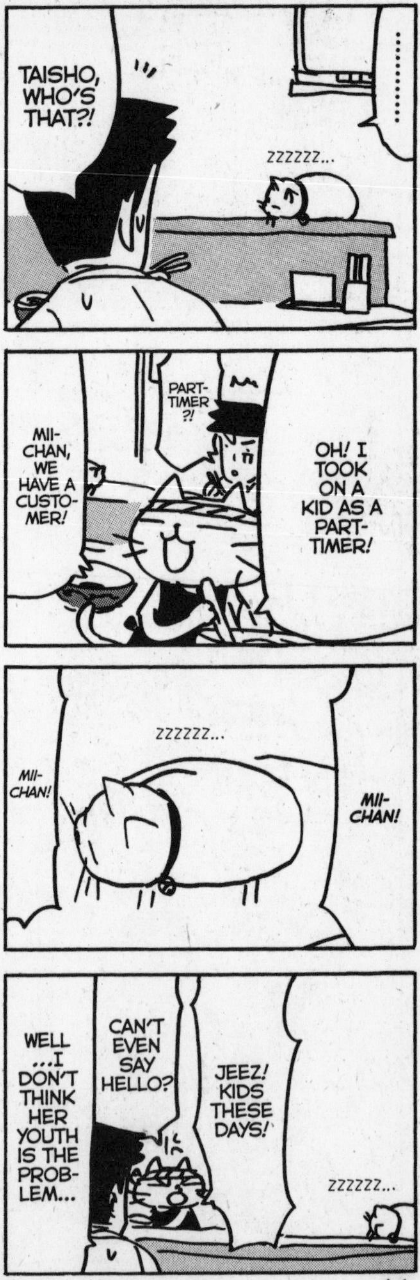
TAISHO, WHO'S THAT?!
......
ZZZZZZ...
OH! I TOOK ON A KID AS A PART-TIMER!
PART-TIMER?!
MII-CHAN, WE HAVE A CUSTOMER!
MII-CHAN!
MII-CHAN!
ZZZZZZ...
JEEZ! KIDS THESE DAYS!
CAN'T EVEN SAY HELLO?
WELL ...I DON'T THINK HER YOUTH IS THE PROBLEM...
ZZZZZZ...

Not Mii-chan?!

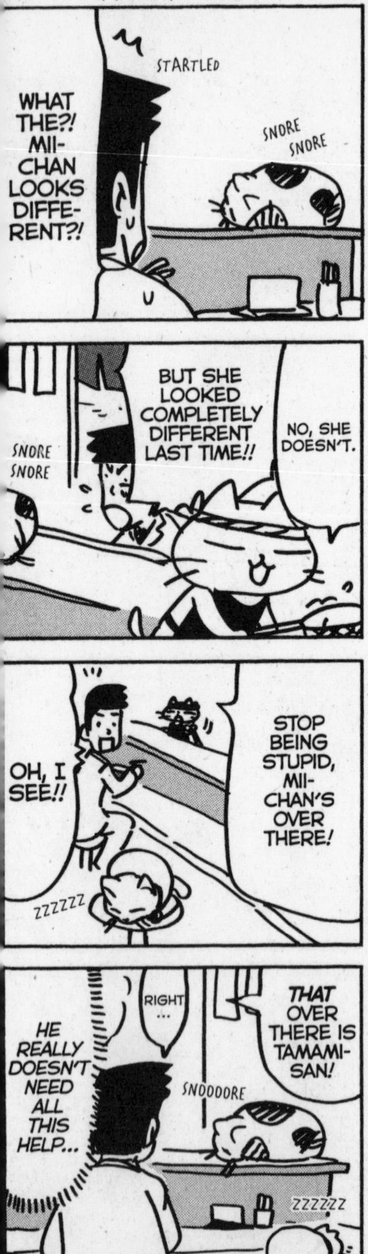
STARTLED
WHAT THE?! MII-CHAN LOOKS DIFFERENT?!
SNORE SNORE
NO, SHE DOESN'T.
BUT SHE LOOKED COMPLETELY DIFFERENT LAST TIME!!
SNORE SNORE
STOP BEING STUPID, MII-CHAN'S OVER THERE!
OH, I SEE!!
ZZZZZZ
THAT OVER THERE IS TAMAMI-SAN!
RIGHT...
HE REALLY DOESN'T NEED ALL THIS HELP...
SNOOOORE
ZZZZZZ

Delivery

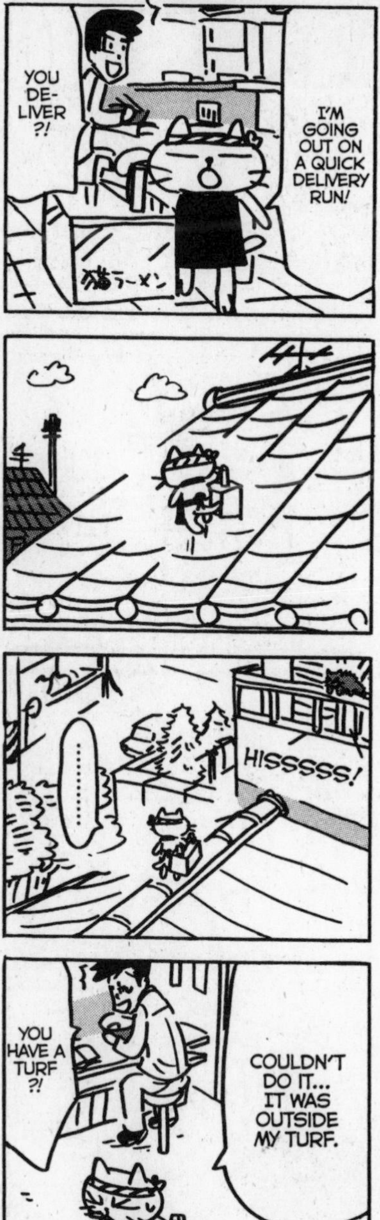
I'M GOING OUT ON A QUICK DELIVERY RUN!
YOU DE-LIVER ?!
猫ラーメン
......
HISSSSS!
COULDN'T DO IT... IT WAS OUTSIDE MY TURF.
YOU HAVE A TURF ?!

Serving Water

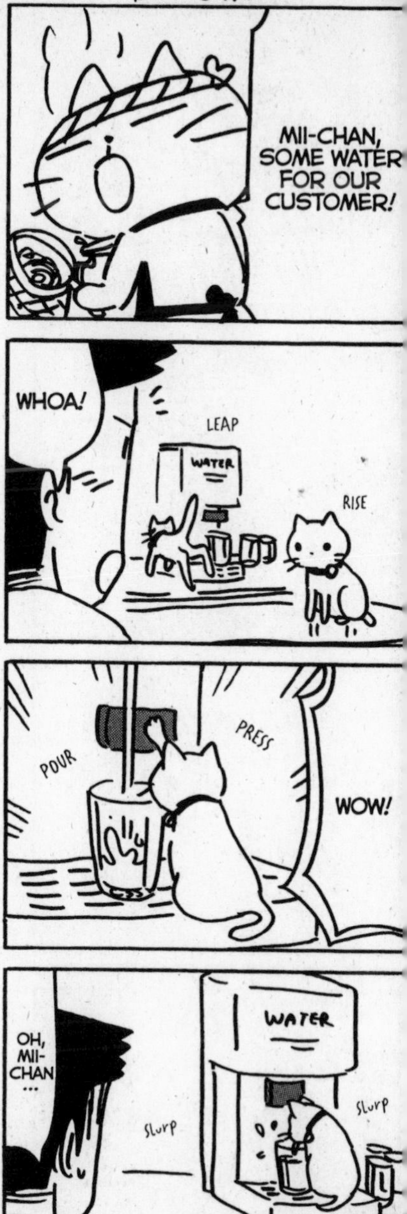
MII-CHAN, SOME WATER FOR OUR CUSTOMER!
LEAP
WATER
RISE
WHOA!
PRESS
POUR
WOW!
WATER
slurp
slurp
OH, MII-CHAN...

Frequent Customer Card

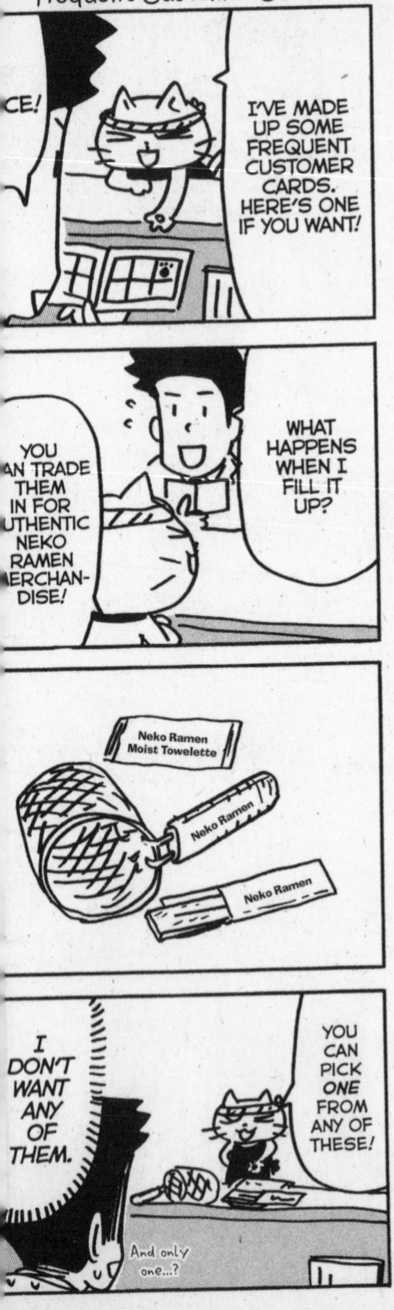
CE!
I'VE MADE UP SOME FREQUENT CUSTOMER CARDS. HERE'S ONE IF YOU WANT!
WHAT HAPPENS WHEN I FILL IT UP?
YOU AN TRADE THEM IN FOR UTHENTIC NEKO RAMEN ERCHAN-DISE!
Neko Ramen Moist Towelette
Neko Ramen
Neko Ramen
YOU CAN PICK ONE FROM ANY OF THESE!
I DON'T WANT ANY OF THEM.
And only one...?

Flattered Purrs

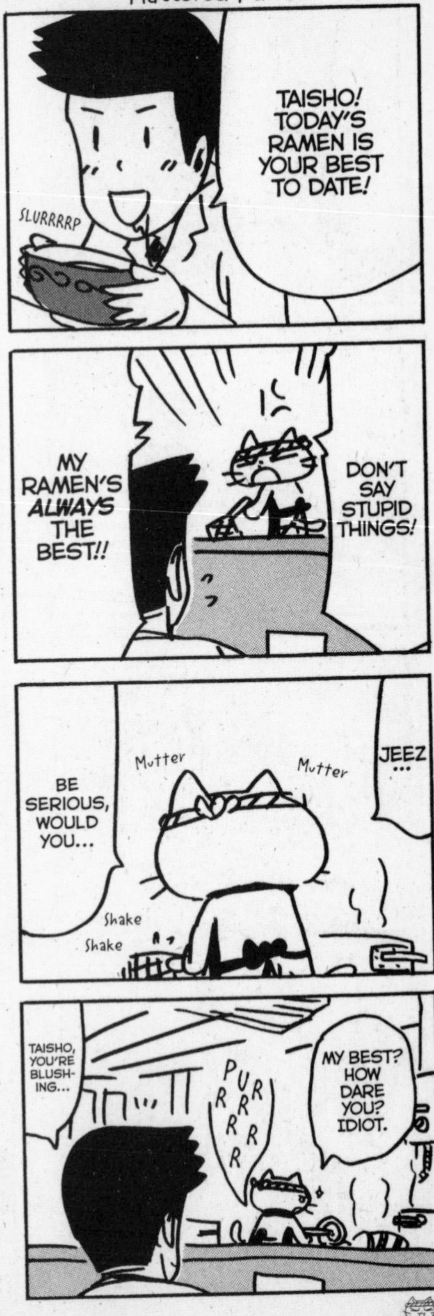
TAISHO! TODAY'S RAMEN IS YOUR BEST TO DATE!
SLURRRRP
DON'T SAY STUPID THINGS!
MY RAMEN'S ALWAYS THE BEST!!
JEEZ...
Mutter
Mutter
BE SERIOUS, WOULD YOU...
Shake
Shake
MY BEST? HOW DARE YOU? IDIOT.
PURRRRRRR
TAISHO, YOU'RE BLUSH-ING...

Studies

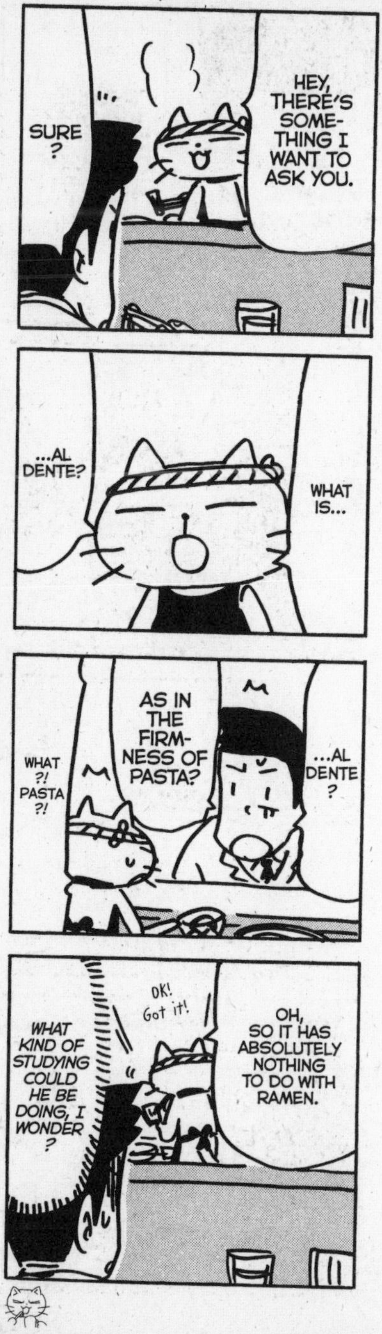
HEY, THERE'S SOMETHING I WANT TO ASK YOU.
SURE?
WHAT IS...
...AL DENTE?
...AL DENTE?
AS IN THE FIRMNESS OF PASTA?
WHAT?! PASTA?!
OH, SO IT HAS ABSOLUTELY NOTHING TO DO WITH RAMEN.
OK! Got it!
WHAT KIND OF STUDYING COULD HE BE DOING, I WONDER?

Long Lines

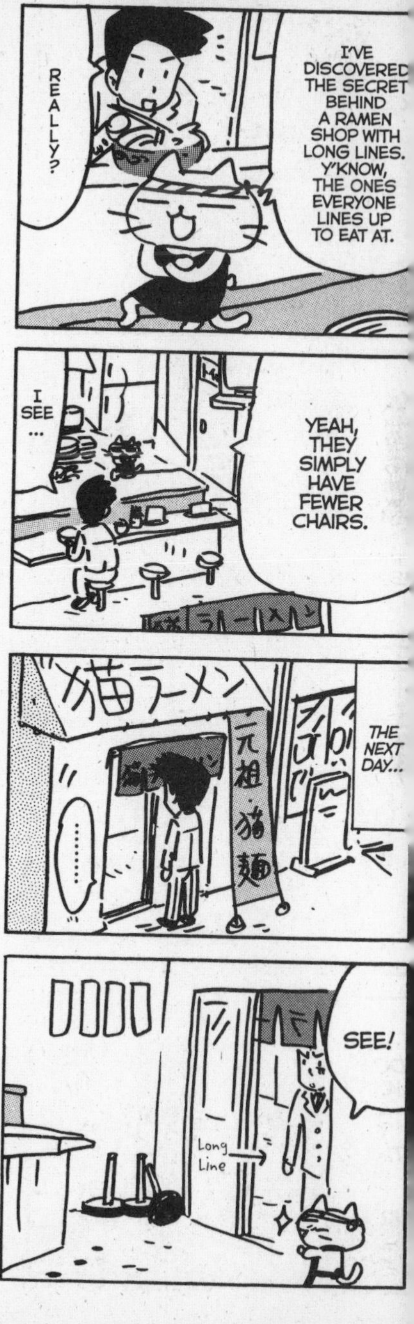
I'VE DISCOVERED THE SECRET BEHIND A RAMEN SHOP WITH LONG LINES. Y'KNOW, THE ONES EVERYONE LINES UP TO EAT AT.
REALLY?
YEAH, THEY SIMPLY HAVE FEWER CHAIRS.
I SEE...
THE NEXT DAY...
猫ラーメン
元祖・猫麺
......
SEE!
Long Line

Kid's Ramen

I'VE BEEN THINKING ABOUT CREATING A RAMEN DISH FOR KIDS AND WANT YOUR OPINION!

...URE...

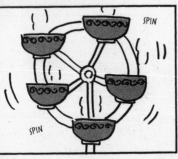

SPIN

SPIN

SPIN

SPIN

SPIN

SPIN

DOESN'T IT GIVE YOU THE FEELING OF A RAMEN AMUSEMENT PARK?

SPIN

SPIN

...OU HINK O?!

HOCKED!

FIRST OF ALL, I DON'T THINK A CHILD COULD EAT ALL THIS...

Free Rice Balls

WANT SOME?

Special: Free Riceballs During Lunch

I'VE DECIDED TO OFFER FREE RICE BALLS WITH LUNCH.

OKAY!

Thanks!

SURE!

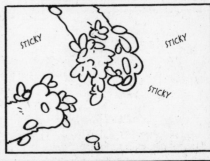

STICKY

STICKY

STICKY

STICKY

UH, NEVER MIND...

ANNOYED

Training

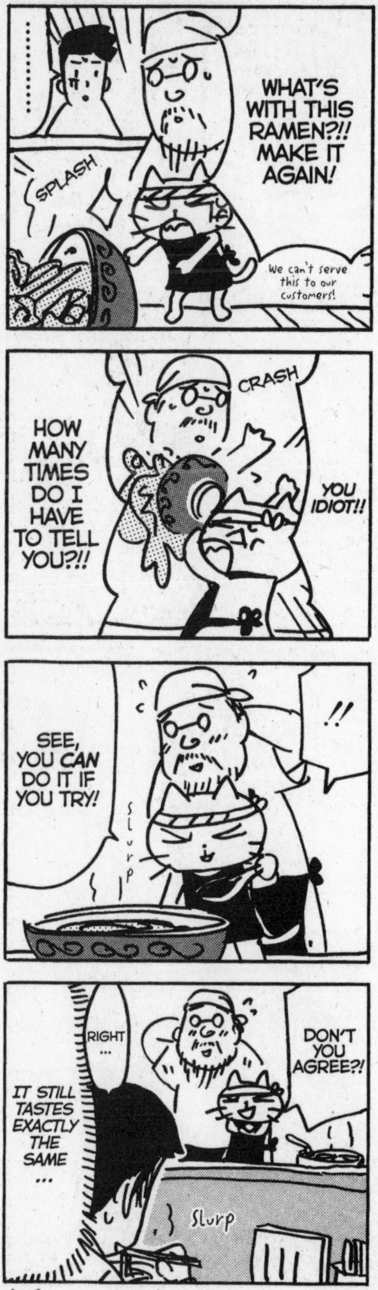
......
WHAT'S WITH THIS RAMEN?!! MAKE IT AGAIN!
SPLASH
We can't serve this to our customers!
CRASH
HOW MANY TIMES DO I HAVE TO TELL YOU?!!
YOU IDIOT!!
!!
SEE, YOU CAN DO IT IF YOU TRY!
Slurp
RIGHT ...
DON'T YOU AGREE?!
IT STILL TASTES EXACTLY THE SAME ...
Slurp

The New Guy

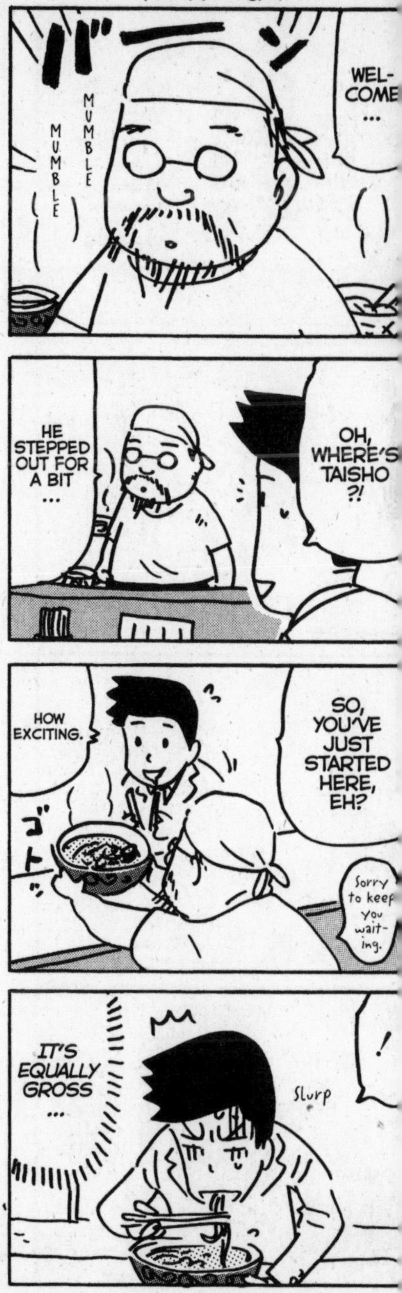
バーン
WEL-COME ...
MUMBLE MUMBLE
OH, WHERE'S TAISHO?!
HE STEPPED OUT FOR A BIT ...
SO, YOU'VE JUST STARTED HERE, EH?
HOW EXCITING.
ゴト
Sorry to keep you wait-ing.
!
IT'S EQUALLY GROSS ...
Slurp

Super Moves

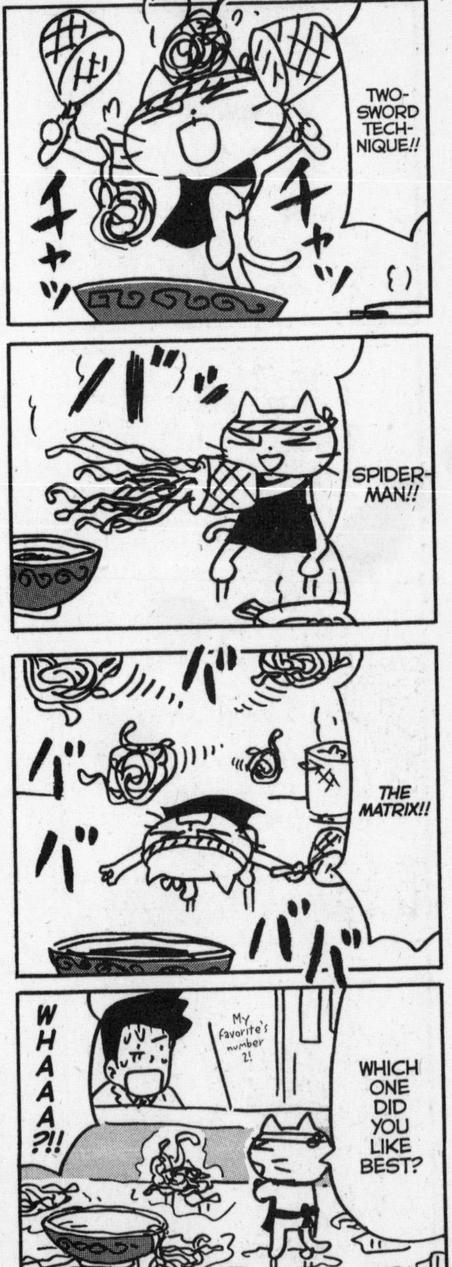
TWO-SWORD TECHNIQUE!!
チャッ
チャッ
SPIDER-MAN!!
THE MATRIX!!
WHAAAA?!!
My favorite's number 2!
WHICH ONE DID YOU LIKE BEST?

Pay Day

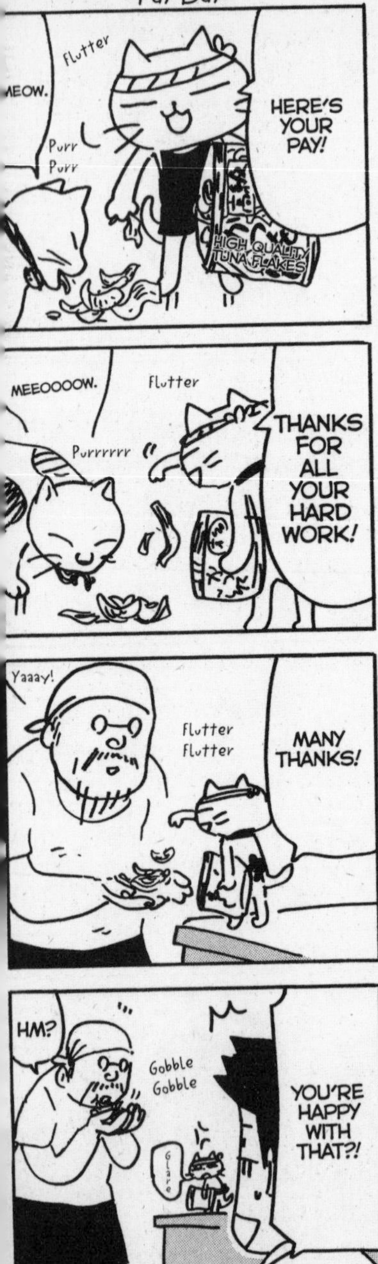
MEOW.
Flutter
Purr Purr
HERE'S YOUR PAY!
HIGH QUALITY TUNA FLAKES
MEEOOOOW.
Flutter
Purrrrrrr
THANKS FOR ALL YOUR HARD WORK!
Yaaay!
Flutter Flutter
MANY THANKS!
HM?
Gobble Gobble
Glare
YOU'RE HAPPY WITH THAT?!

Where's Mii-chan?

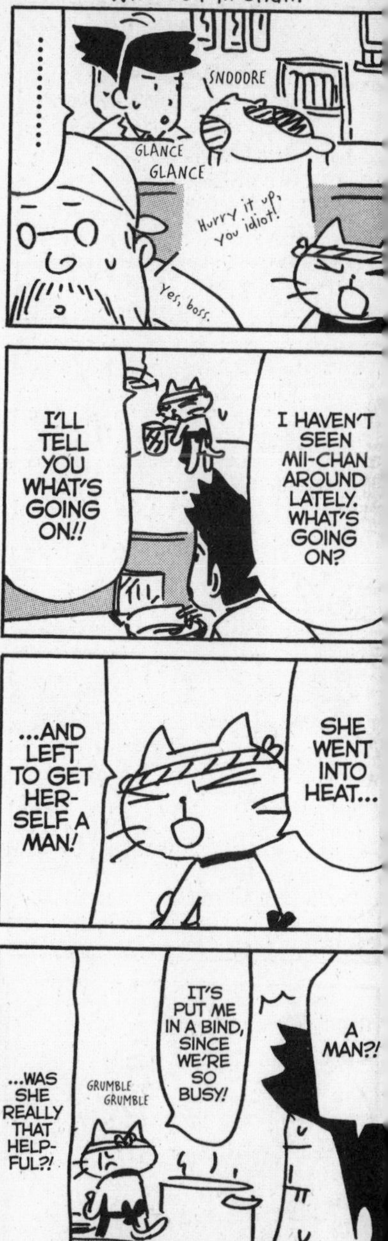
SNOOORE
Hurry it up, you idiot!
GLANCE
GLANCE
Yes, boss.
....
I HAVEN'T SEEN MII-CHAN AROUND LATELY. WHAT'S GOING ON?
I'LL TELL YOU WHAT'S GOING ON!!
SHE WENT INTO HEAT...
...AND LEFT TO GET HER-SELF A MAN!
A MAN?!
IT'S PUT ME IN A BIND, SINCE WE'RE SO BUSY!
GRUMBLE GRUMBLE
...WAS SHE REALLY THAT HELPFUL?!

Mii-chan Returns

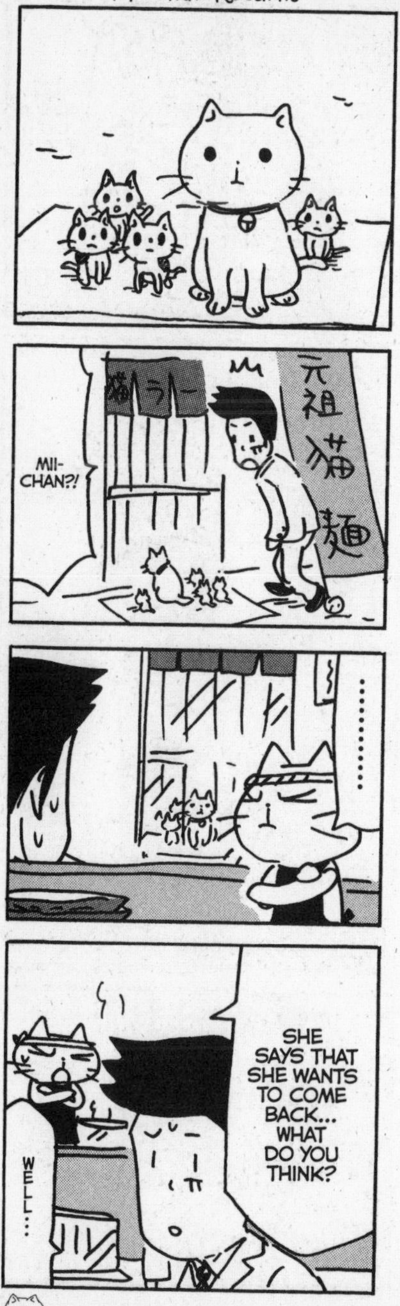
元祖猫麺
MII-CHAN?!
....
SHE SAYS THAT SHE WANTS TO COME BACK... WHAT DO YOU THINK?
WELL...

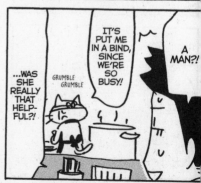

The Second Location

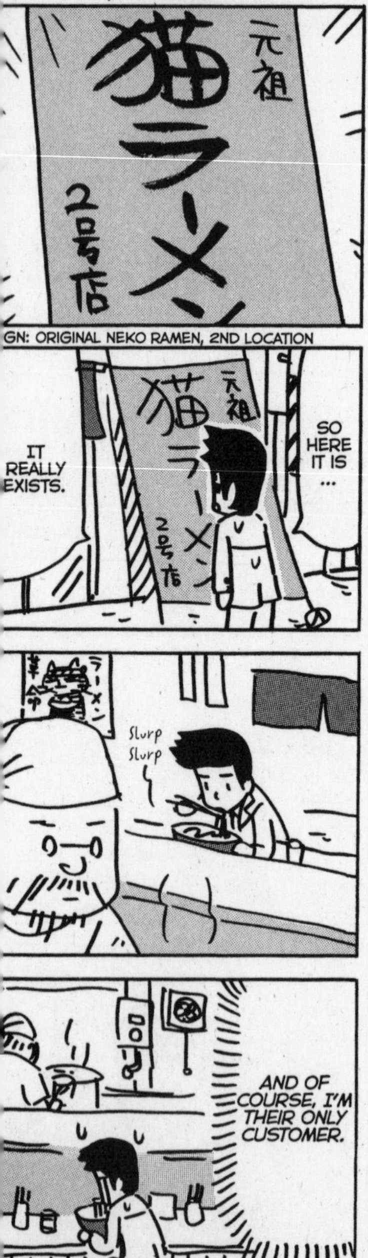
元祖
猫ラーメン
2号店
GN: ORIGINAL NEKO RAMEN, 2ND LOCATION
SO HERE IT IS ...
IT REALLY EXISTS.
Slurp Slurp
AND OF COURSE, I'M THEIR ONLY CUSTOMER.

He Quit?

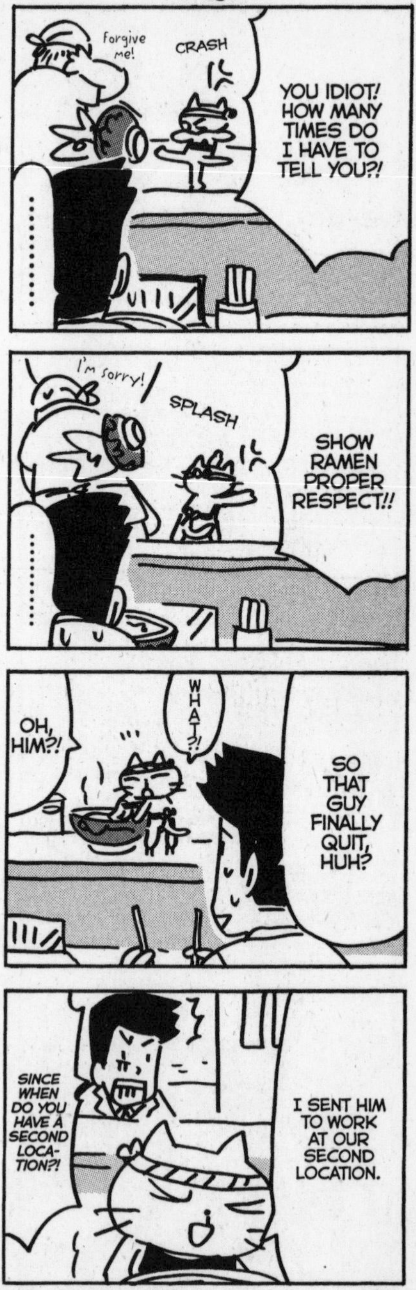
YOU IDIOT! HOW MANY TIMES DO I HAVE TO TELL YOU?!
CRASH
Forgive me!
SHOW RAMEN PROPER RESPECT!!
SPLASH
I'm sorry!
SO THAT GUY FINALLY QUIT, HUH?
WHAT?!
OH, HIM?!
I SENT HIM TO WORK AT OUR SECOND LOCATION.
SINCE WHEN DO YOU HAVE A SECOND LOCATION?!

Ultimate

RIP
Chicken
POUR~
Tic Tic
Tic
HERE! SORRY TO KEEP YOU WAITING!
THIS IS INSTANT RAMEN!!
SLAM
AFTER ALL MY RESEARCH, I FINALLY ACCEPTED THAT NOTHING BEATS INSTANT RAMEN!!
AND YOU'RE CHARING ME $8?!

猫ラーメン

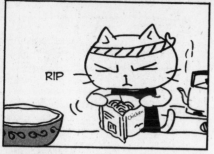

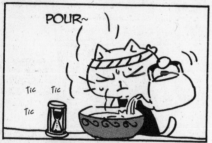

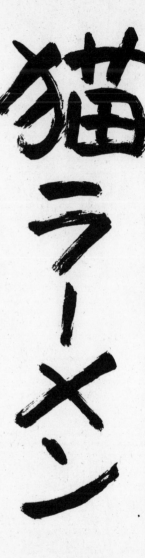

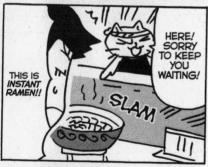

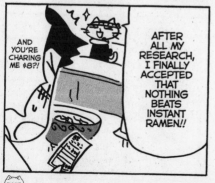

Chapter 2

Do It Yourself
Ramen $7
*Self Serve $5
WHAT IS "SELF SERVE"?!
YOU DON'T KNOW?! IT MEANS YOU MAKE IT YOURSELF!
Self serve is very trendy right now.
Ramen $7
* Self Serve $5
WELL... I KNOW THAT, BUT...
HERE!
WHAT?! SERIOUSLY?!
ALL RIGHT, I'M HEADING OUT FOR A COUPLE OF HOURS! SEE YA!
WHAAT?!
Message
HUH?
TAISHO, S THERE SOME-THING WRITTEN AT THE BOTTOM?!
YUP!
FINISH ALL THE BROTH AND A FABULOUS MESSAGE WILL APPEAR!
OH, EAT.
SLURRRRP
How cool.
!!
YOU WIN ANOTHER BOWL OF RAMEN!
WHAT DOES IT SAY?!
Swipe
OH... NOTHING REALLY...

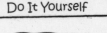

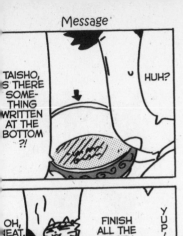

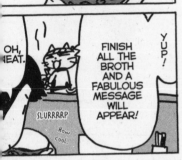

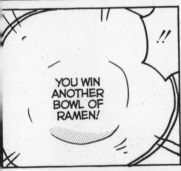

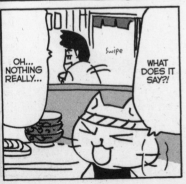

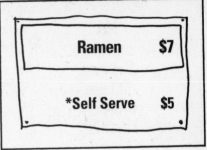

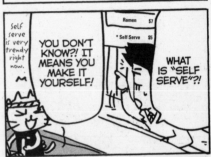

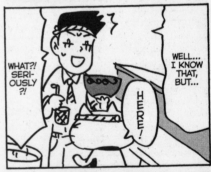

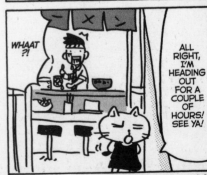

Chilled Chinese Noodles

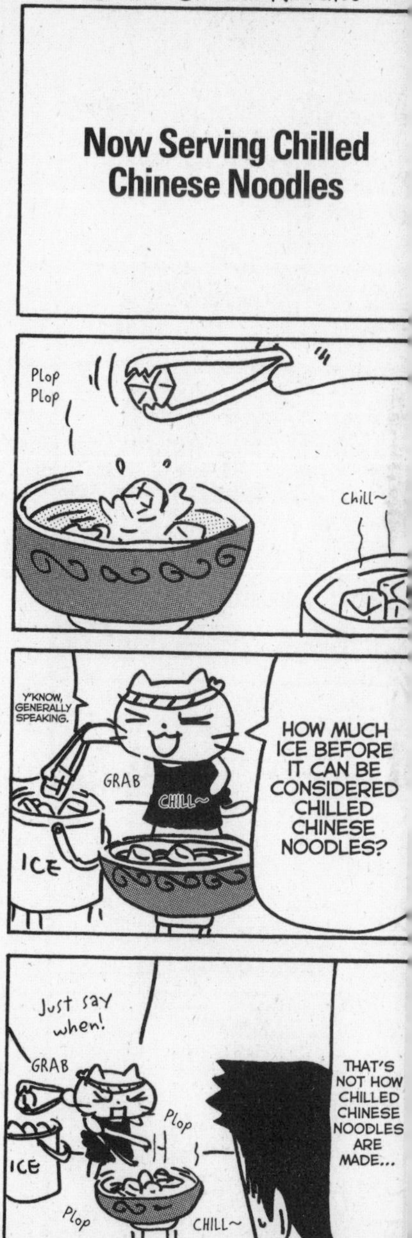

Now Serving Chilled Chinese Noodles
Chill~
Plop Plop
HOW MUCH ICE BEFORE IT CAN BE CONSIDERED CHILLED CHINESE NOODLES?
Y'KNOW, GENERALLY SPEAKING.
GRAB
CHILL~
ICE
THAT'S NOT HOW CHILLED CHINESE NOODLES ARE MADE...
Just say when!
GRAB
Plop
ICE
Plop
CHILL~

Quit

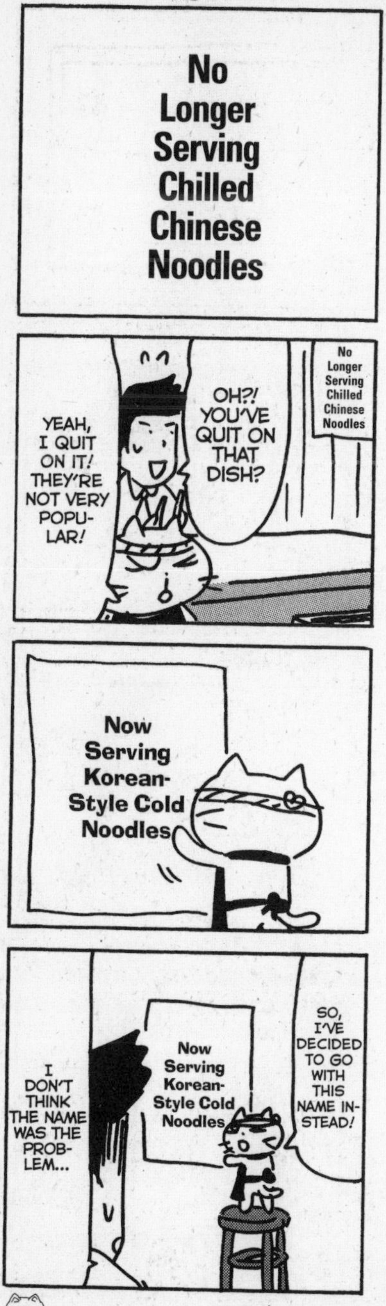

No Longer Serving Chilled Chinese Noodles
No Longer Serving Chilled Chinese Noodles
OH?! YOU'VE QUIT ON THAT DISH?
YEAH, I QUIT ON IT! THEY'RE NOT VERY POPU-LAR!
Now Serving Korean-Style Cold Noodles
SO, I'VE DECIDED TO GO WITH THIS NAME IN-STEAD!
Now Serving Korean-Style Cold Noodles
I DON'T THINK THE NAME WAS THE PROB-LEM...

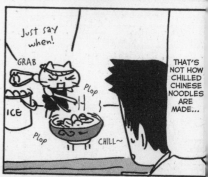

Assessment

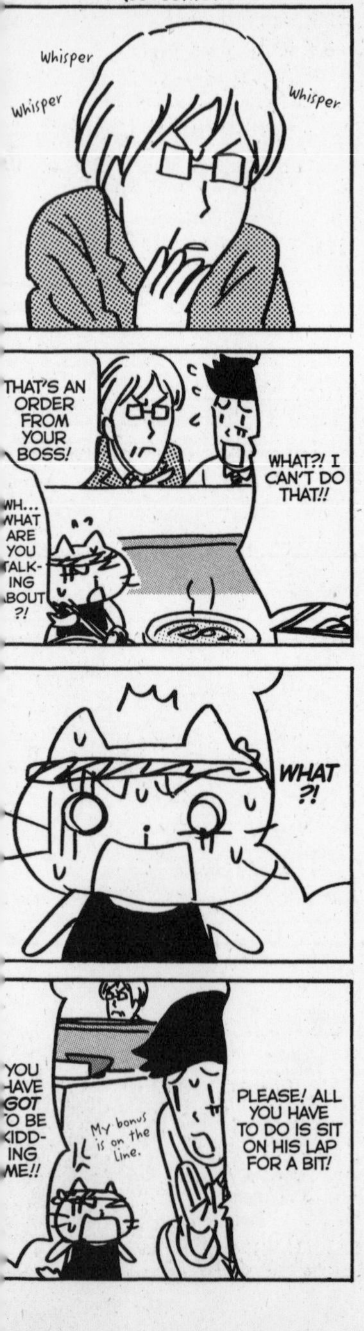
Whisper
Whisper
Whisper
THAT'S AN ORDER FROM YOUR BOSS!
WHAT?! I CAN'T DO THAT!!
WH... WHAT ARE YOU TALKING ABOUT?!
WHAT?!
YOU HAVE GOT TO BE KIDDING ME!!
My bonus is on the line.
PLEASE! ALL YOU HAVE TO DO IS SIT ON HIS LAP FOR A BIT!

Boss

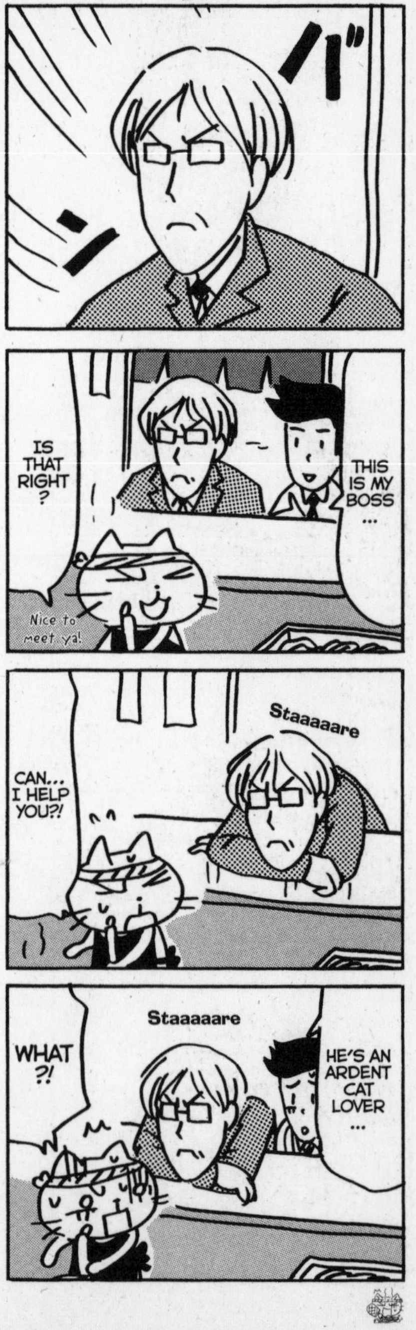
IS THAT RIGHT?
THIS IS MY BOSS...
Nice to meet ya!
Staaaaare
CAN... I HELP YOU?!
Staaaaare
WHAT?!
HE'S AN ARDENT CAT LOVER...

Kaiten Ramen (Conveyer-Belt Ramen)

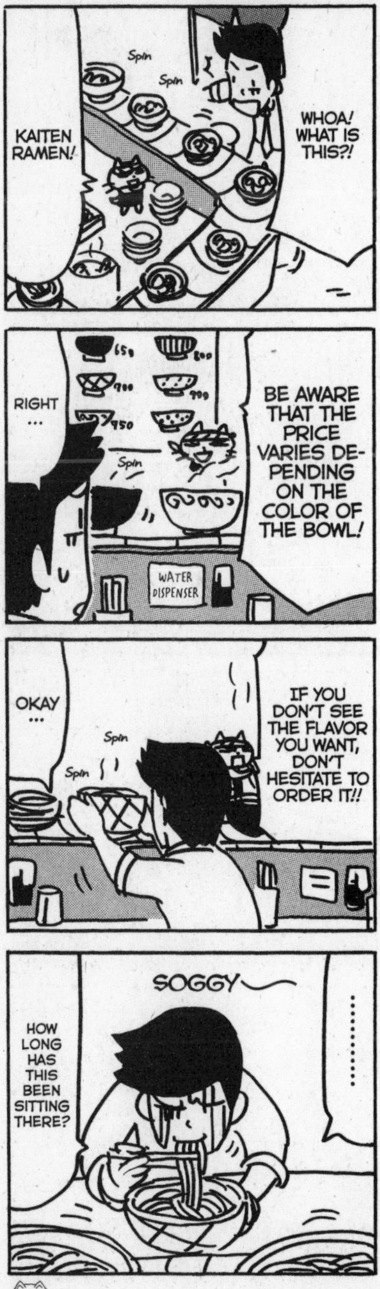
Spin
Spin
WHOA! WHAT IS THIS?!
KAITEN RAMEN!
RIGHT ...
BE AWARE THAT THE PRICE VARIES DE-PENDING ON THE COLOR OF THE BOWL!
Spin
WATER DISPENSER
OKAY ...
IF YOU DON'T SEE THE FLAVOR YOU WANT, DON'T HESITATE TO ORDER IT!!
Spin
Spin
SOGGY~
HOW LONG HAS THIS BEEN SITTING THERE?
....

Natural Predator

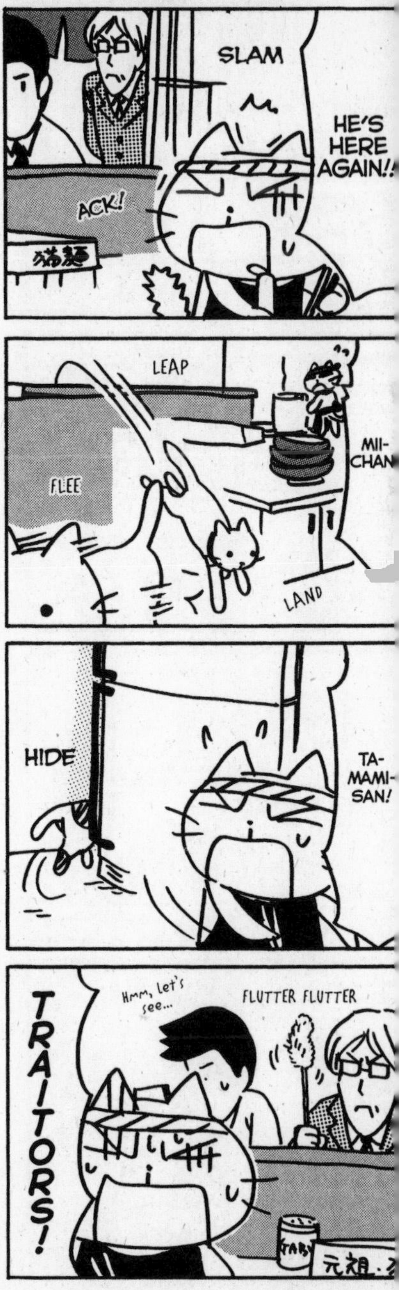
SLAM
HE'S HERE AGAIN!!
ACK!
LEAP
MII-CHAN
FLEE
LAND
HIDE
TA-MAMI-SAN!
TRAITORS!
Hmm, let's see...
FLUTTER FLUTTER

Cancelled

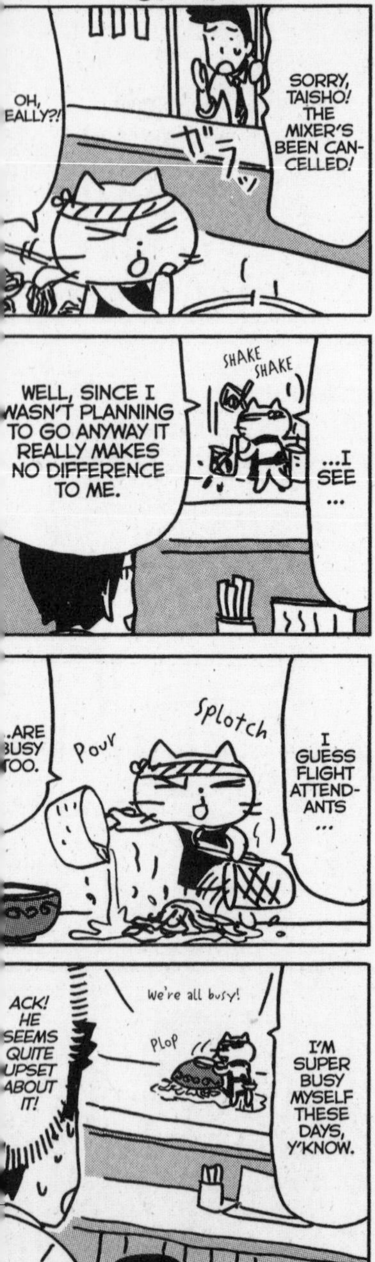
SORRY, TAISHO! THE MIXER'S BEEN CANCELLED!
OH, EALLY?!
SHAKE SHAKE
...I SEE ...
WELL, SINCE I WASN'T PLANNING TO GO ANYWAY IT REALLY MAKES NO DIFFERENCE TO ME.
Splotch
I GUESS FLIGHT ATTENDANTS ...
Pour
.ARE BUSY TOO.
I'M SUPER BUSY MYSELF THESE DAYS, Y'KNOW.
We're all busy!
PLOP
ACK! HE SEEMS QUITE UPSET ABOUT IT!

Mixers

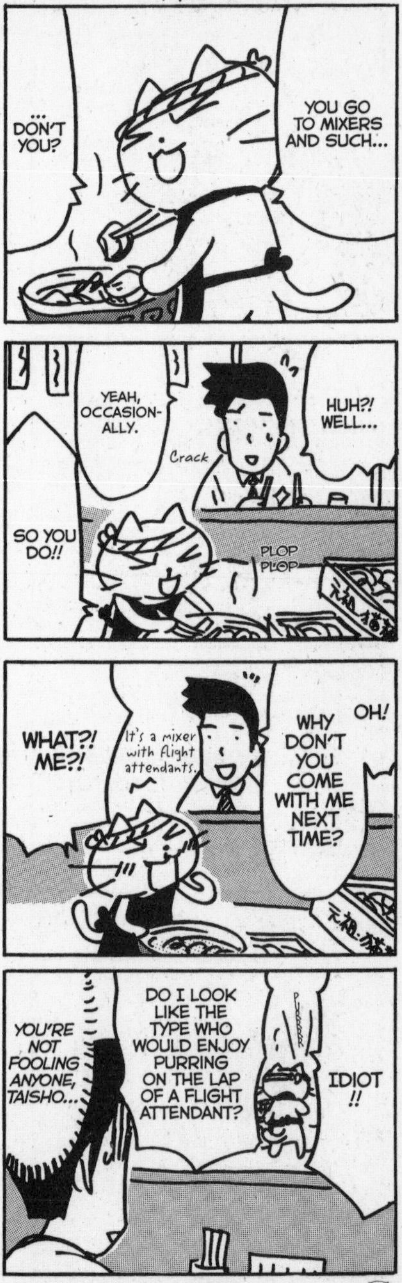
YOU GO TO MIXERS AND SUCH...
... DON'T YOU?
HUH?! WELL...
YEAH, OCCASIONALLY.
Crack
SO YOU DO!!
PLOP PLOP
OH!
WHY DON'T YOU COME WITH ME NEXT TIME?
It's a mixer with flight attendants.
WHAT?! ME?!
IDIOT !!
DO I LOOK LIKE THE TYPE WHO WOULD ENJOY PURRING ON THE LAP OF A FLIGHT ATTENDANT?
YOU'RE NOT FOOLING ANYONE, TAISHO...

Animal Rescue

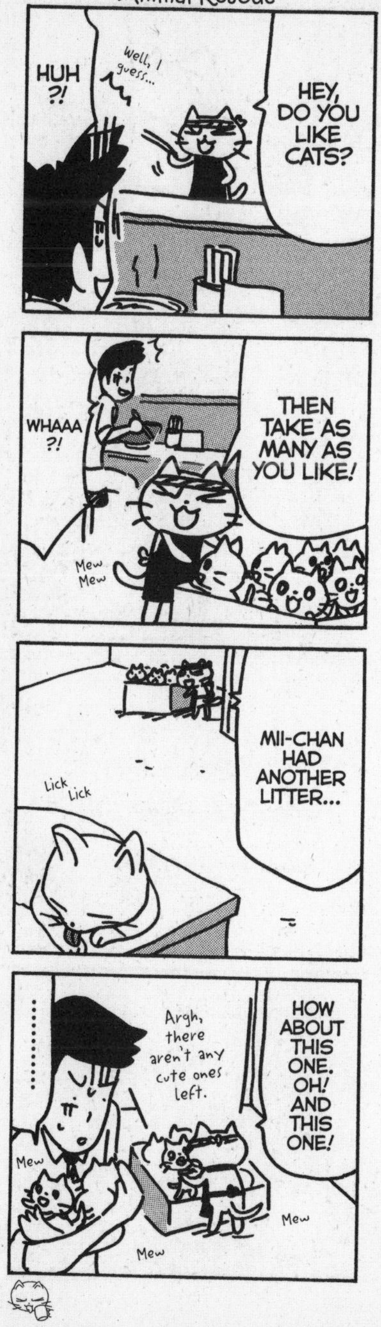
HEY, DO YOU LIKE CATS?
Well, I guess...
HUH?!
THEN TAKE AS MANY AS YOU LIKE!
WHAAA?!
Mew Mew
MII-CHAN HAD ANOTHER LITTER...
Lick Lick
HOW ABOUT THIS ONE. OH! AND THIS ONE!
Argh, there aren't any cute ones left.
....
Mew
Mew
Mew

New Taste

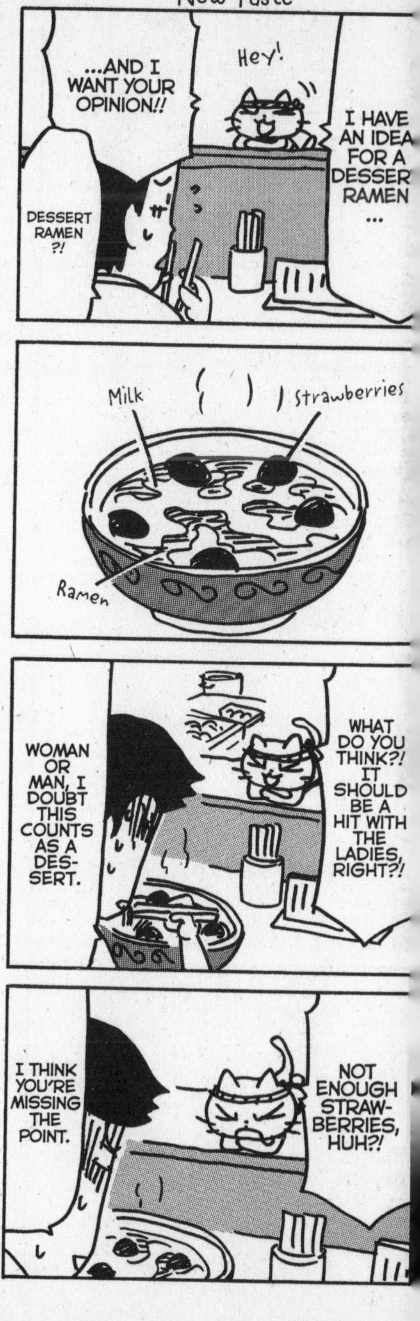
I HAVE AN IDEA FOR A DESSERT RAMEN...
Hey!
...AND I WANT YOUR OPINION!!
DESSERT RAMEN?!
Strawberries
Milk
Ramen
WHAT DO YOU THINK?! IT SHOULD BE A HIT WITH THE LADIES, RIGHT?!
WOMAN OR MAN, I DOUBT THIS COUNTS AS A DES-SERT.
NOT ENOUGH STRAW-BERRIES, HUH?!
I THINK YOU'RE MISSING THE POINT.

TV Coverage

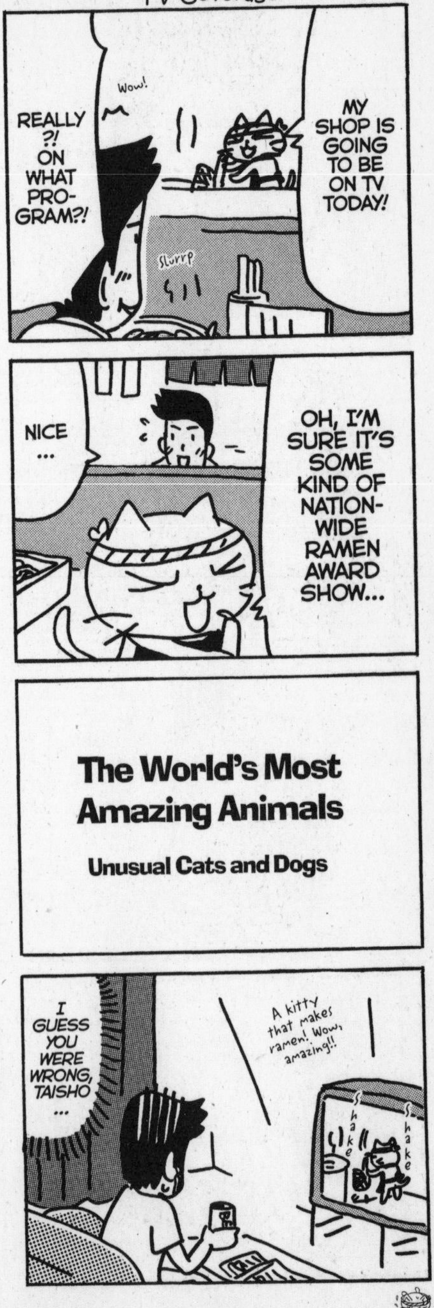
MY SHOP IS GOING TO BE ON TV TODAY!
Wow!
REALLY?! ON WHAT PRO-GRAM?!
Slurrp
OH, I'M SURE IT'S SOME KIND OF NATION-WIDE RAMEN AWARD SHOW...
NICE ...
The World's Most Amazing Animals
Unusual Cats and Dogs
A kitty that makes ramen! Wow, amazing!!
shake
shake
I GUESS YOU WERE WRONG, TAISHO ...

Unusual

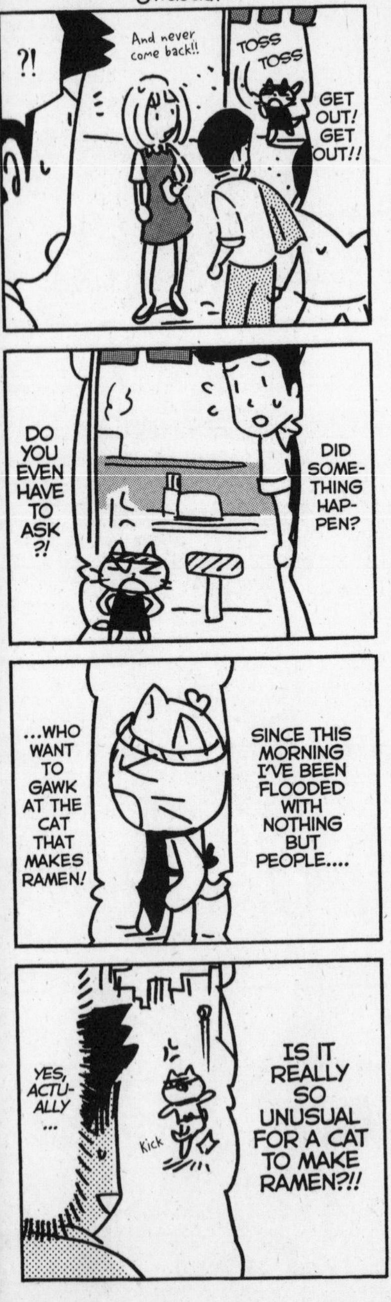
GET OUT! GET OUT!!
TOSS TOSS
And never come back!!
?!
DID SOME-THING HAP-PEN?
DO YOU EVEN HAVE TO ASK?!
SINCE THIS MORNING I'VE BEEN FLOODED WITH NOTHING BUT PEOPLE....
...WHO WANT TO GAWK AT THE CAT THAT MAKES RAMEN!
IS IT REALLY SO UNUSUAL FOR A CAT TO MAKE RAMEN?!!
Kick
YES, ACTU-ALLY ...

Solution

SHOULD I HAVE MISO...
...OR SHOYU ...?
OH! TROUBLE DECIDING?!
I HAVE JUST THE THING FOR YOU!
WHAT IS IT?
Miso
Shoyu
HALF AND HALF!
EAT IT CAREFULLY!
THAT'S IMPOSSIBLE!!

猫ラーメン

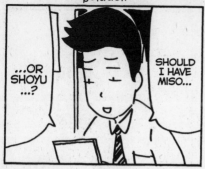

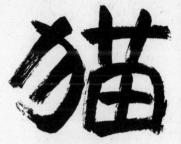

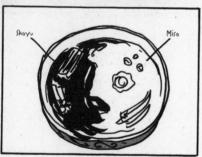

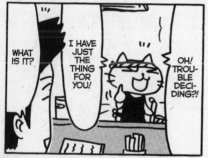

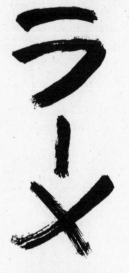

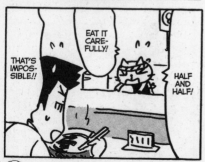

Chapter 3

Supplements

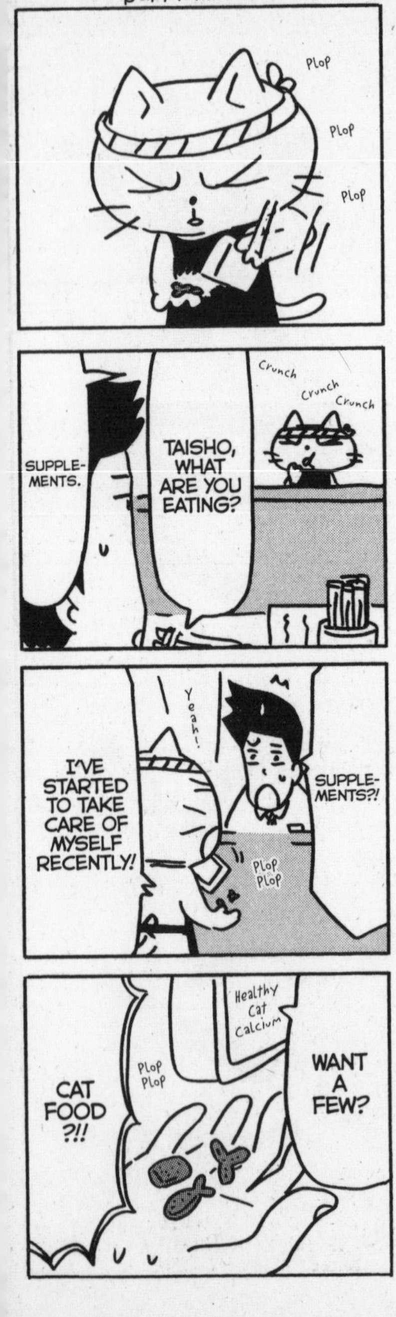
Plop
Plop
Plop
Crunch
Crunch
Crunch
TAISHO, WHAT ARE YOU EATING?
SUPPLEMENTS.
Yeah!
SUPPLEMENTS?!
I'VE STARTED TO TAKE CARE OF MYSELF RECENTLY!
Plop Plop
Healthy Cat Calcium
Plop Plop
WANT A FEW?
CAT FOOD ?!!

Choice

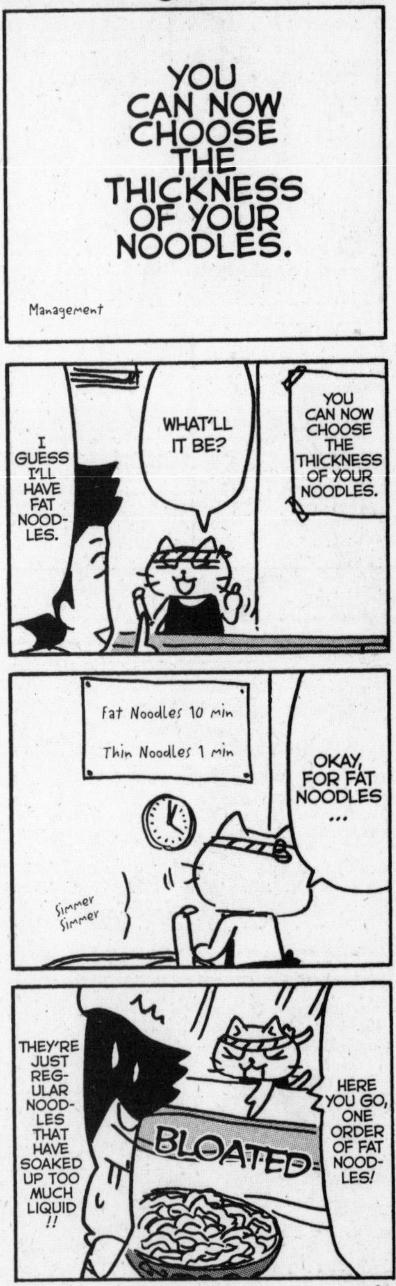
YOU CAN NOW CHOOSE THE THICKNESS OF YOUR NOODLES.
Management
YOU CAN NOW CHOOSE THE THICKNESS OF YOUR NOODLES.
WHAT'LL IT BE?
I GUESS I'LL HAVE FAT NOODLES.
Fat Noodles 10 min
Thin Noodles 1 min
OKAY, FOR FAT NOODLES ...
Simmer Simmer
HERE YOU GO, ONE ORDER OF FAT NOODLES!
BLOATED
THEY'RE JUST REGULAR NOODLES THAT HAVE SOAKED UP TOO MUCH LIQUID !!

Rival Shop

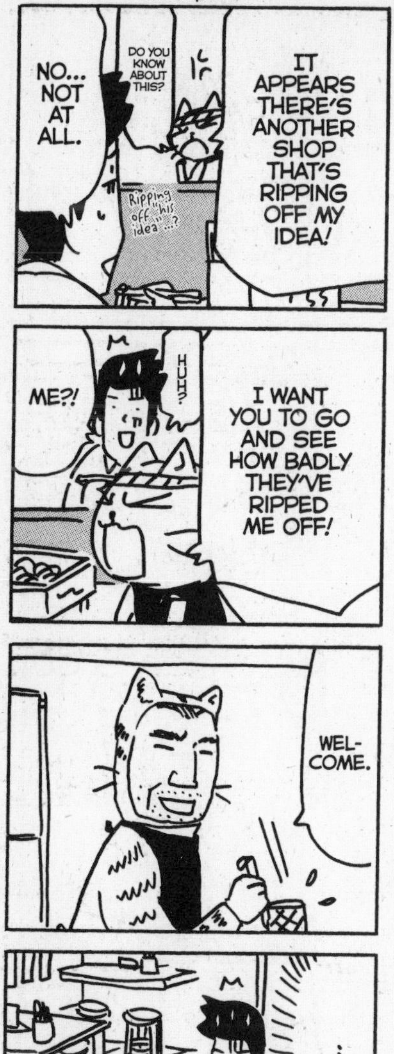
IT APPEARS THERE'S ANOTHER SHOP THAT'S RIPPING OFF MY IDEA!
DO YOU KNOW ABOUT THIS?
NO... NOT AT ALL.
Ripping off "his idea"...?
I WANT YOU TO GO AND SEE HOW BADLY THEY'VE RIPPED ME OFF!
HUH?
ME?!
WEL-COME.
Shake
....
Shake

New Proposal

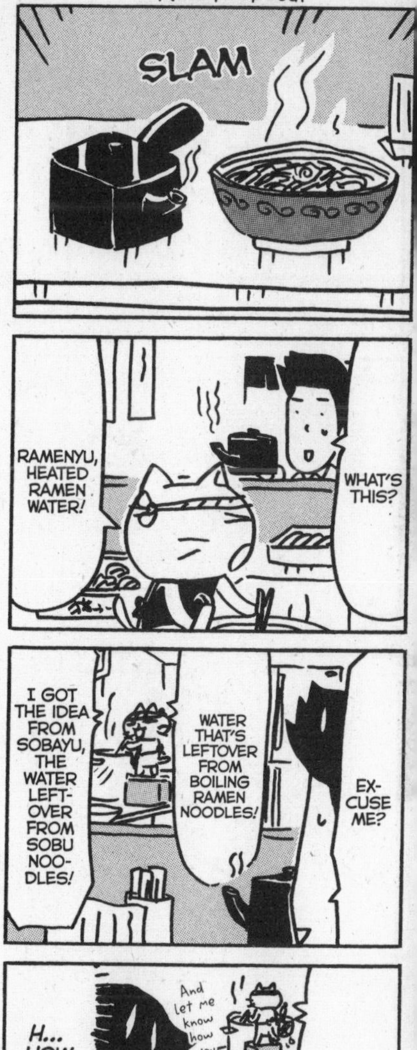
SLAM
WHAT'S THIS?
RAMENYU, HEATED RAMEN WATER!
EX-CUSE ME?
WATER THAT'S LEFTOVER FROM BOILING RAMEN NOODLES!
I GOT THE IDEA FROM SOBAYU, THE WATER LEFT-OVER FROM SOBU NOO-DLES!
GIVE IT A TRY!
And let me know how you like it!
H... HOW DO I EAT THIS?!

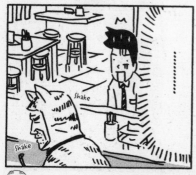

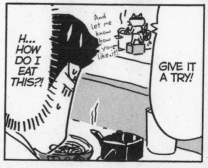

What Style?

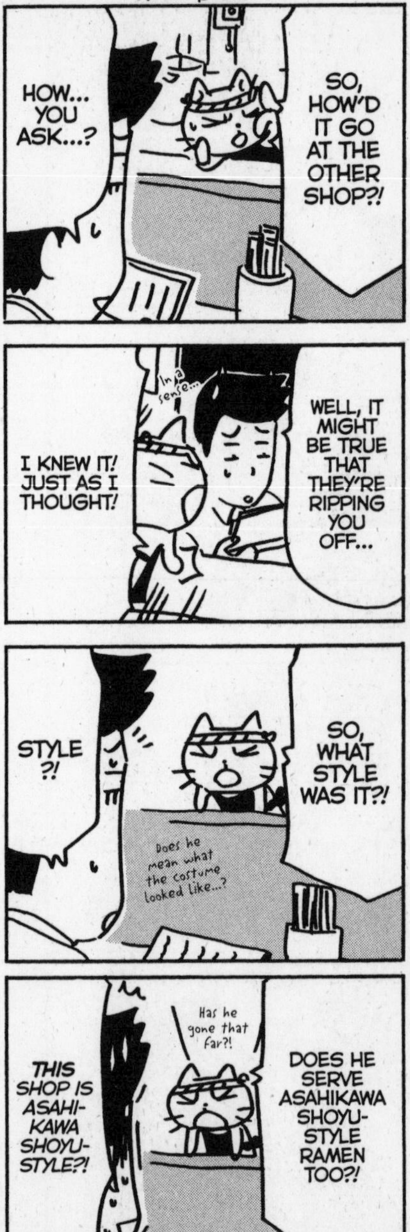

SO, HOW'D IT GO AT THE OTHER SHOP?!
HOW... YOU ASK...?
WELL, IT MIGHT BE TRUE THAT THEY'RE RIPPING YOU OFF...
In a sense...
I KNEW IT! JUST AS I THOUGHT!
SO, WHAT STYLE WAS IT?!
STYLE?!
Does he mean what the costume looked like...?
DOES HE SERVE ASAHIKAWA SHOYU-STYLE RAMEN TOO?!
Has he gone that far?!
THIS SHOP IS ASAHIKAWA SHOYU-STYLE?!

Countermeasures

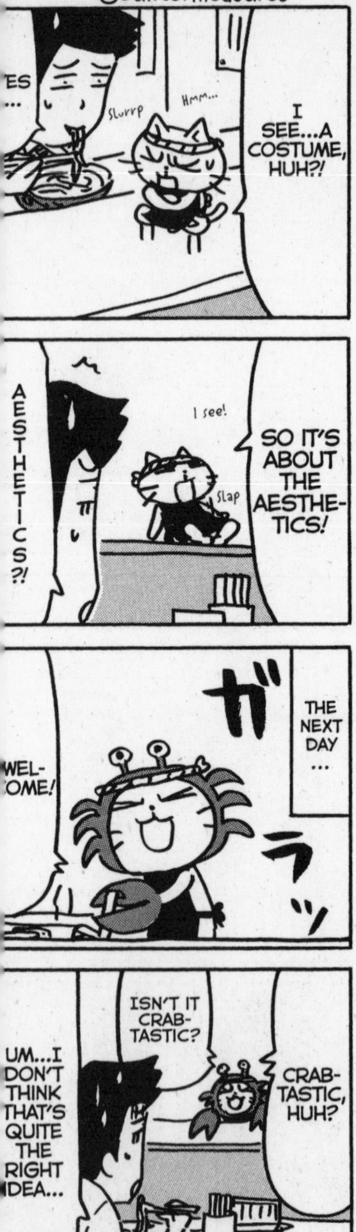

I SEE...A COSTUME, HUH?!
Hmm...
Slurrp
ES ...
SO IT'S ABOUT THE AESTHETICS!
I see!
Slap
AESTHETICS?!
THE NEXT DAY ...
ガラッ
WEL- OME!
CRAB-TASTIC, HUH?
ISN'T IT CRAB-TASTIC?
UM...I DON'T THINK THAT'S QUITE THE RIGHT IDEA...

Runs in the Family

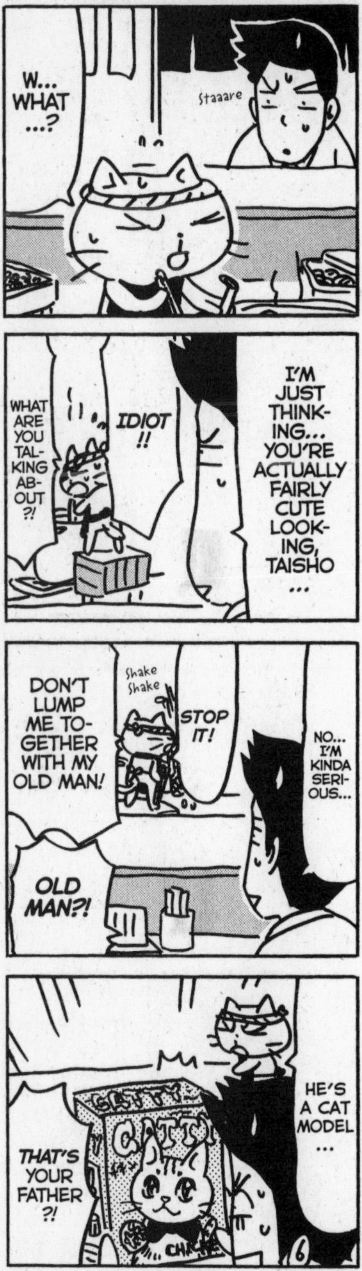
W... WHAT ...?
Staaare
WHAT ARE YOU TALKING ABOUT ?!
IDIOT !!
I'M JUST THINKING... YOU'RE ACTUALLY FAIRLY CUTE LOOKING, TAISHO ...
DON'T LUMP ME TOGETHER WITH MY OLD MAN!
Shake Shake
STOP IT!
NO... I'M KINDA SERIOUS...
OLD MAN?!
THAT'S YOUR FATHER ?!
HE'S A CAT MODEL ...

Afternoon Nap

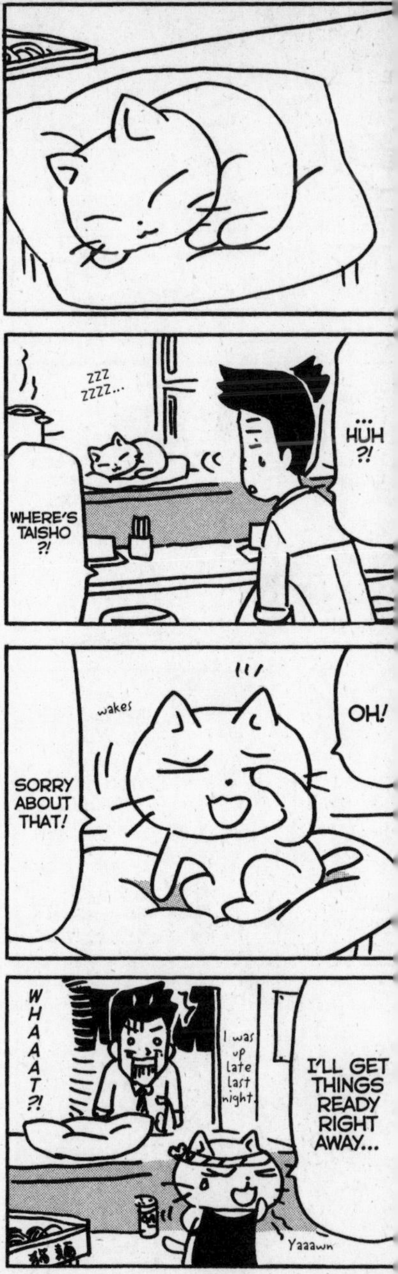
ZZZ ZZZZ...
WHERE'S TAISHO ?!
... HUH ?!
wakes
SORRY ABOUT THAT!
OH!
WHAAAAT ?!
I was up late last night.
I'LL GET THINGS READY RIGHT AWAY...
Yaaawn

Father

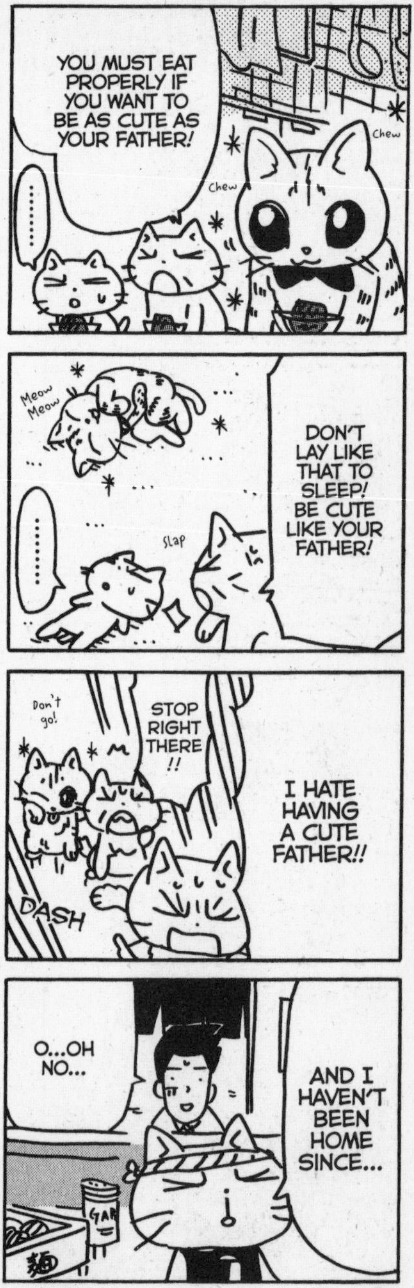
Chew
Chew
YOU MUST EAT PROPERLY IF YOU WANT TO BE AS CUTE AS YOUR FATHER!
......
DON'T LAY LIKE THAT TO SLEEP! BE CUTE LIKE YOUR FATHER!
Slap
Meow Meow
......
I HATE HAVING A CUTE FATHER!!
STOP RIGHT THERE!!
Don't go!
DASH
AND I HAVEN'T BEEN HOME SINCE...
O...OH NO...

Copycat Defense

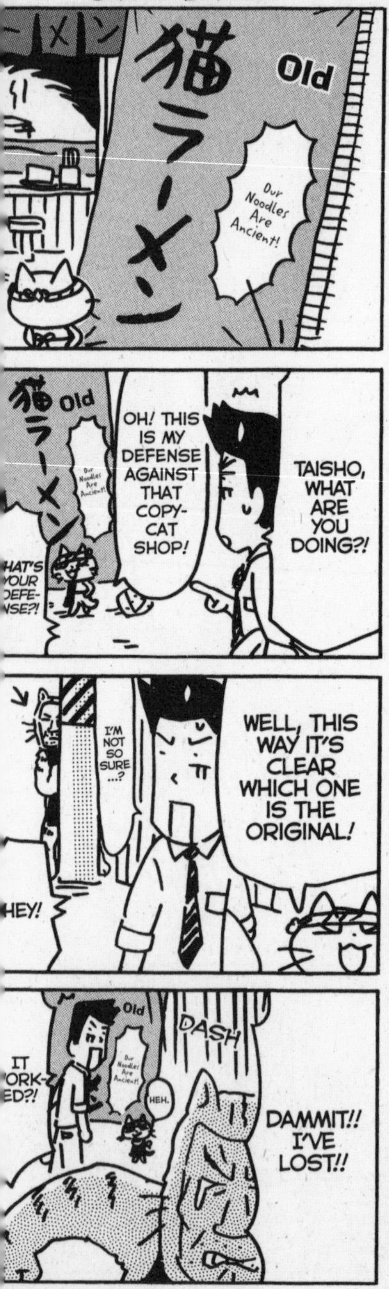
Old
猫ラーメン
Our Noodles Are Ancient!
TAISHO, WHAT ARE YOU DOING?!
OH! THIS IS MY DEFENSE AGAINST THAT COPY-CAT SHOP!
猫 Old ラーメン
Our Noodles Are Ancient!
WELL, THIS WAY IT'S CLEAR WHICH ONE IS THE ORIGINAL!
I'M NOT SO SURE ...?
HEY!
DAMMIT!! I'VE LOST!!
DASH
HEH.
Old
Our Noodles Are Ancient!

Coupon

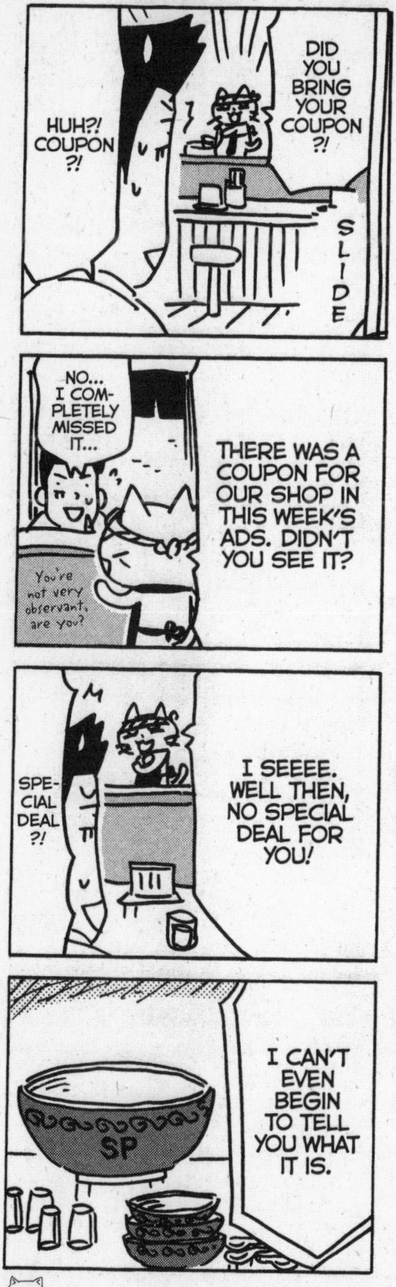
DID YOU BRING YOUR COUPON?!
HUH?! COUPON?!
SLIDE
NO... I COMPLETELY MISSED IT...
THERE WAS A COUPON FOR OUR SHOP IN THIS WEEK'S ADS. DIDN'T YOU SEE IT?
You're not very observant, are you?
I SEEEE. WELL THEN, NO SPECIAL DEAL FOR YOU!
SPECIAL DEAL?!
I CAN'T EVEN BEGIN TO TELL YOU WHAT IT IS.
SP

Super Spicy Ramen

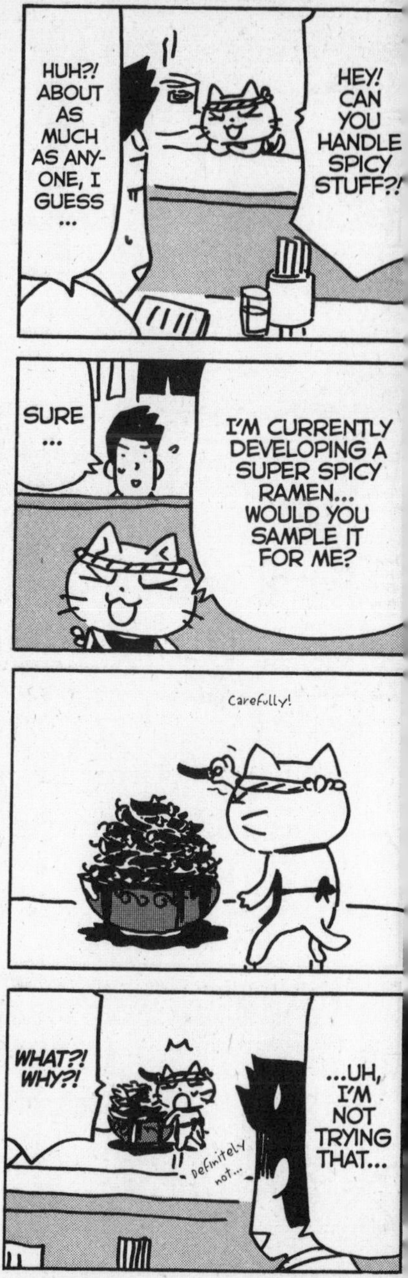
HEY! CAN YOU HANDLE SPICY STUFF?!
HUH?! ABOUT AS MUCH AS ANYONE, I GUESS...
I'M CURRENTLY DEVELOPING A SUPER SPICY RAMEN... WOULD YOU SAMPLE IT FOR ME?
SURE...
Carefully!
...UH, I'M NOT TRYING THAT...
WHAT?! WHY?!
Definitely not...

The Second Location

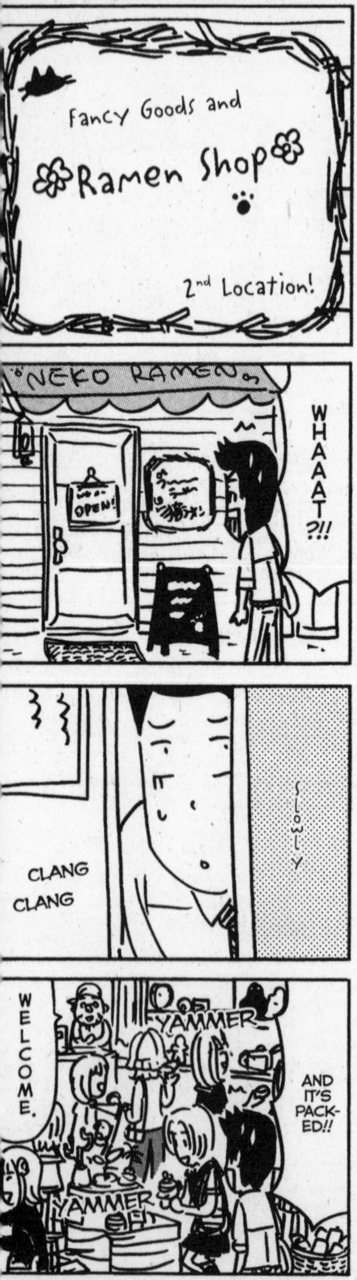

Fancy Goods and
Ramen Shop
2nd Location!
NEKO RAMEN
OPEN!
WHAAAAT?!!
SLOWLY
CLANG
CLANG
AND IT'S PACKED!!
WELCOME.
YAMMER
YAMMER

Chain

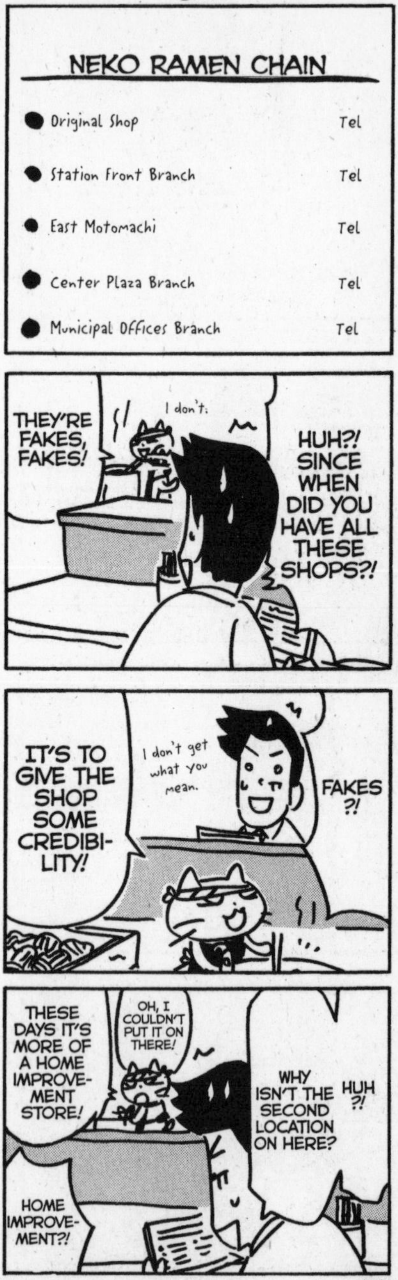

NEKO RAMEN CHAIN
Original Shop Tel
Station Front Branch Tel
East Motomachi Tel
Center Plaza Branch Tel
Municipal Offices Branch Tel
HUH?! SINCE WHEN DID YOU HAVE ALL THESE SHOPS?!
I don't.
THEY'RE FAKES, FAKES!
FAKES?!
I don't get what you mean.
IT'S TO GIVE THE SHOP SOME CREDIBILITY!
HUH?!
WHY ISN'T THE SECOND LOCATION ON HERE?
OH, I COULDN'T PUT IT ON THERE!
THESE DAYS IT'S MORE OF A HOME IMPROVEMENT STORE!
HOME IMPROVEMENT?!

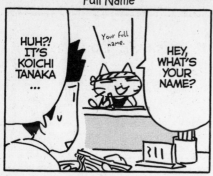

Full Name

HEY, WHAT'S YOUR NAME?
HUH?! IT'S KOICHI TANAKA ...
Your full name.
HOW DO YOU SPELL IT?
Well...
Scribble
Scribble
TANAKA USES "PADDY FIELD" AND "CENTER" KANJI CHARACTERS. KOICHI IS THE "HEALTH" AND "NUMBER ONE" CHARACTER.
To everyone at Neko Ramen
Koichi Tanaka
田中康一
12・10
HOW DOES IT LOOK?
WHA... WHAT IS THAT SUPPOSED TO BE?!

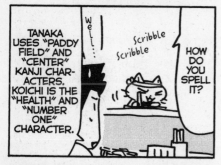

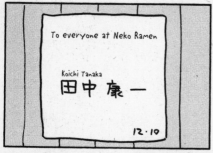

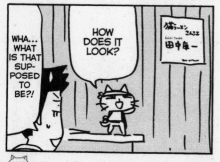

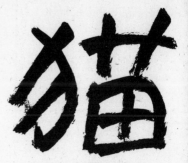

猫ラーメン

Chapter 4

Fried Rice and Ramen

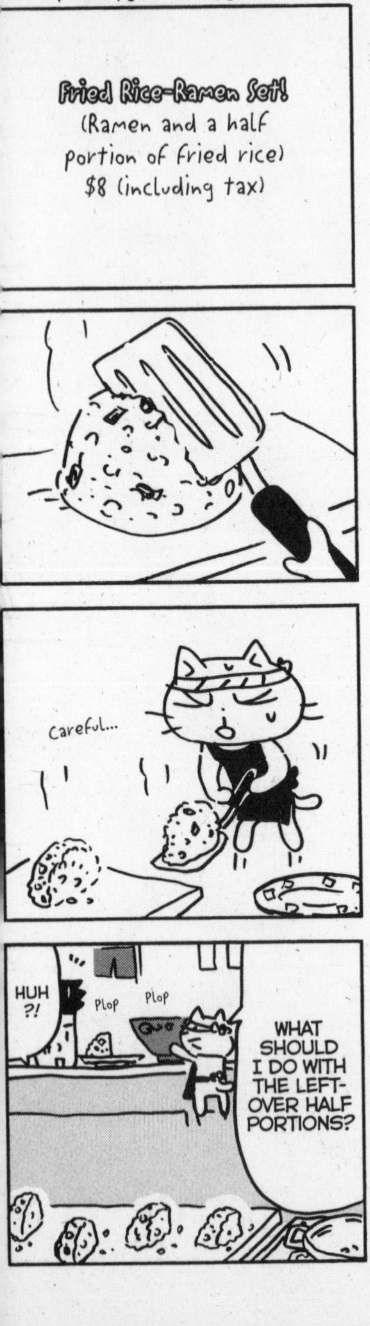

Fried Rice-Ramen Set!
(Ramen and a half portion of fried rice) $8 (including tax)
Careful...
HUH ?!
Plop
Plop
WHAT SHOULD I DO WITH THE LEFT-OVER HALF PORTIONS?

Autographs

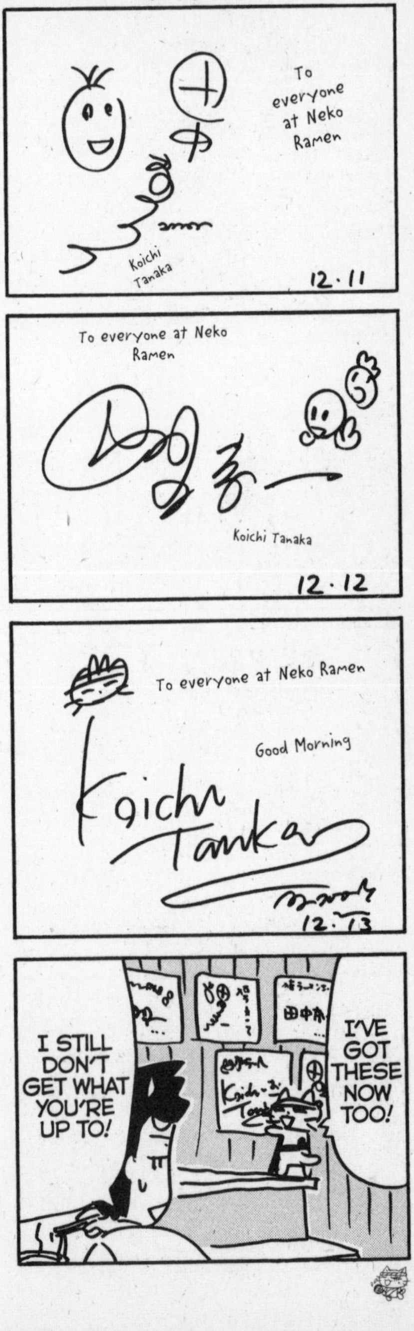

To everyone at Neko Ramen
Koichi Tanaka
12. 11
To everyone at Neko Ramen
Koichi Tanaka
12. 12
To everyone at Neko Ramen
Good Morning
Koichi Tanaka
12. 13
I STILL DON'T GET WHAT YOU'RE UP TO!
I'VE GOT THESE NOW TOO!

Article

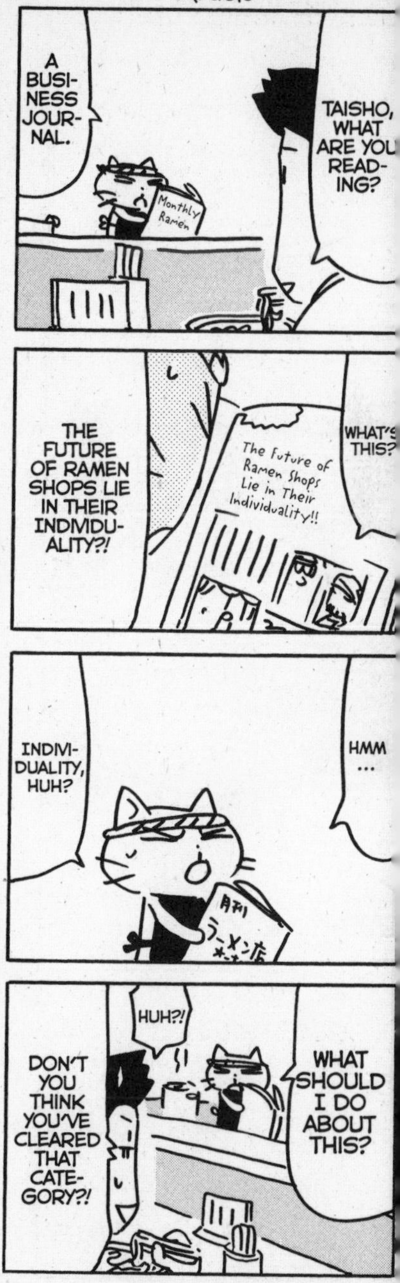
TAISHO, WHAT ARE YOU READING?
A BUSINESS JOURNAL.
Monthly Ramen
WHAT'S THIS?
The Future of Ramen Shops Lie in Their Individuality!!
THE FUTURE OF RAMEN SHOPS LIE IN THEIR INDIVIDUALITY?!
HMM...
INDIVIDUALITY, HUH?
月刊
ラーメン店
WHAT SHOULD I DO ABOUT THIS?
HUH?!
DON'T YOU THINK YOU'VE CLEARED THAT CATEGORY?!

Individuality

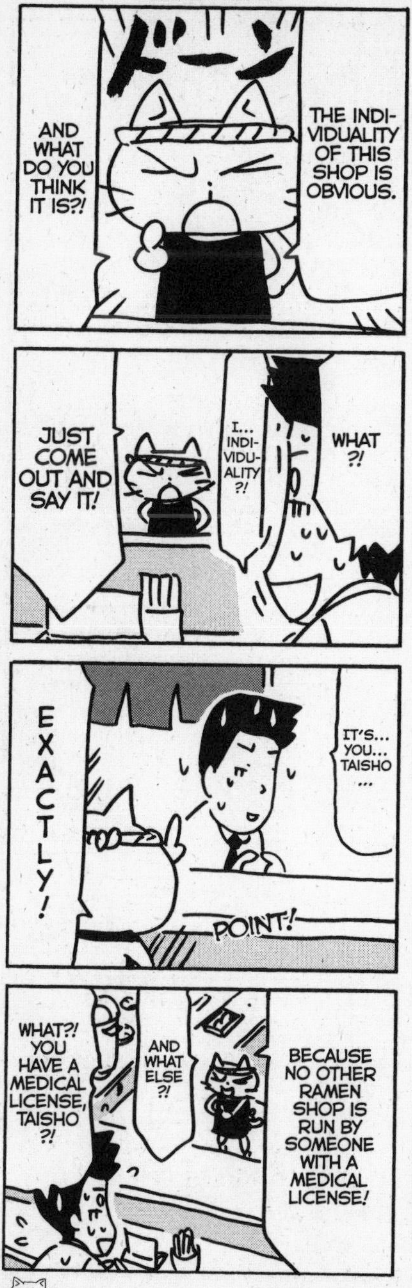
ドーン
THE INDIVIDUALITY OF THIS SHOP IS OBVIOUS.
AND WHAT DO YOU THINK IT IS?!
WHAT?!
I... INDIVIDUALITY?!
JUST COME OUT AND SAY IT!
IT'S... YOU... TAISHO...
EXACTLY!
POINT!
BECAUSE NO OTHER RAMEN SHOP IS RUN BY SOMEONE WITH A MEDICAL LICENSE!
AND WHAT ELSE?!
WHAT?! YOU HAVE A MEDICAL LICENSE, TAISHO?!

Security Measures

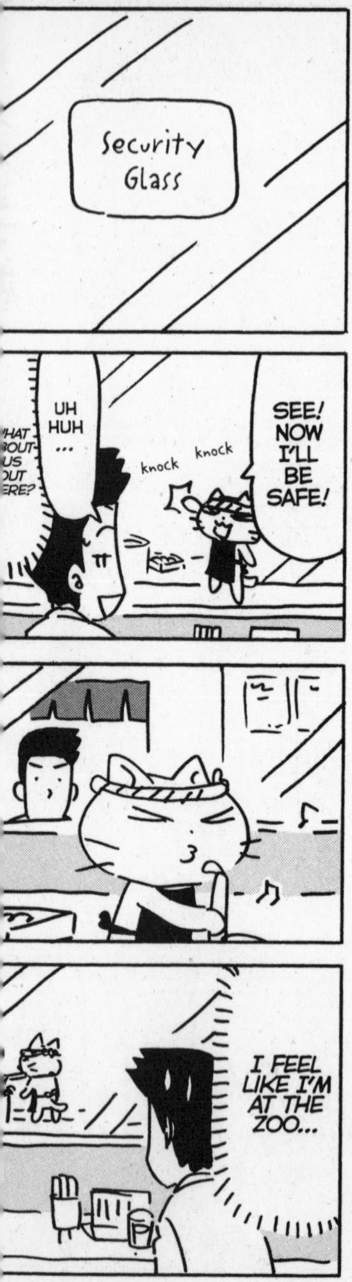
Security Glass
knock
knock
SEE! NOW I'LL BE SAFE!
UH HUH ...
I FEEL LIKE I'M AT THE ZOO...

Act

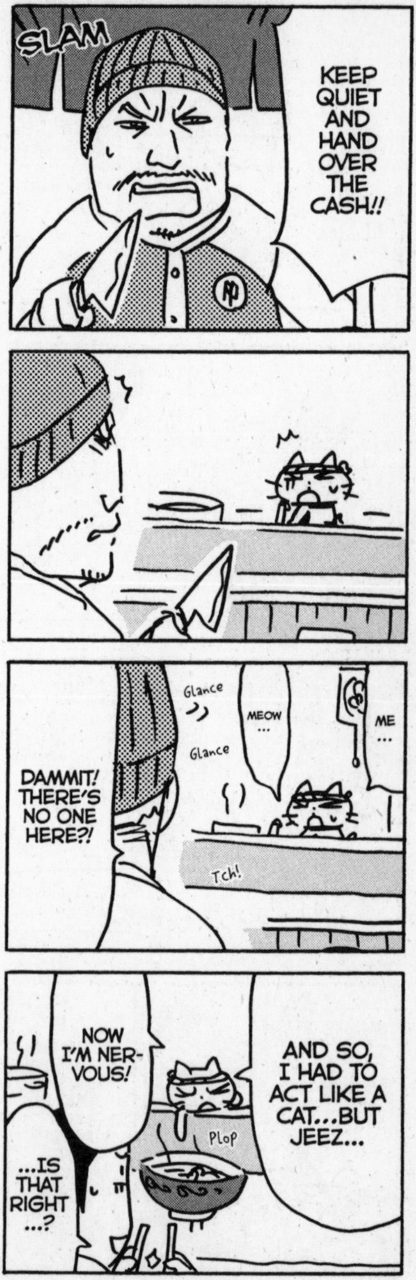
SLAM
KEEP QUIET AND HAND OVER THE CASH!!
DAMMIT! THERE'S NO ONE HERE?!
Glance
Glance
MEOW ...
ME ...
Tch!
AND SO, I HAD TO ACT LIKE A CAT...BUT JEEZ...
NOW I'M NERVOUS!
Plop
...IS THAT RIGHT ...?

The Process of Elimination

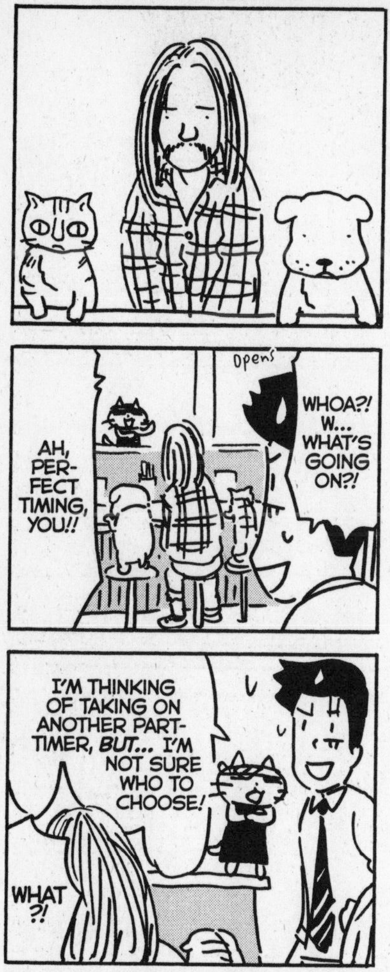
Opens
WHOA?! W... WHAT'S GOING ON?!
AH, PER-FECT TIMING, YOU!!
I'M THINKING OF TAKING ON ANOTHER PART-TIMER, *BUT*... I'M NOT SURE WHO TO CHOOSE!
WHAT?!
FOR START-ERS...I THINK THE DOG IS DEFI-NITELY OUT...
Pant
Pant
Slap
I KNEW YOU'D AGREE WITH ME!!

Improvements

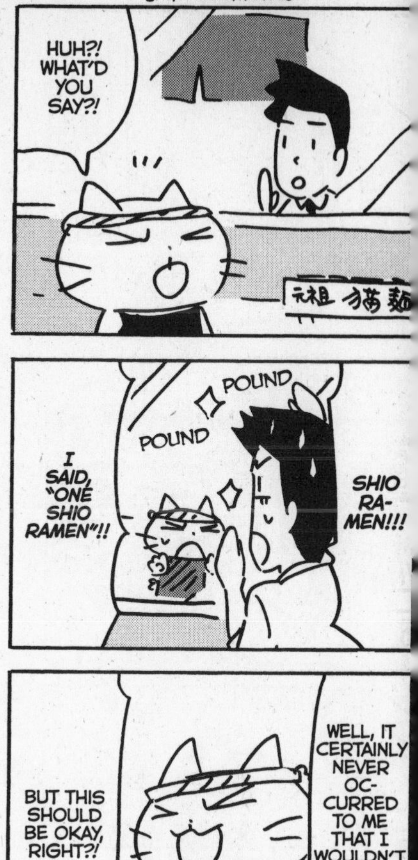
HUH?! WHAT'D YOU SAY?!
POUND
POUND
I SAID, "ONE SHIO RAMEN"!!
SHIO RA-MEN!!!
WELL, IT CERTAINLY NEVER OC-CURRED TO ME THAT I WOULDN'T BE ABLE TO HEAR YOU.
BUT THIS SHOULD BE OKAY, RIGHT?!
IT'S PER-FECT!
THIS IS EVEN MORE LIKE A ZOO...

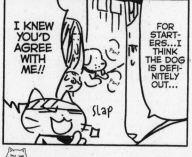

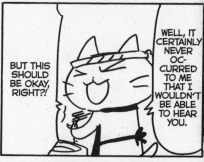

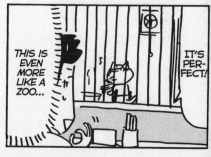

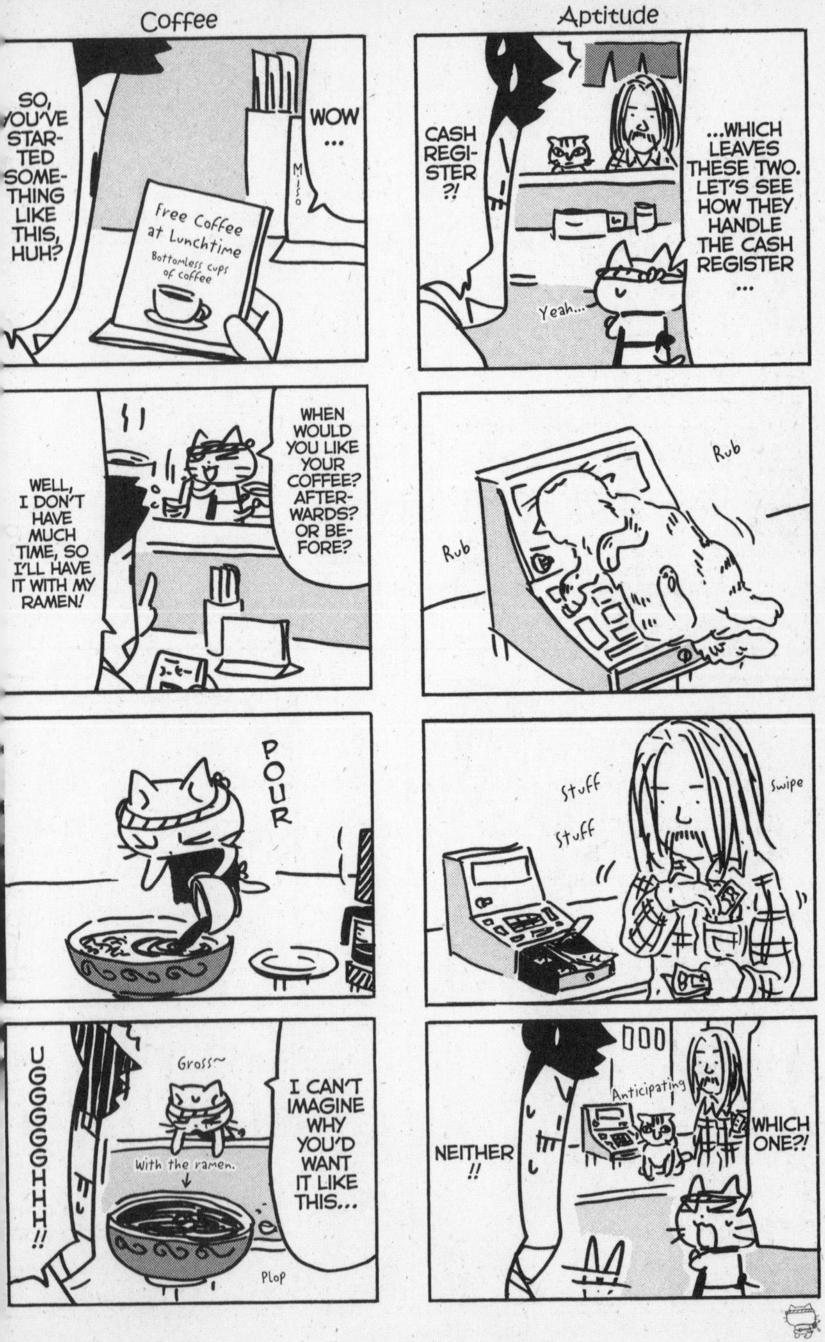
Coffee
SO, YOU'VE STARTED SOMETHING LIKE THIS, HUH?
WOW...
M I S O
Free Coffee at Lunchtime
Bottomless cups of coffee
WHEN WOULD YOU LIKE YOUR COFFEE? AFTERWARDS? OR BEFORE?
WELL, I DON'T HAVE MUCH TIME, SO I'LL HAVE IT WITH MY RAMEN!
POUR
Gross~
With the ramen.
UGGGGGHHH!!
I CAN'T IMAGINE WHY YOU'D WANT IT LIKE THIS...
Plop
Aptitude
CASH REGISTER?!
...WHICH LEAVES THESE TWO. LET'S SEE HOW THEY HANDLE THE CASH REGISTER...
Yeah...
Rub
Rub
Stuff
Stuff
Swipe
Anticipating
NEITHER!!
WHICH ONE?!

Quick Thinking

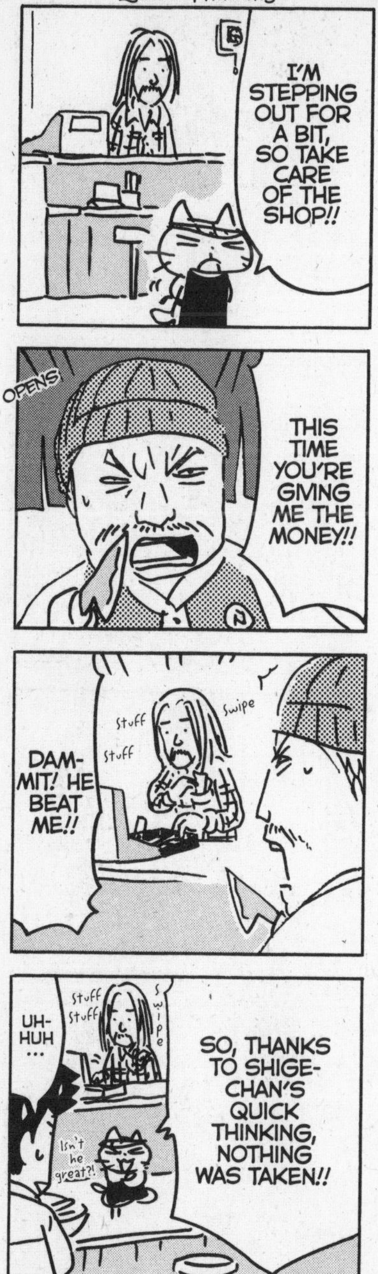
I'M STEPPING OUT FOR A BIT, SO TAKE CARE OF THE SHOP!!
OPENS
THIS TIME YOU'RE GIVING ME THE MONEY!!
Stuff
Stuff
Swipe
DAMMIT! HE BEAT ME!!
UH-HUH...
Stuff
Stuff
Swipe
Isn't he great?!
SO, THANKS TO SHIGE-CHAN'S QUICK THINKING, NOTHING WAS TAKEN!!

Shige-chan

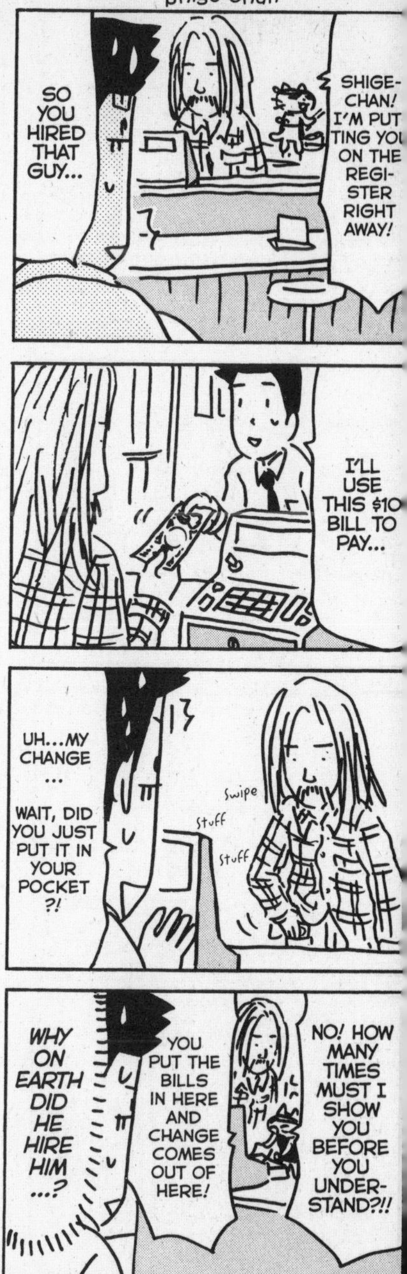
SHIGE-CHAN! I'M PUTTING YOU ON THE REGISTER RIGHT AWAY!
SO YOU HIRED THAT GUY...
I'LL USE THIS $10 BILL TO PAY...
UH...MY CHANGE...
WAIT, DID YOU JUST PUT IT IN YOUR POCKET?!
Swipe
Stuff
Stuff
NO! HOW MANY TIMES MUST I SHOW YOU BEFORE YOU UNDERSTAND?!!
YOU PUT THE BILLS IN HERE AND CHANGE COMES OUT OF HERE!
WHY ON EARTH DID HE HIRE HIM...?

Parental Love

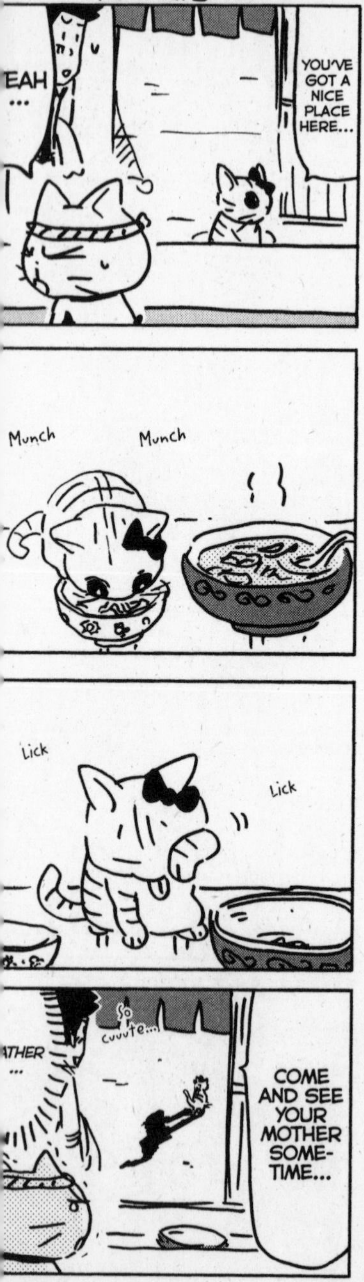
EAH
...
YOU'VE GOT A NICE PLACE HERE...
Munch
Munch
Lick
Lick
ATHER
...
So cuuute...
COME AND SEE YOUR MOTHER SOME-TIME...

The Mysterious Beautiful Cat

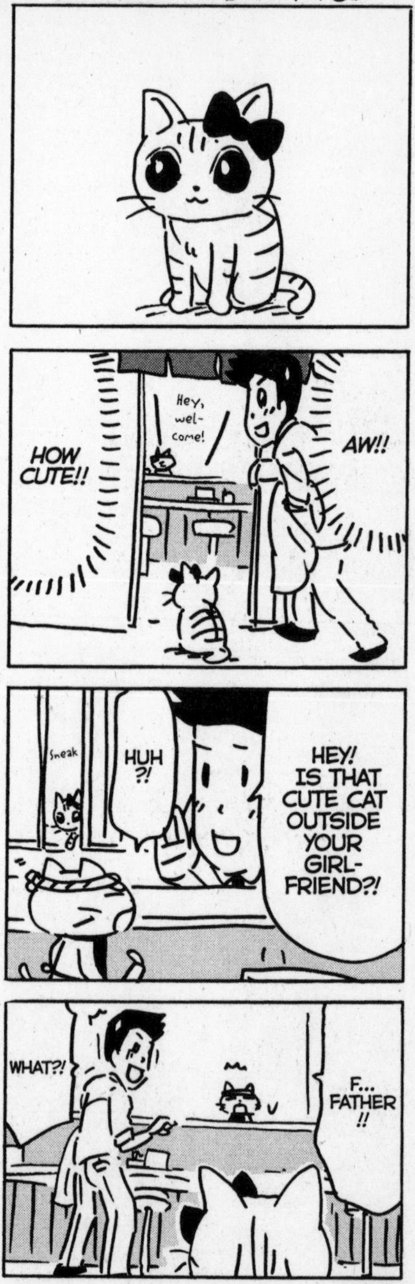
Hey, wel-come!
HOW CUTE!!
AW!!
Sneak
HUH ?!
HEY! IS THAT CUTE CAT OUTSIDE YOUR GIRL-FRIEND?!
WHAT?!
F... FATHER !!

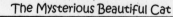

Special Menu

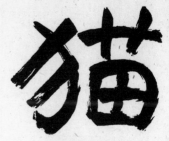

Chef's Special
Ramen
$7.80
IT'S A SIMPLE DISH. WANT IT?
AH! THAT SOUNDS GOOD!
DEFINI-TELY!
Chef's Special Ramen $7.80
Peel
Canned Cat Food
Tuna
Um...
Plop
Plop
Plop
IS IT TOO LATE TO CHANGE MY OR-DER?
祖猫麺

猫ラーメン

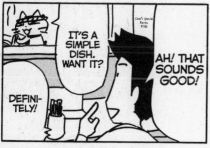

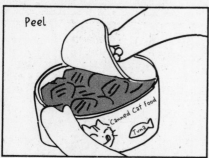

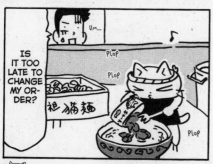

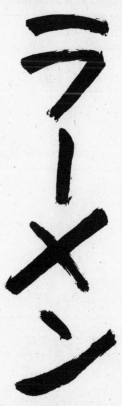

Chapter 5

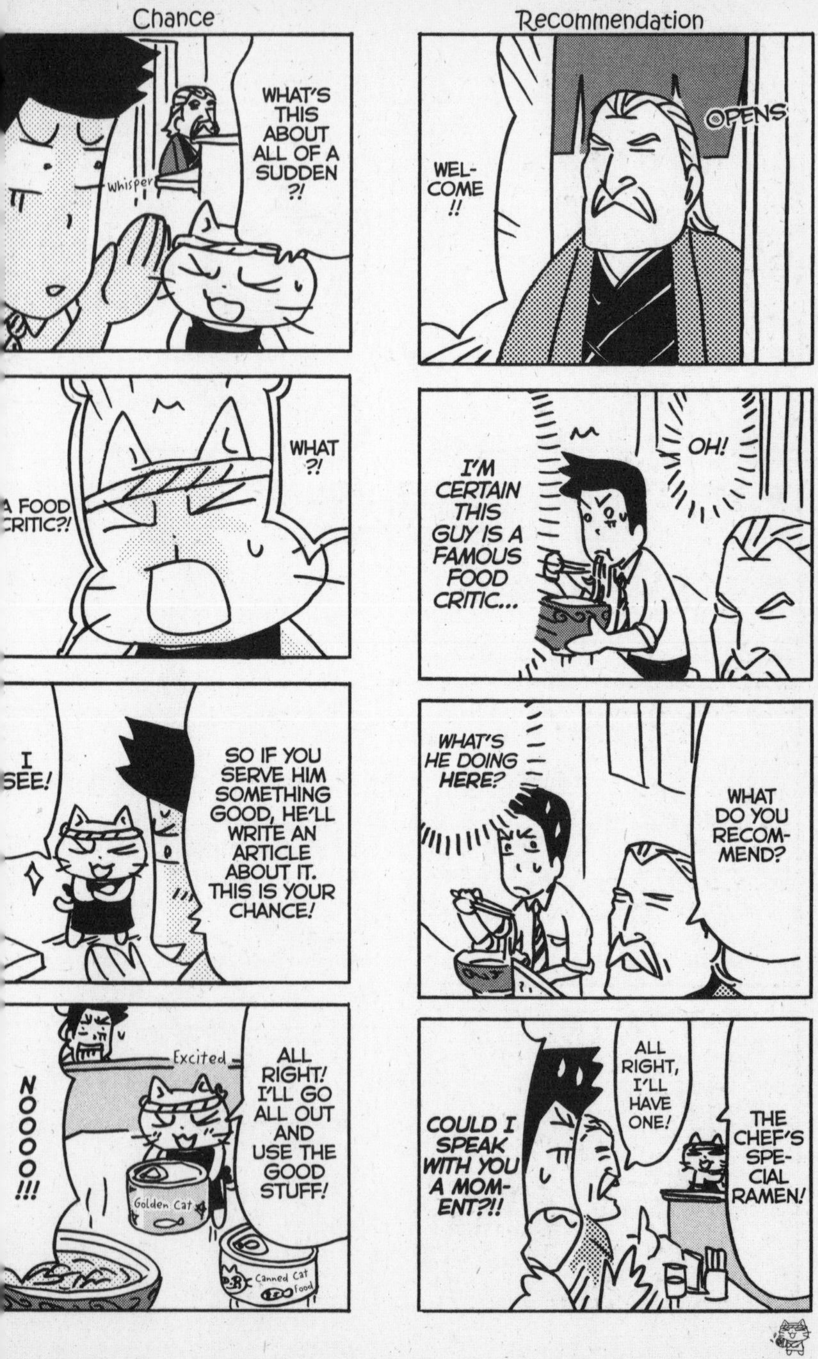
Recommendation
OPENS
WEL-COME!!
OH!
I'M CERTAIN THIS GUY IS A FAMOUS FOOD CRITIC...
WHAT DO YOU RECOM-MEND?
WHAT'S HE DOING HERE?
THE CHEF'S SPE-CIAL RAMEN!
ALL RIGHT, I'LL HAVE ONE!
COULD I SPEAK WITH YOU A MOM-ENT?!!
Chance
WHAT'S THIS ABOUT ALL OF A SUDDEN?!
Whisper
WHAT?!
A FOOD CRITIC?!
SO IF YOU SERVE HIM SOMETHING GOOD, HE'LL WRITE AN ARTICLE ABOUT IT. THIS IS YOUR CHANCE!
I SEE!
ALL RIGHT! I'LL GO ALL OUT AND USE THE GOOD STUFF!
Excited
Golden Cat
Canned Cat Food
NOOOOO!!!

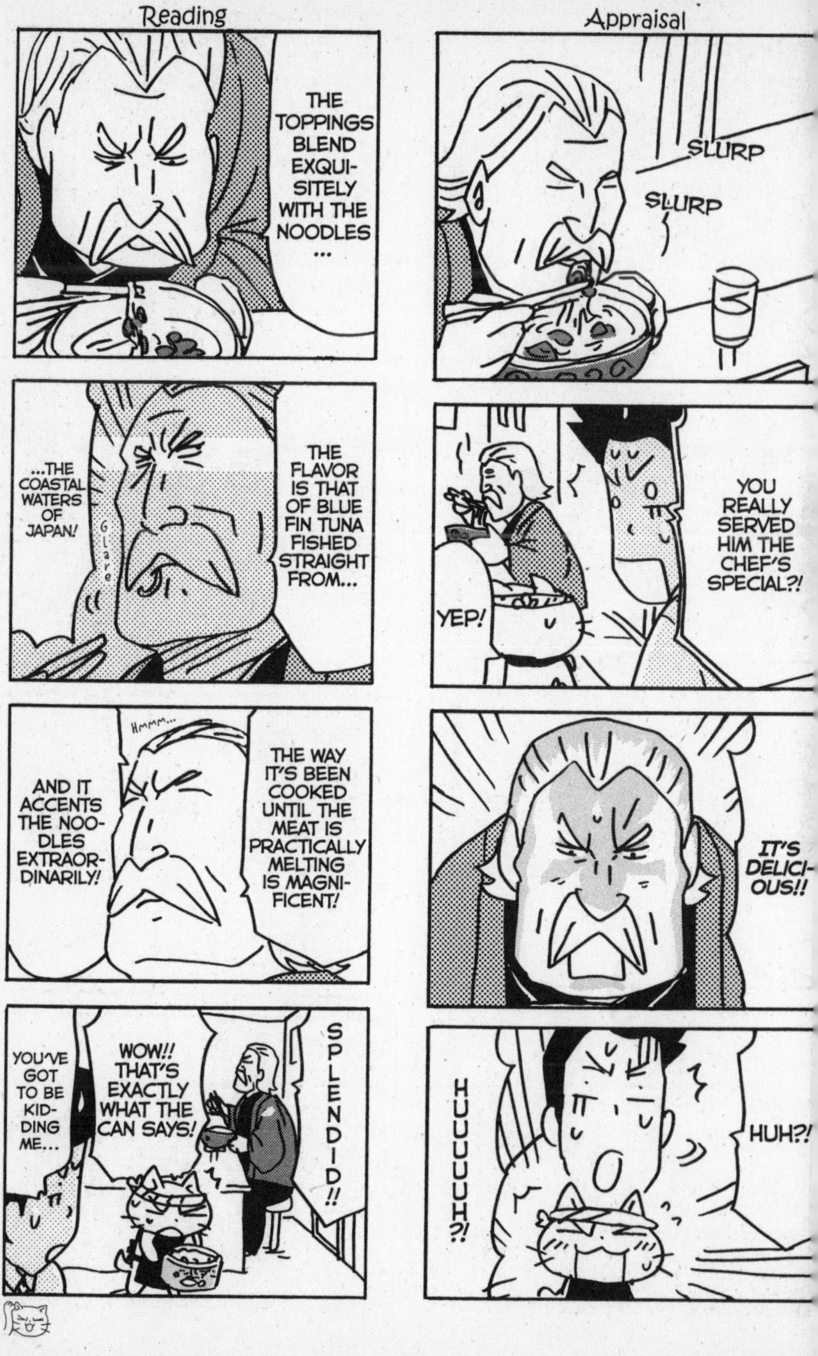
Appraisal
SLURP
SLURP
YOU REALLY SERVED HIM THE CHEF'S SPECIAL?!
YEP!
IT'S DELICIOUS!!
HUH?!
HUUUUUH?!
Reading
THE TOPPINGS BLEND EXQUISITELY WITH THE NOODLES...
THE FLAVOR IS THAT OF BLUE FIN TUNA FISHED STRAIGHT FROM...
Glare
...THE COASTAL WATERS OF JAPAN!
THE WAY IT'S BEEN COOKED UNTIL THE MEAT IS PRACTICALLY MELTING IS MAGNIFICENT!
HMMM...
AND IT ACCENTS THE NOODLES EXTRAORDINARILY!
SPLENDID!!
WOW!! THAT'S EXACTLY WHAT THE CAN SAYS!
YOU'VE GOT TO BE KIDDING ME...

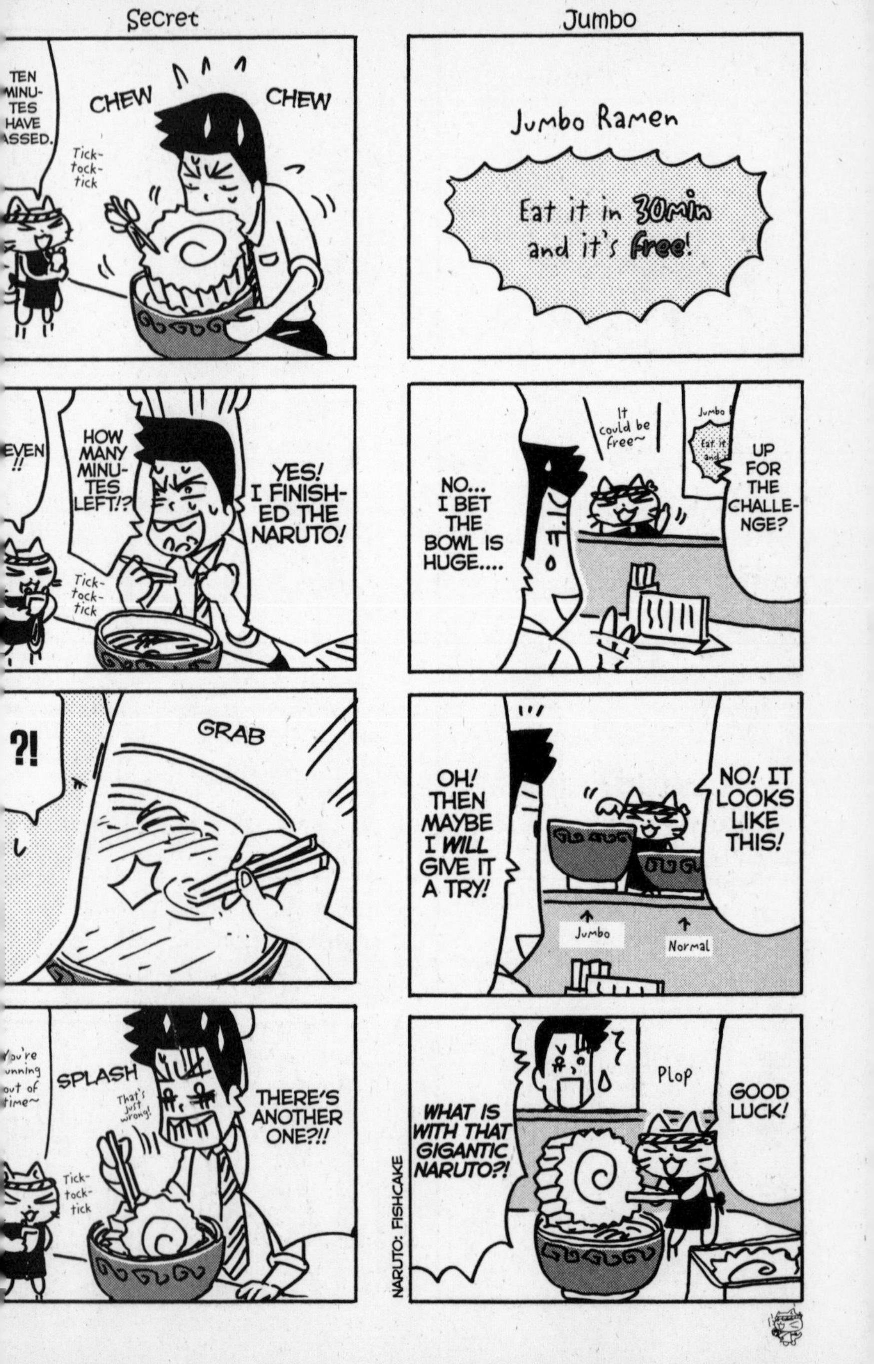
Jumbo
Jumbo Ramen
Eat it in 30min and it's free!
UP FOR THE CHALLENGE?
Jumbo
It could be free~
NO... I BET THE BOWL IS HUGE....
NO! IT LOOKS LIKE THIS!
OH! THEN MAYBE I WILL GIVE IT A TRY!
Jumbo
Normal
GOOD LUCK!
Plop
WHAT IS WITH THAT GIGANTIC NARUTO?!
NARUTO: FISHCAKE
Secret
CHEW CHEW
TEN MINU-TES HAVE ASSED.
Tick-tock-tick
YES! I FINISHED THE NARUTO!
HOW MANY MINUTES LEFT!?
EVEN !!
Tick-tock-tick
GRAB
?!
THERE'S ANOTHER ONE?!!
That's just wrong!
SPLASH
ou're unning out of time~
Tick-tock-tick

Weakness

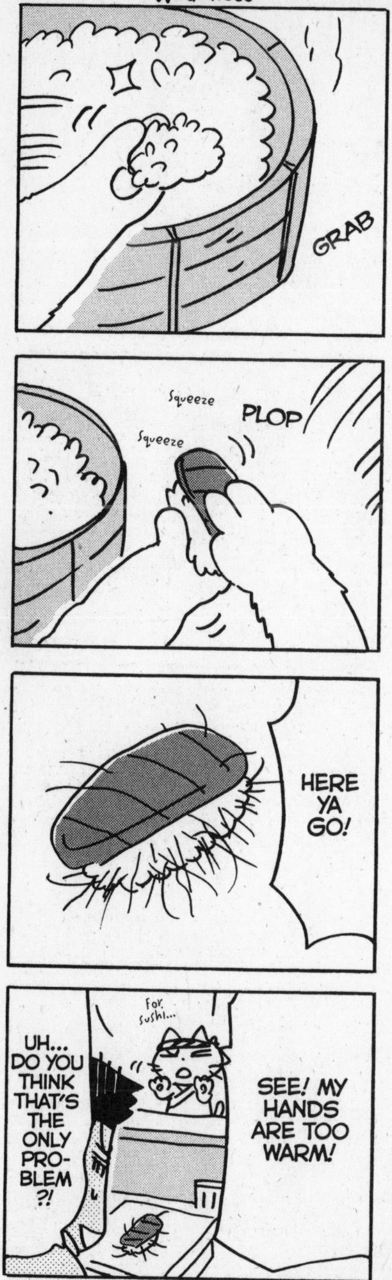
GRAB
Squeeze
Squeeze
PLOP
HERE YA GO!
For sushi...
SEE! MY HANDS ARE TOO WARM!
UH... DO YOU THINK THAT'S THE ONLY PRO-BLEM ?!

Taisho's Dreams

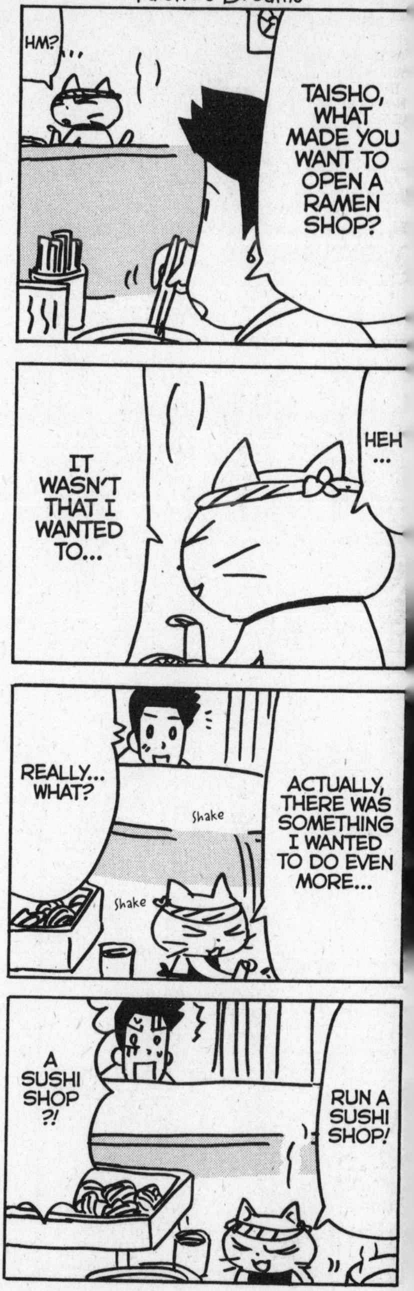
HM?
TAISHO, WHAT MADE YOU WANT TO OPEN A RAMEN SHOP?
HEH ...
IT WASN'T THAT I WANTED TO...
ACTUALLY, THERE WAS SOMETHING I WANTED TO DO EVEN MORE...
Shake
Shake
REALLY... WHAT?
RUN A SUSHI SHOP!
A SUSHI SHOP ?!

Longing

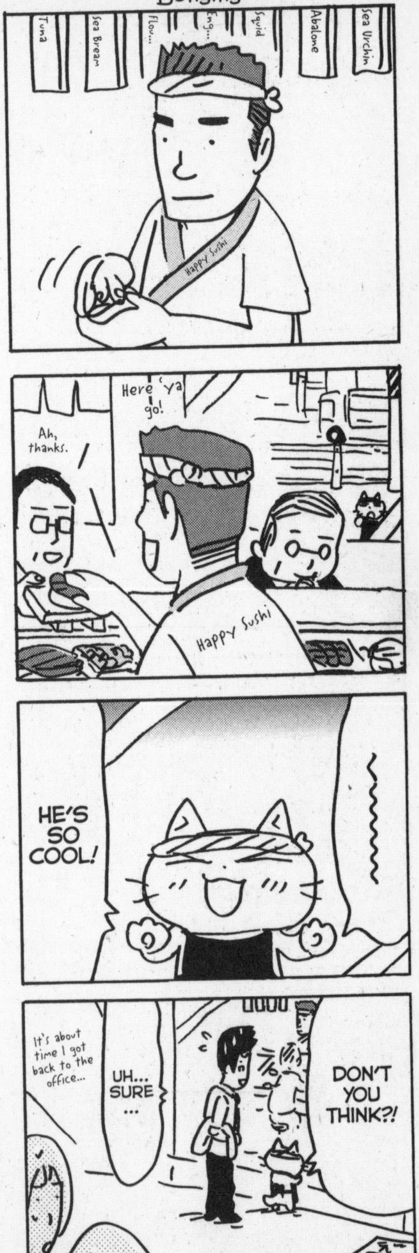

Sea Urchin
Abalone
Squid
Eng...
Flou...
Sea Bream
Tuna
Happy Sushi
Here 'ya go!
Ah, thanks.
Happy Sushi
HE'S SO COOL!
DON'T YOU THINK?!
UH... SURE ...
It's about time I got back to the office...

Neko-ani, the Big Brother Cat

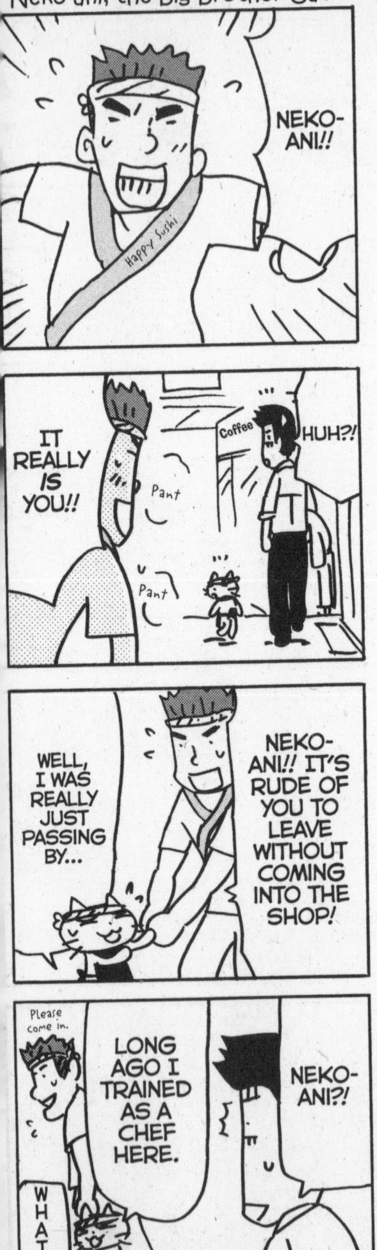

NEKO-ANI!!
Happy Sushi
HUH?!
Coffee
Pant
Pant
IT REALLY IS YOU!!
NEKO-ANI!! IT'S RUDE OF YOU TO LEAVE WITHOUT COMING INTO THE SHOP!
WELL, I WAS REALLY JUST PASSING BY...
NEKO-ANI?!
LONG AGO I TRAINED AS A CHEF HERE.
Please come in.
WHAT?!

The Training Days

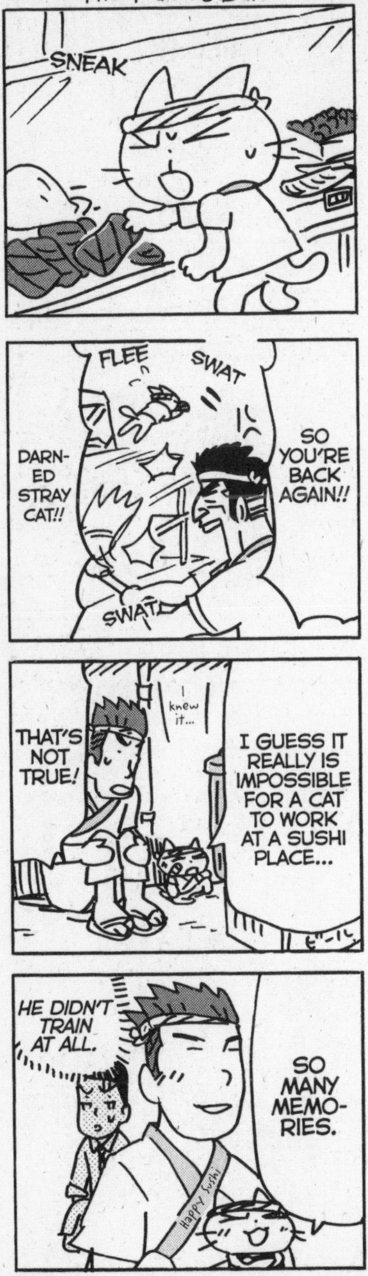
SNEAK
FLEE
SWAT
SO YOU'RE BACK AGAIN!!
DARNED STRAY CAT!!
SWAT
I knew it...
I GUESS IT REALLY IS IMPOSSIBLE FOR A CAT TO WORK AT A SUSHI PLACE...
THAT'S NOT TRUE!
SO MANY MEMORIES.
HE DIDN'T TRAIN AT ALL.
Happy Sushi

Memories

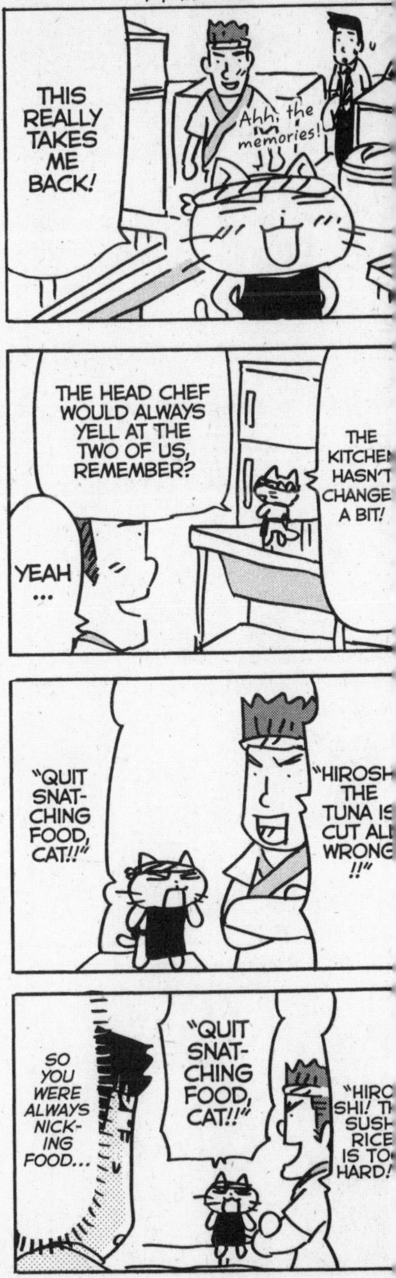
Ahh, the memories!
THIS REALLY TAKES ME BACK!
THE KITCHE HASN'T CHANGE A BIT!
THE HEAD CHEF WOULD ALWAYS YELL AT THE TWO OF US, REMEMBER?
YEAH ...
"HIROSH THE TUNA IS CUT AL WRONG !!"
"QUIT SNATCHING FOOD, CAT!!"
"HIRO SHI! T SUSH RICE IS TO HARD!
"QUIT SNATCHING FOOD, CAT!!"
SO YOU WERE ALWAYS NICKING FOOD...

Appraisal

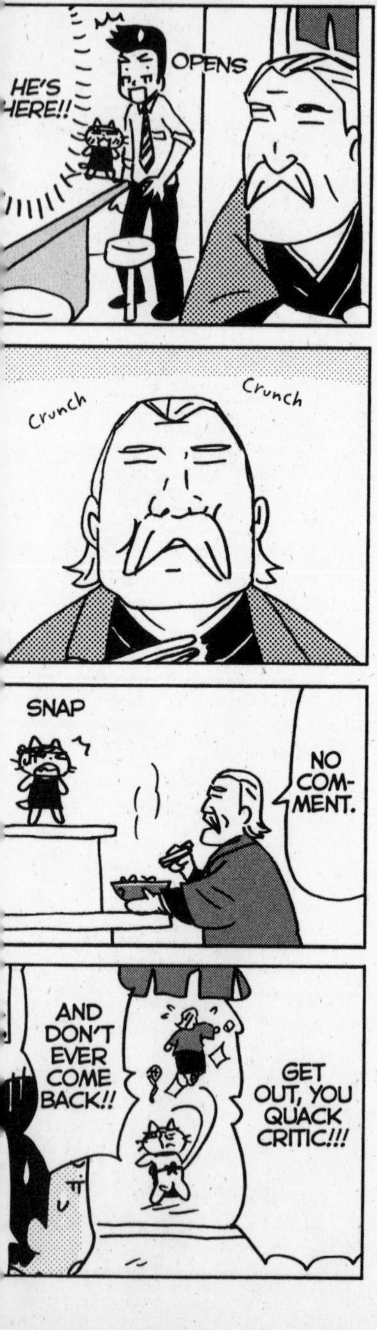
HE'S HERE!!
OPENS
Crunch
Crunch
SNAP
NO COM-MENT.
AND DON'T EVER COME BACK!!
GET OUT, YOU QUACK CRITIC!!!

Two!

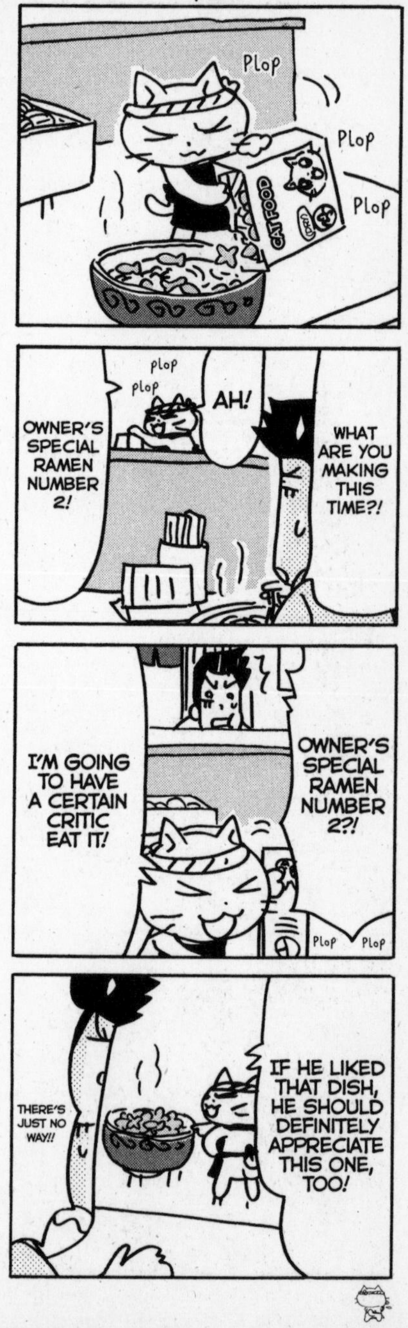
Plop
Plop
Plop
CATFOOD
plop
plop
AH!
OWNER'S SPECIAL RAMEN NUMBER 2!
WHAT ARE YOU MAKING THIS TIME?!
I'M GOING TO HAVE A CERTAIN CRITIC EAT IT!
OWNER'S SPECIAL RAMEN NUMBER 2?!
Plop
Plop
THERE'S JUST NO WAY!!
IF HE LIKED THAT DISH, HE SHOULD DEFINITELY APPRECIATE THIS ONE, TOO!

Mini Ramen

Extra-Value Lunch Combo
$8
Comes with mini-ramen
I recommend it!
UP FOR IT?! IT'S PRETTY FILLING!
SURE !!
Here you go!
HUH ?!
Mini Ramen
Ramen
SLAM
SLURP
JUST GREAT... THEY TASTE EXACTLY THE SAME...

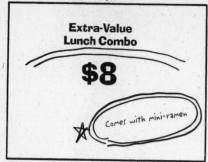

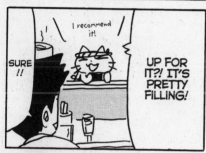

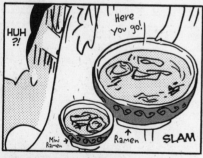

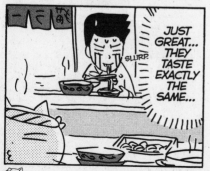

猫ラーメン

Chapter 6

Buffet Style

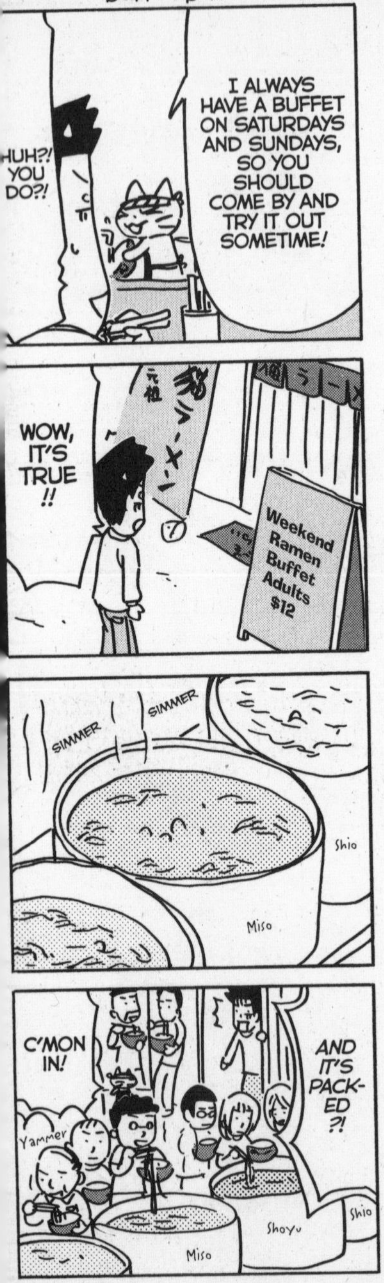
I ALWAYS HAVE A BUFFET ON SATURDAYS AND SUNDAYS, SO YOU SHOULD COME BY AND TRY IT OUT SOMETIME!
HUH?! YOU DO?!
WOW, IT'S TRUE!!
Weekend Ramen Buffet Adults $12
SIMMER
SIMMER
Shio
Miso
AND IT'S PACKED?!
C'MON IN!
Yammer
Shio
Shoyu
Miso

Which one?

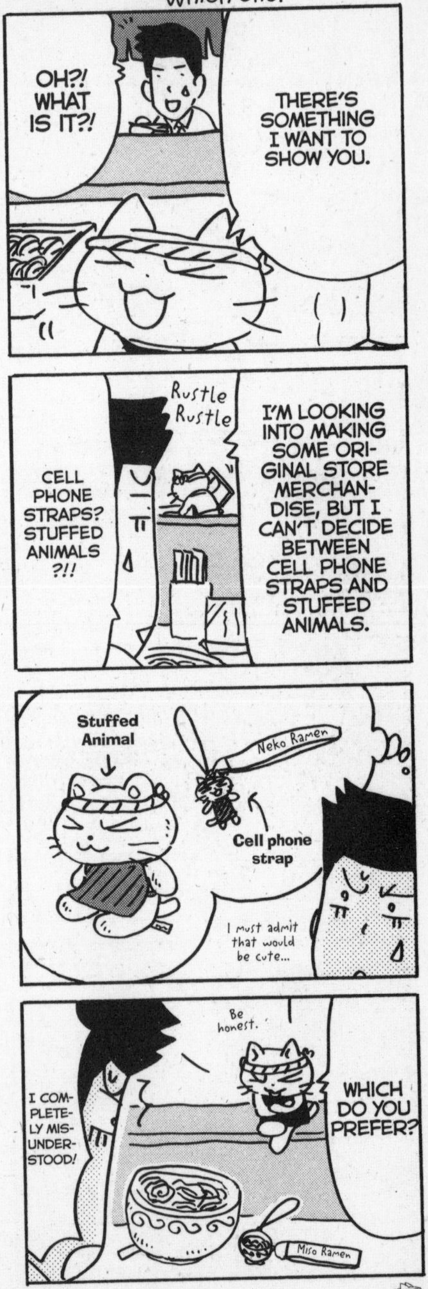
THERE'S SOMETHING I WANT TO SHOW YOU.
OH?! WHAT IS IT?!
I'M LOOKING INTO MAKING SOME ORIGINAL STORE MERCHANDISE, BUT I CAN'T DECIDE BETWEEN CELL PHONE STRAPS AND STUFFED ANIMALS.
Rustle Rustle
CELL PHONE STRAPS? STUFFED ANIMALS?!!
Stuffed Animal
Neko Ramen
Cell phone strap
I must admit that would be cute...
WHICH DO YOU PREFER?
Be honest.
I COMPLETELY MISUNDERSTOOD!
Miso Ramen

Little Brothers

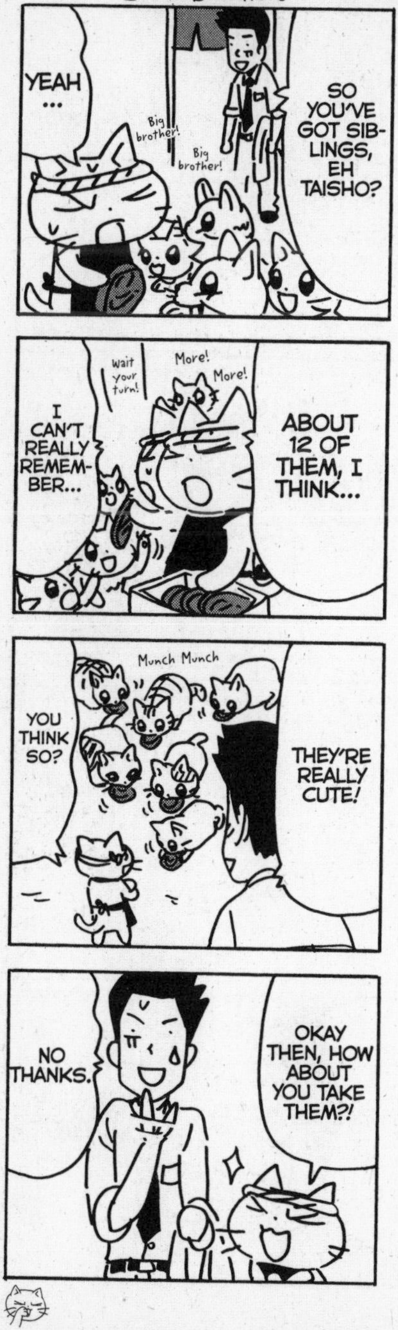
SO YOU'VE GOT SIBLINGS, EH TAISHO?
Big brother!
Big brother!
YEAH...
ABOUT 12 OF THEM, I THINK...
More!
More!
Wait your turn!
I CAN'T REALLY REMEMBER...
THEY'RE REALLY CUTE!
Munch Munch
YOU THINK SO?
OKAY THEN, HOW ABOUT YOU TAKE THEM?!
NO THANKS.

Big Brother!

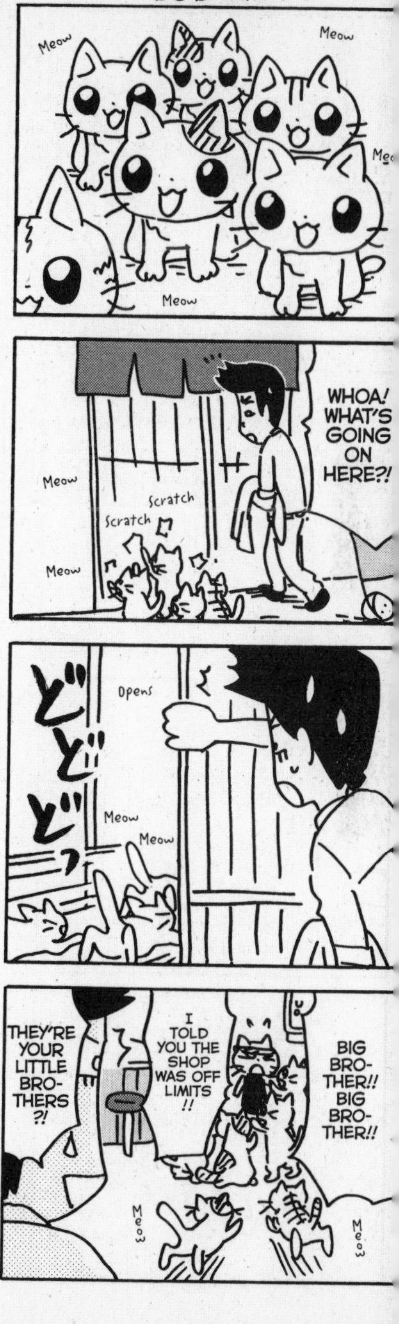
Meow
Meow
Meow
WHOA! WHAT'S GOING ON HERE?!
Scratch
Scratch
Meow
Meow
Opens
どどどどっ
Meow
Meow
BIG BROTHER!! BIG BROTHER!!
I TOLD YOU THE SHOP WAS OFF LIMITS!!
THEY'RE YOUR LITTLE BROTHERS?!
Meow
Meow

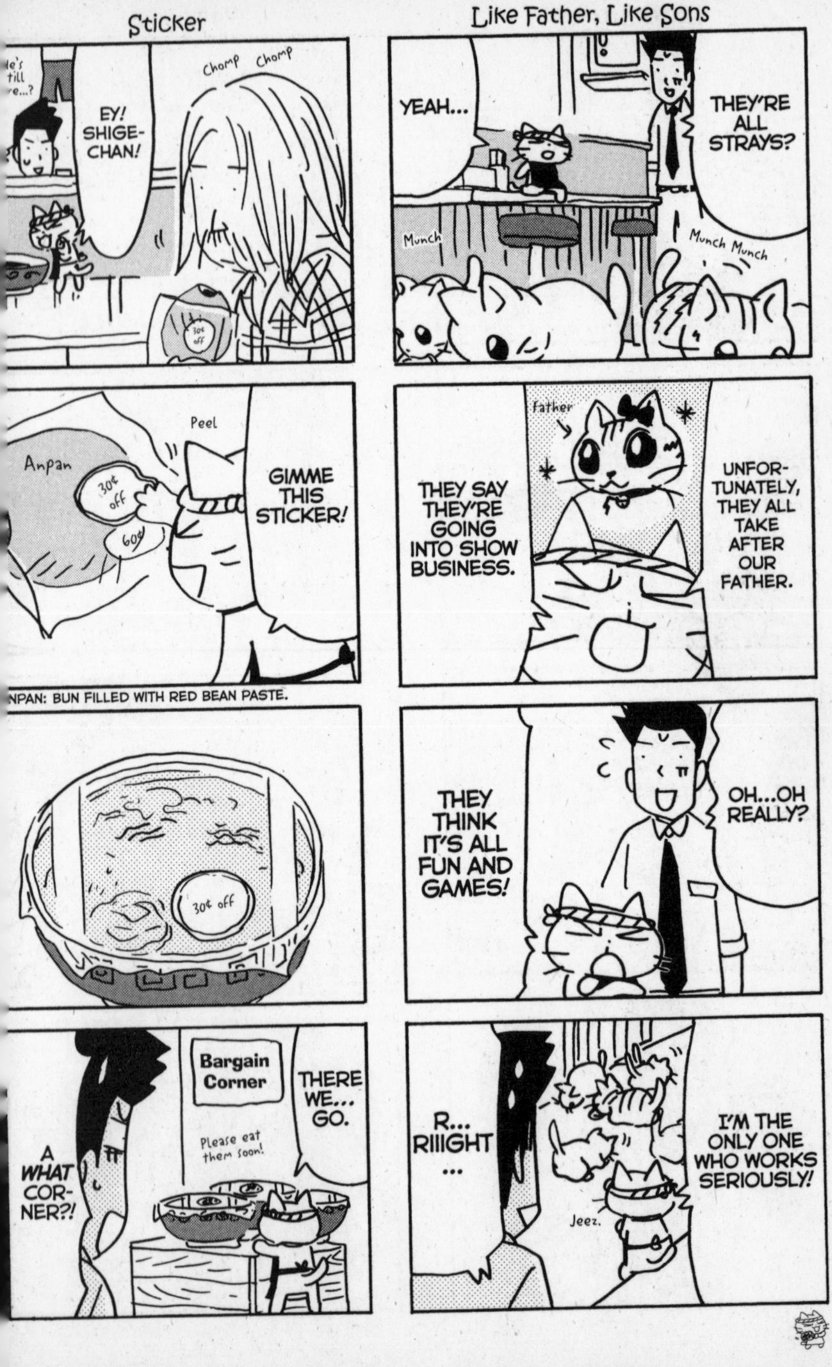
Like Father, Like Sons
YEAH...
THEY'RE ALL STRAYS?
Munch
Munch Munch
Father
THEY SAY THEY'RE GOING INTO SHOW BUSINESS.
UNFOR-TUNATELY, THEY ALL TAKE AFTER OUR FATHER.
THEY THINK IT'S ALL FUN AND GAMES!
OH...OH REALLY?
R... RIIIGHT ...
I'M THE ONLY ONE WHO WORKS SERIOUSLY!
Jeez.
Sticker
He's still here...?
EY! SHIGE-CHAN!
Chomp Chomp
30¢ off
Peel
Anpan
30¢ off
60¢
GIMME THIS STICKER!
NPAN: BUN FILLED WITH RED BEAN PASTE.
30¢ off
Bargain Corner
Please eat them soon!
THERE WE... GO.
A WHAT CORNER?!

Easy

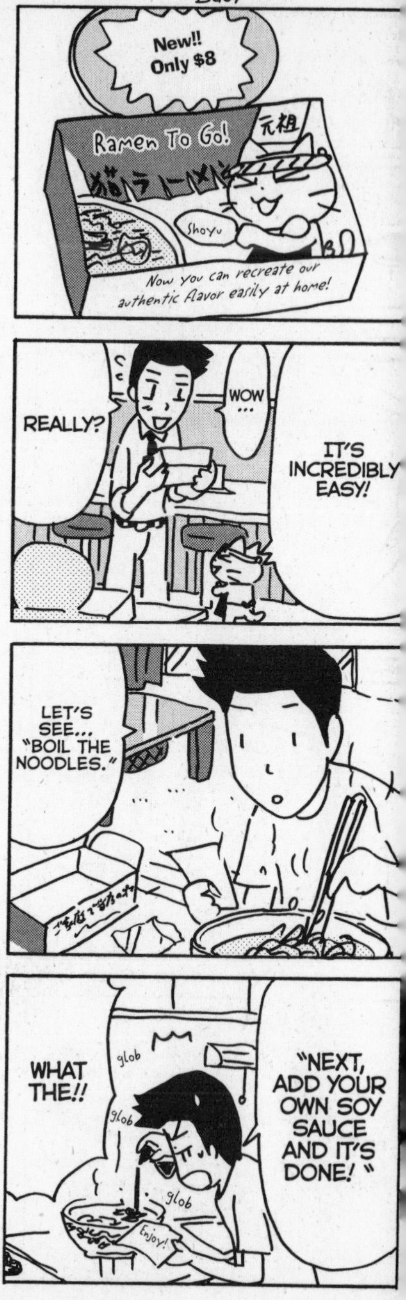

New!! Only $8
Ramen To Go!
元祖
Shoyu
Now you can recreate our authentic flavor easily at home!
IT'S INCREDIBLY EASY!
WOW...
REALLY?
LET'S SEE... "BOIL THE NOODLES."
...
...
...
"NEXT, ADD YOUR OWN SOY SAUCE AND IT'S DONE!"
WHAT THE!!
glob
glob
glob
Enjoy!

Xylitol

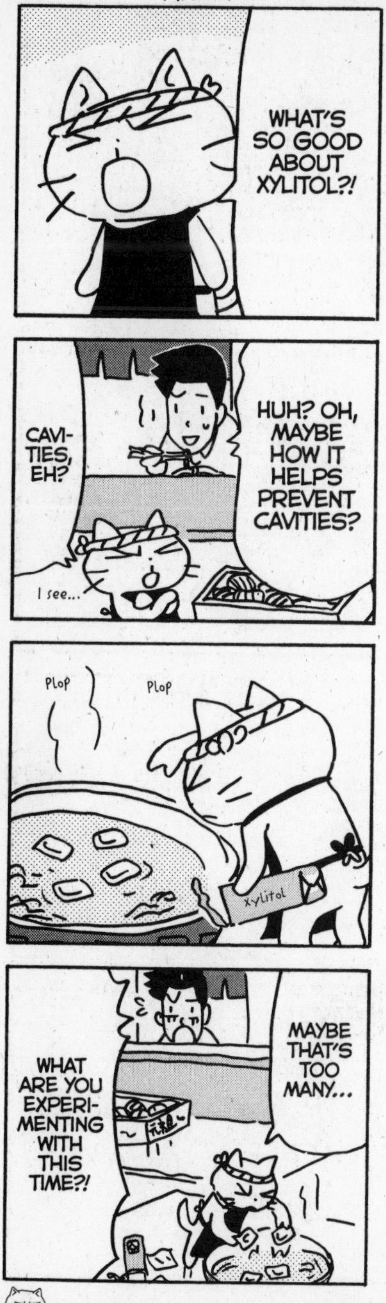

WHAT'S SO GOOD ABOUT XYLITOL?!
HUH? OH, MAYBE HOW IT HELPS PREVENT CAVITIES?
CAVITIES, EH?
I see...
Plop
Plop
Xylitol
MAYBE THAT'S TOO MANY...
WHAT ARE YOU EXPERIMENTING WITH THIS TIME?!
元祖

Driver's License

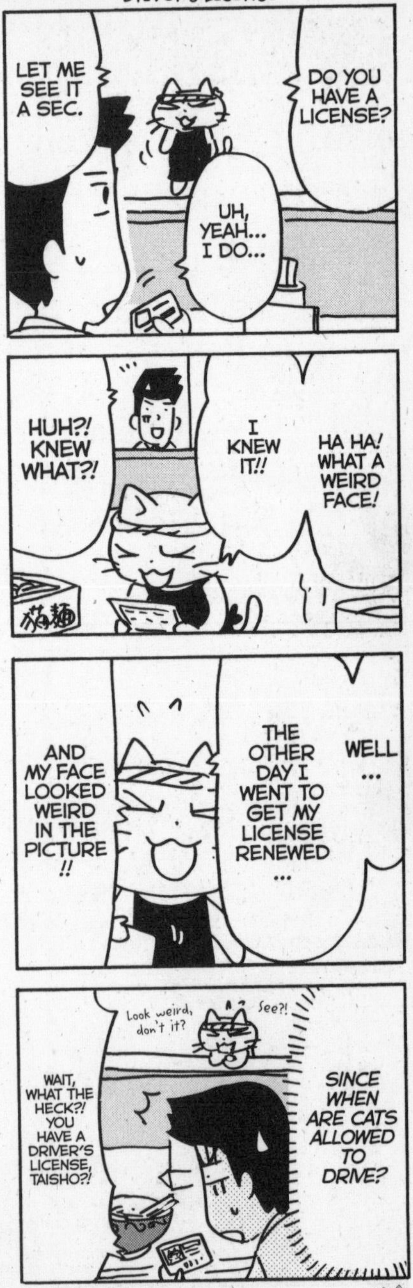
DO YOU HAVE A LICENSE?
UH, YEAH... I DO...
LET ME SEE IT A SEC.
HA HA! WHAT A WEIRD FACE!
I KNEW IT!!
HUH?! KNEW WHAT?!
WELL...
THE OTHER DAY I WENT TO GET MY LICENSE RENEWED...
AND MY FACE LOOKED WEIRD IN THE PICTURE!!
SINCE WHEN ARE CATS ALLOWED TO DRIVE?
See?!
Look weird, don't it?
WAIT, WHAT THE HECK?! YOU HAVE A DRIVER'S LICENSE, TAISHO?!

Stamps

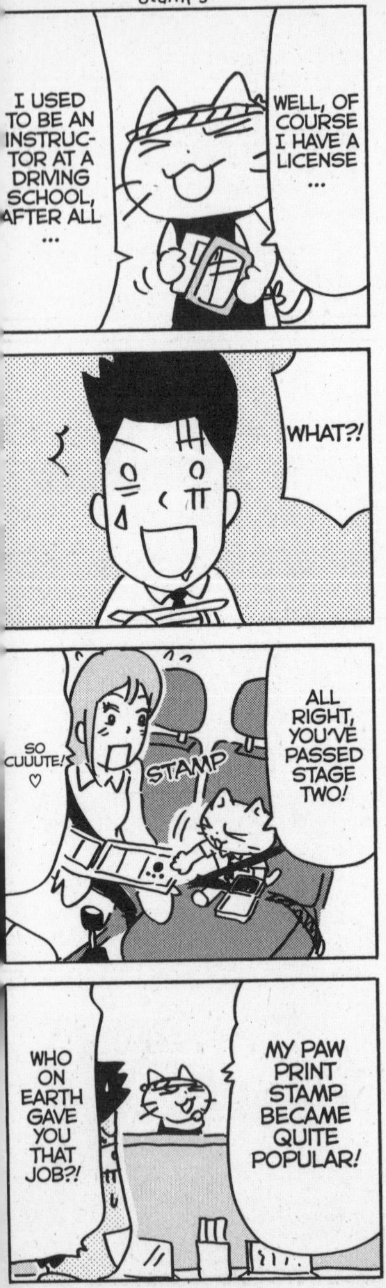
WELL, OF COURSE I HAVE A LICENSE...
I USED TO BE AN INSTRUCTOR AT A DRIVING SCHOOL, AFTER ALL...
WHAT?!
ALL RIGHT, YOU'VE PASSED STAGE TWO!
STAMP
SO CUUUTE! ♡
MY PAW PRINT STAMP BECAME QUITE POPULAR!
WHO ON EARTH GAVE YOU THAT JOB?!

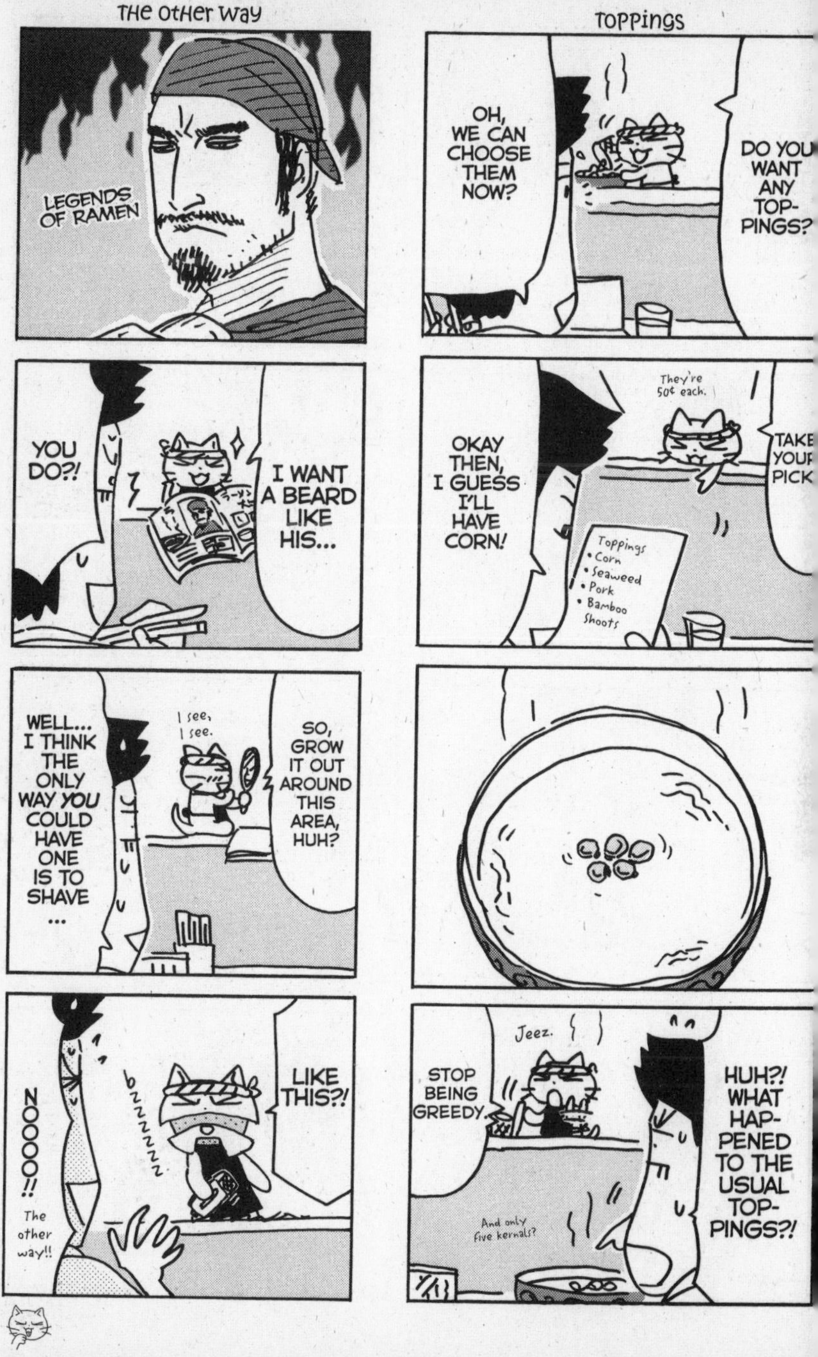

Toppings
DO YOU WANT ANY TOP-PINGS?
OH, WE CAN CHOOSE THEM NOW?
TAKE YOUR PICK
They're 50¢ each.
OKAY THEN, I GUESS I'LL HAVE CORN!
Toppings
• Corn
• Seaweed
• Pork
• Bamboo Shoots
HUH?! WHAT HAP-PENED TO THE USUAL TOP-PINGS?!
Jeez.
STOP BEING GREEDY.
And only five kernals?
The Other Way
LEGENDS OF RAMEN
I WANT A BEARD LIKE HIS...
YOU DO?!
SO, GROW IT OUT AROUND THIS AREA, HUH?
I see, I see.
WELL... I THINK THE ONLY WAY YOU COULD HAVE ONE IS TO SHAVE ...
LIKE THIS?!
bZZZZZZ
NOOOO!!
The other way!!

Purchasing

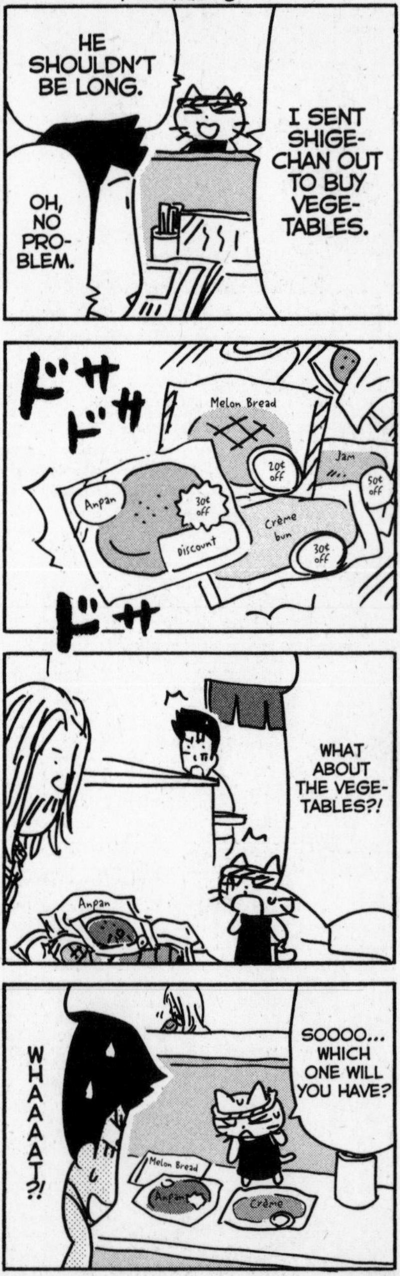

I SENT SHIGE-CHAN OUT TO BUY VEGE-TABLES.
HE SHOULDN'T BE LONG.
OH, NO PRO-BLEM.
ドサ
ドサ
Melon Bread
20¢ off
Jam
50¢ off
Anpan
30¢ off
Discount
Crème bun
30¢ off
ドサ
WHAT ABOUT THE VEGE-TABLES?!
Anpan
SOOOO... WHICH ONE WILL YOU HAVE?
WHAAAAAT?!
Melon Bread
Anpan
Crème

Cat Food

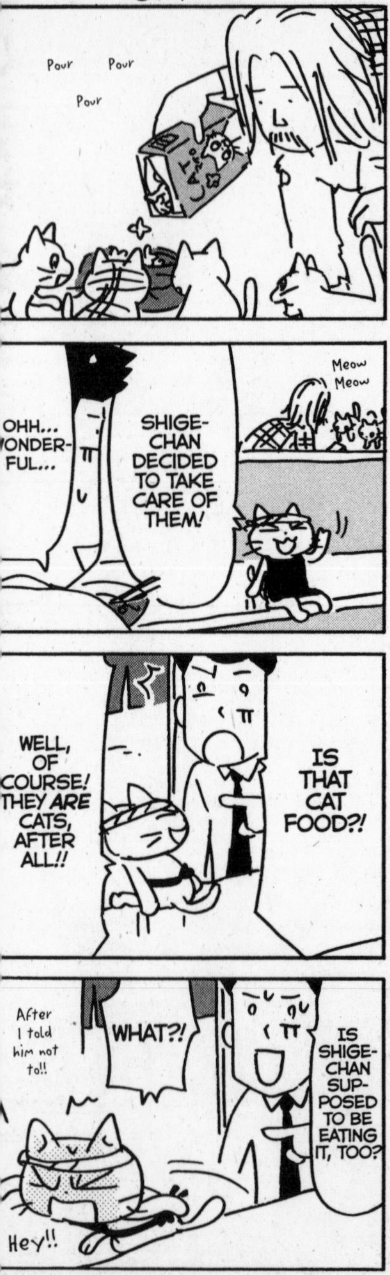

Pour
Pour
Pour
Meow
Meow
SHIGE-CHAN DECIDED TO TAKE CARE OF THEM!
OHH... ONDER-FUL...
IS THAT CAT FOOD?!
WELL, OF COURSE! THEY *ARE* CATS, AFTER ALL!!
IS SHIGE-CHAN SUP-POSED TO BE EATING IT, TOO?
WHAT?!
After I told him not to!!
Hey!!

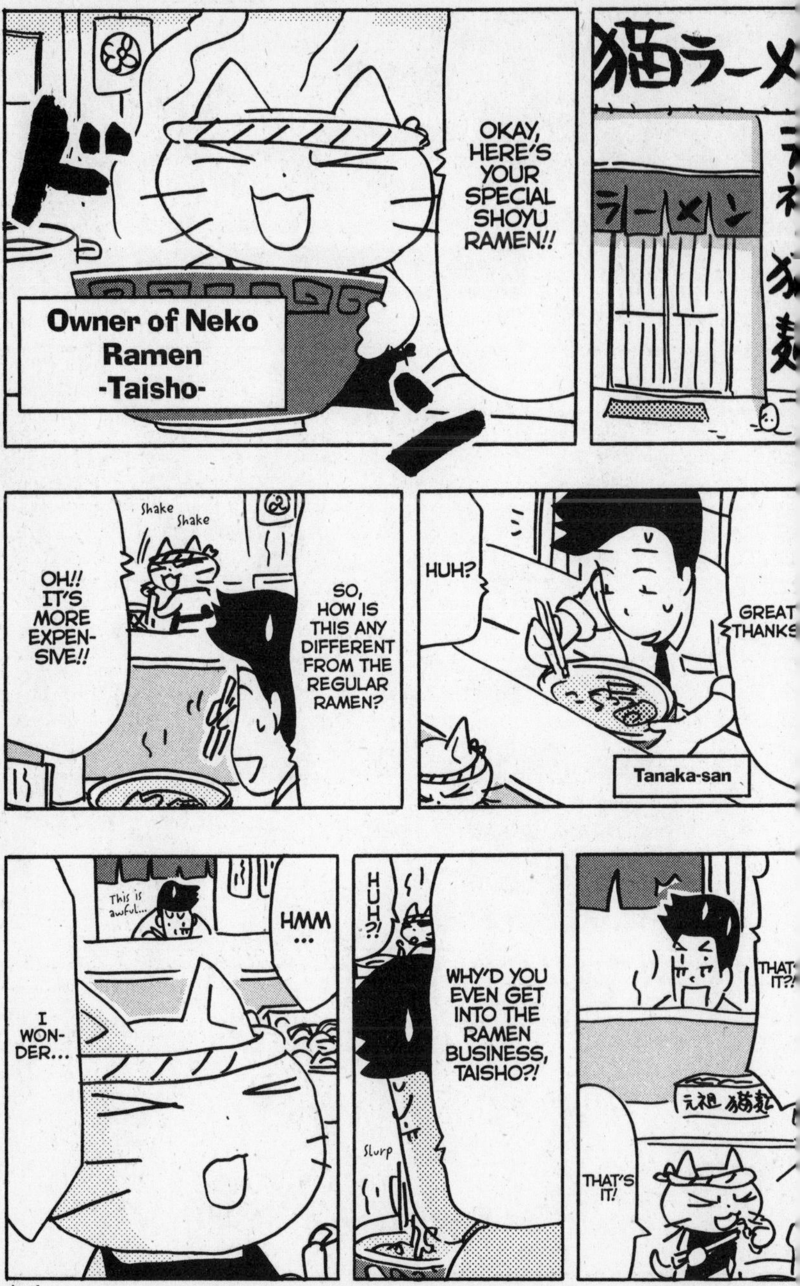
ラーメン
OKAY, HERE'S YOUR SPECIAL SHOYU RAMEN!!
Owner of Neko Ramen -Taisho-
GREAT THANKS
HUH?
Tanaka-san
SO, HOW IS THIS ANY DIFFERENT FROM THE REGULAR RAMEN?
Shake Shake
OH!! IT'S MORE EXPEN-SIVE!!
THAT'S IT?!
元祖 猫麺
THAT'S IT!
HUH?!
WHY'D YOU EVEN GET INTO THE RAMEN BUSINESS, TAISHO?!
Slurp
HMM...
This is awful...
I WON-DER...

猫ラーメン

Short Comic Special

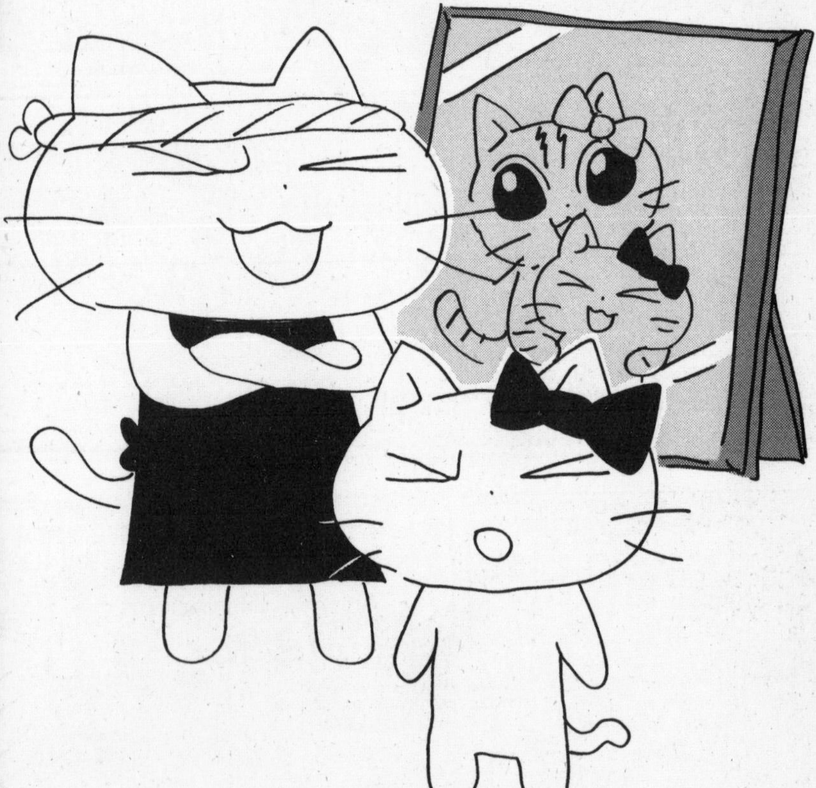

The Beginning of it All

Six years ago...

Tokyo

Taisho
(6 months old)

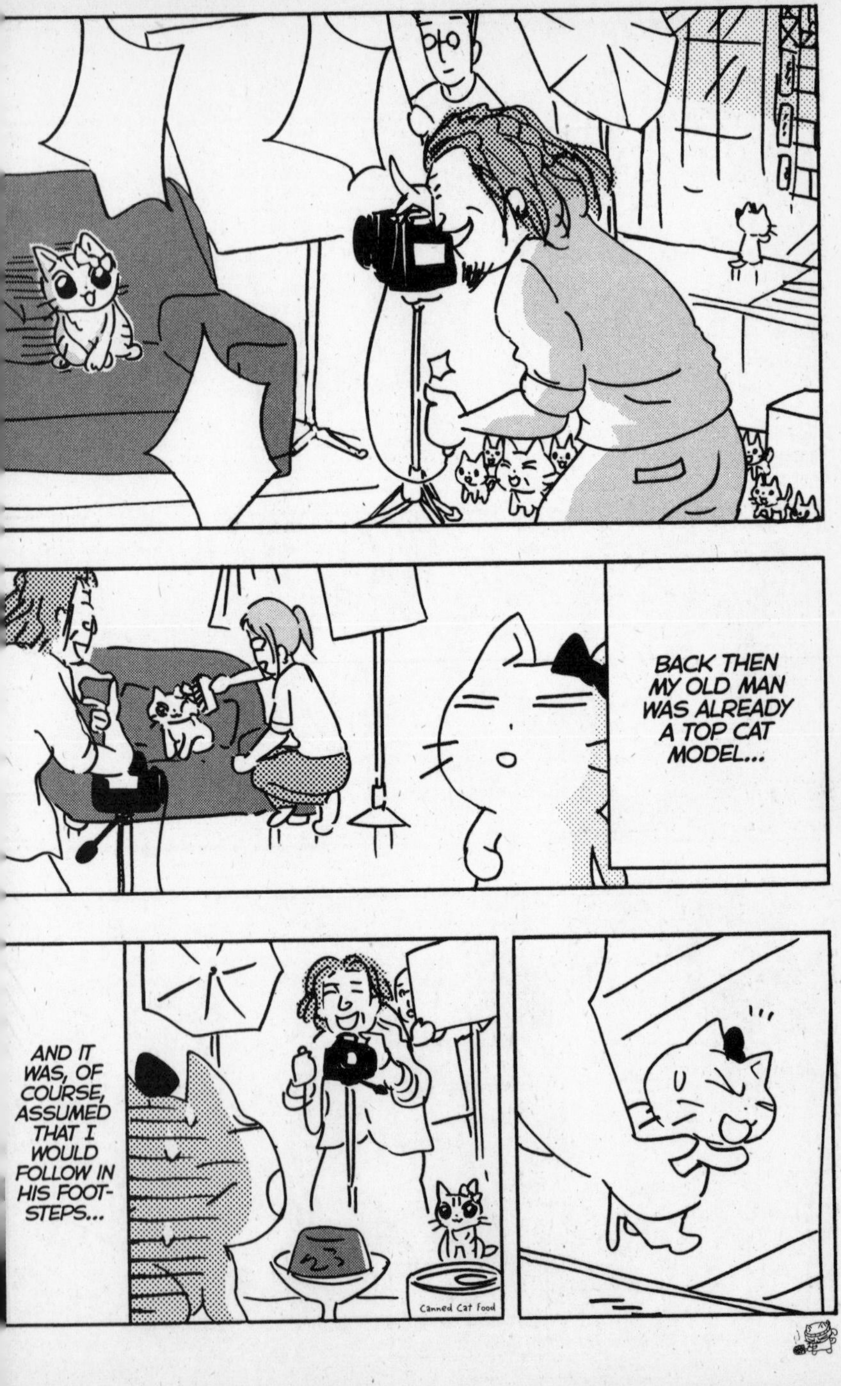
BACK THEN MY OLD MAN WAS ALREADY A TOP CAT MODEL...
AND IT WAS, OF COURSE, ASSUMED THAT I WOULD FOLLOW IN HIS FOOT-STEPS...
Canned Cat Food

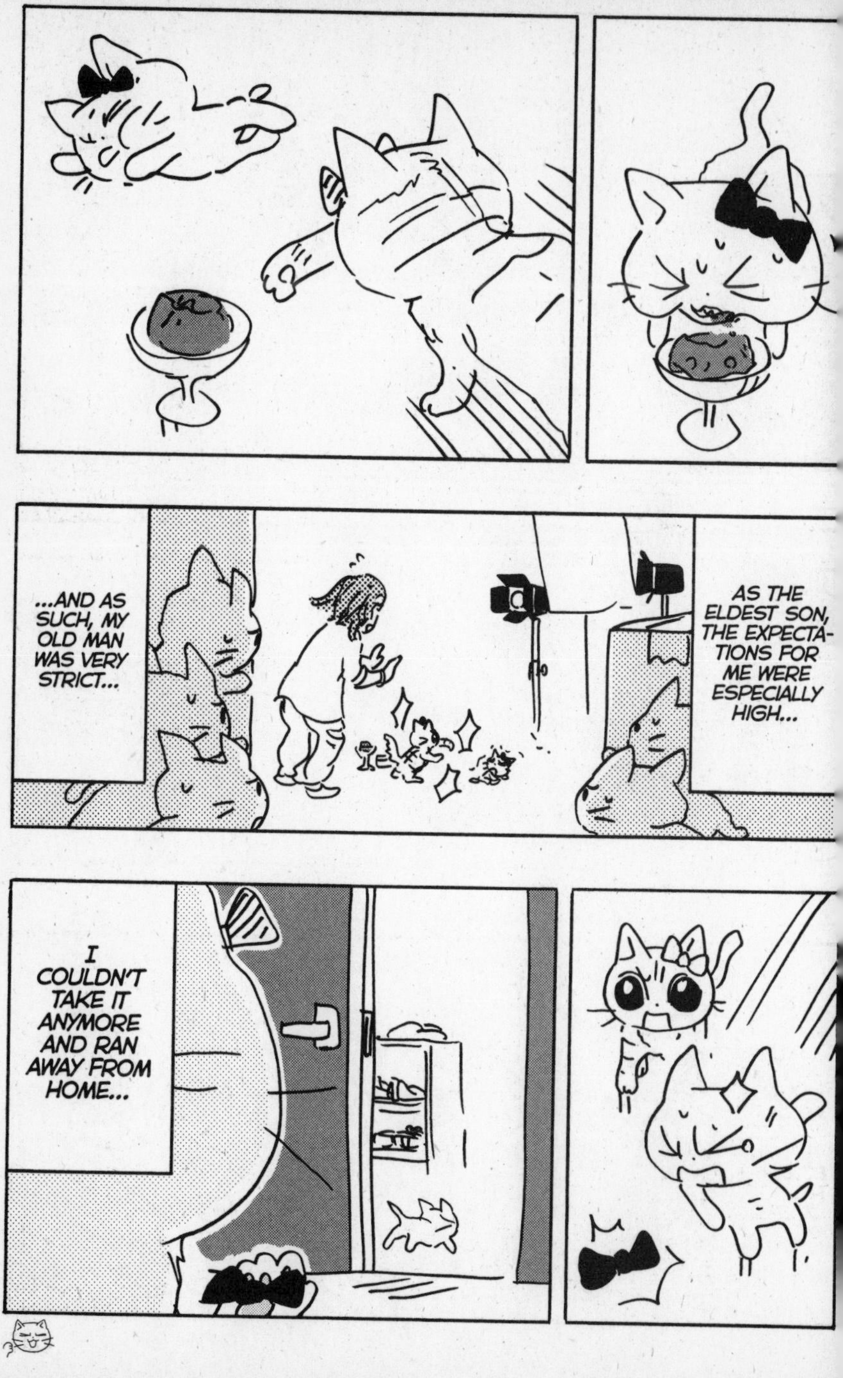
AS THE ELDEST SON, THE EXPECTATIONS FOR ME WERE ESPECIALLY HIGH...
...AND AS SUCH, MY OLD MAN WAS VERY STRICT...
I COULDN'T TAKE IT ANYMORE AND RAN AWAY FROM HOME...

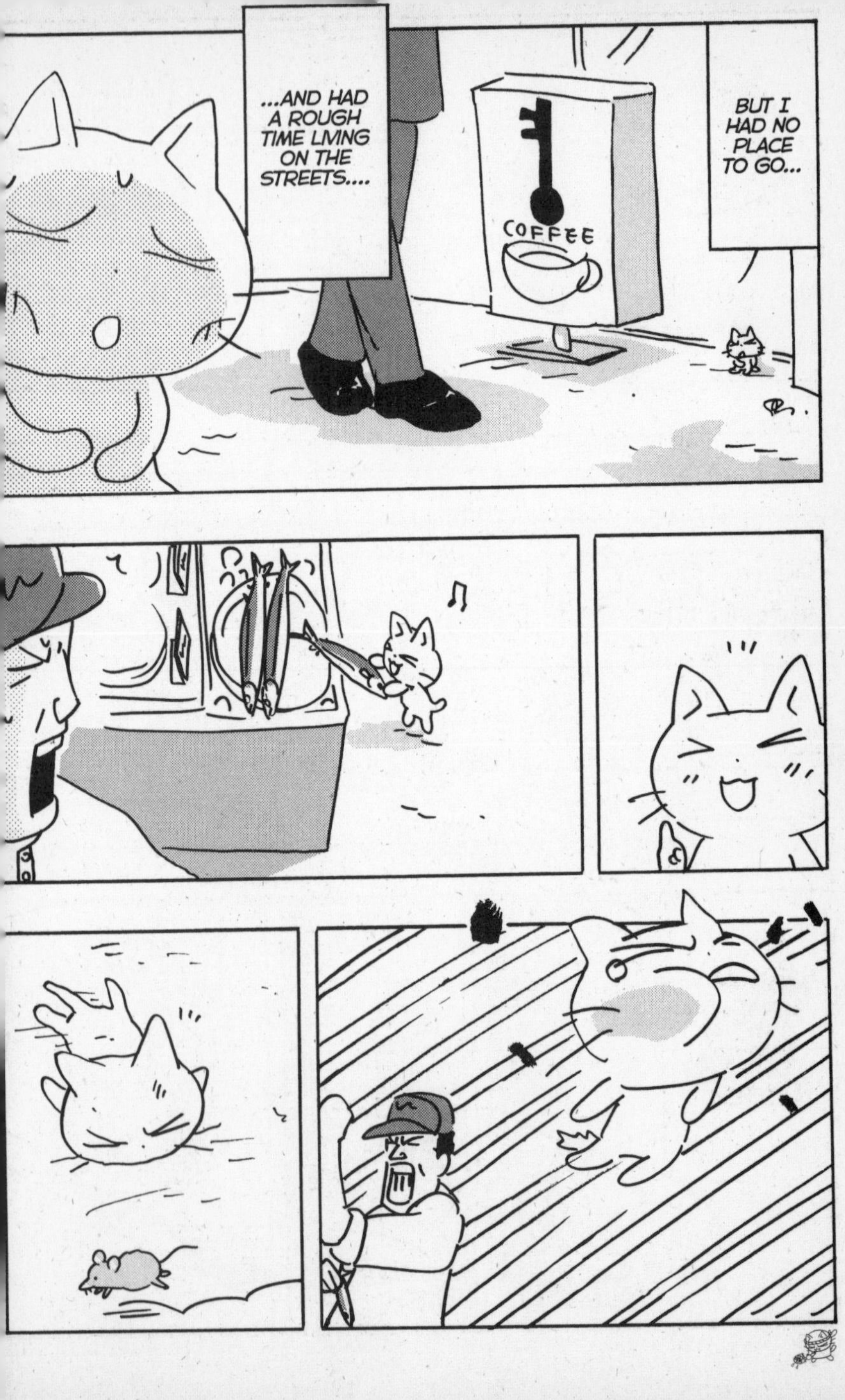
...AND HAD A ROUGH TIME LIVING ON THE STREETS....
BUT I HAD NO PLACE TO GO...

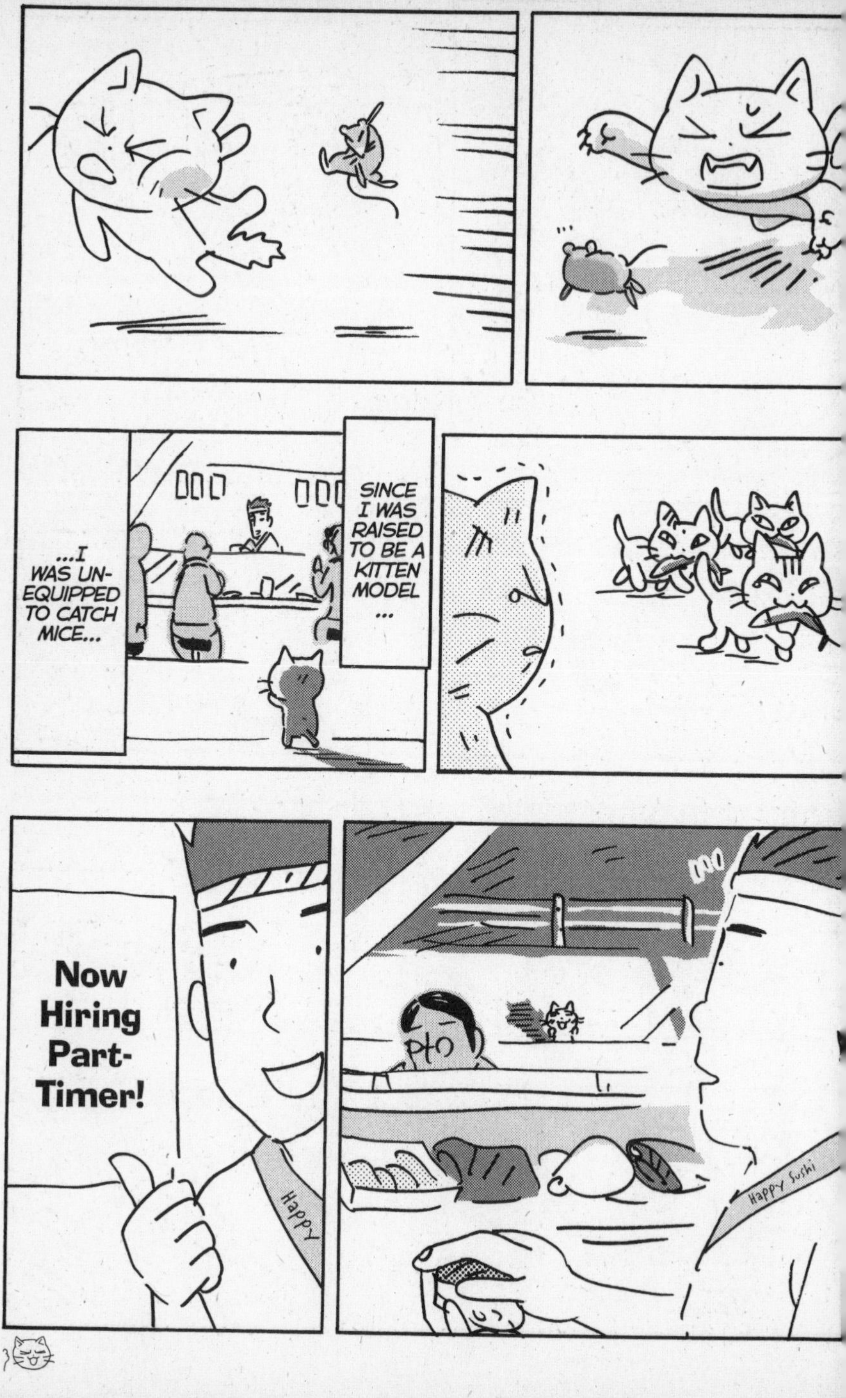
SINCE I WAS RAISED TO BE A KITTEN MODEL ...
...I WAS UN-EQUIPPED TO CATCH MICE...
Happy Sushi
Now Hiring Part-Timer!
Happy

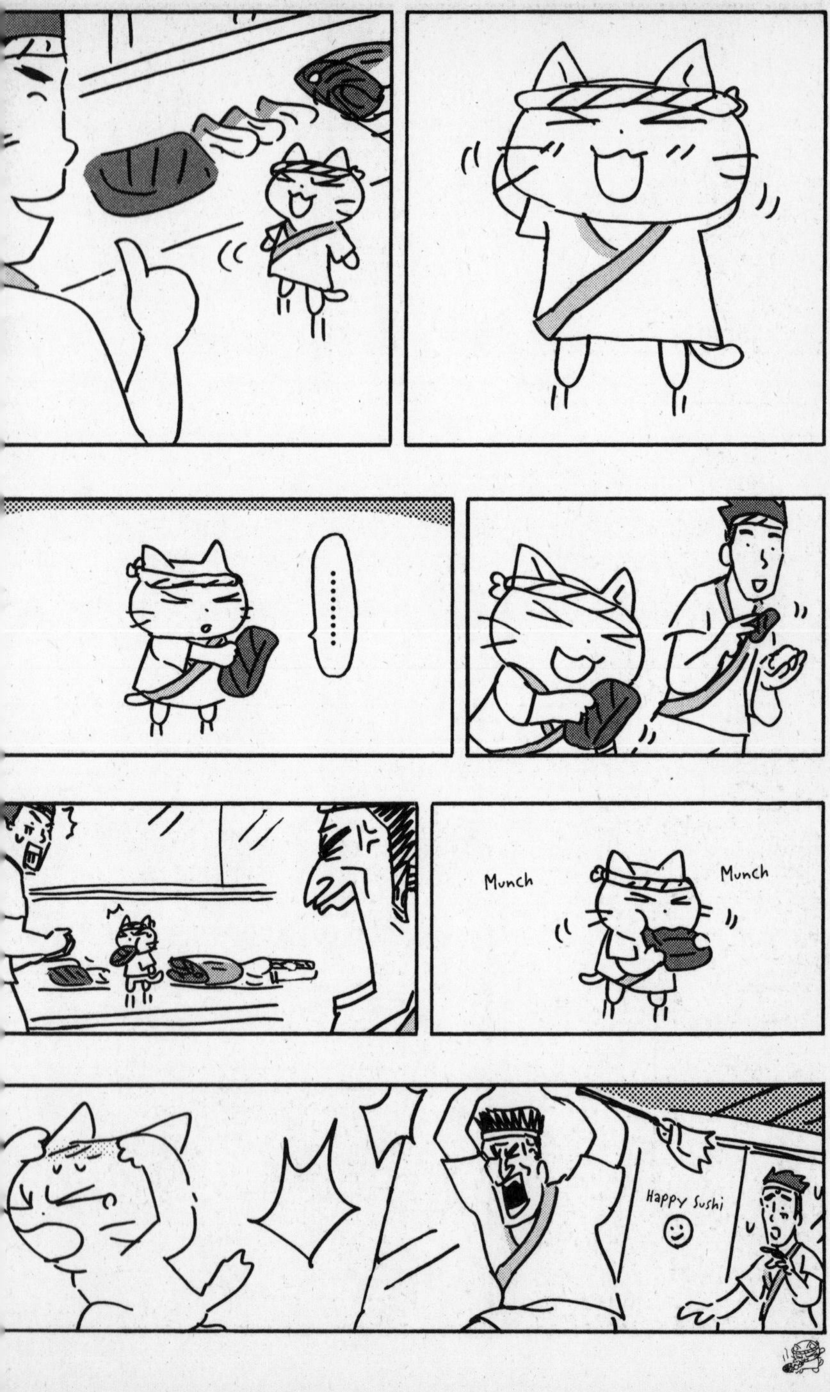
....
Munch
Munch
Happy Sushi

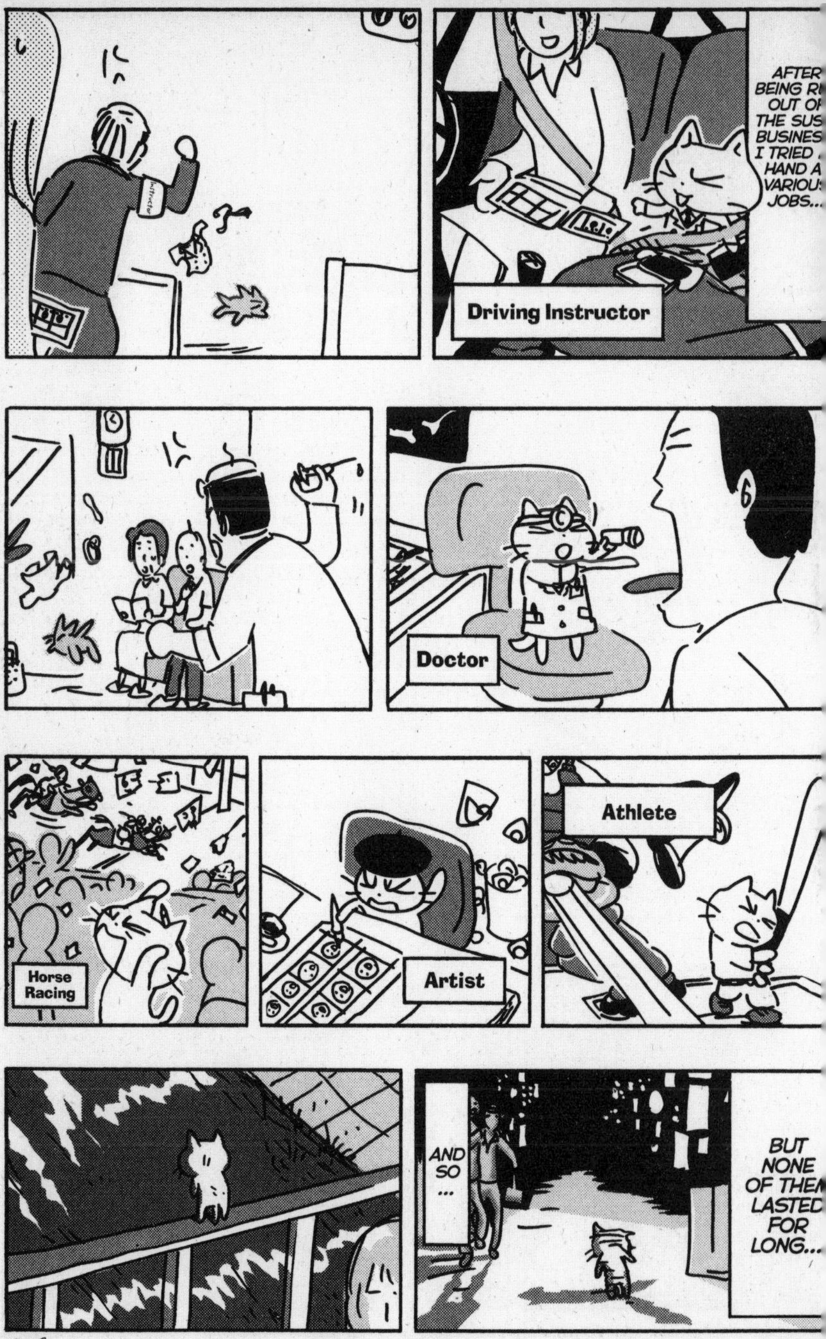

AFTER BEING R OUT OF THE SUS BUSINES I TRIED HAND A VARIOUS JOBS...
Driving Instructor
Instructor
Doctor
Athlete
Artist
Horse Racing
BUT NONE OF THEM LASTED FOR LONG...
AND SO ...

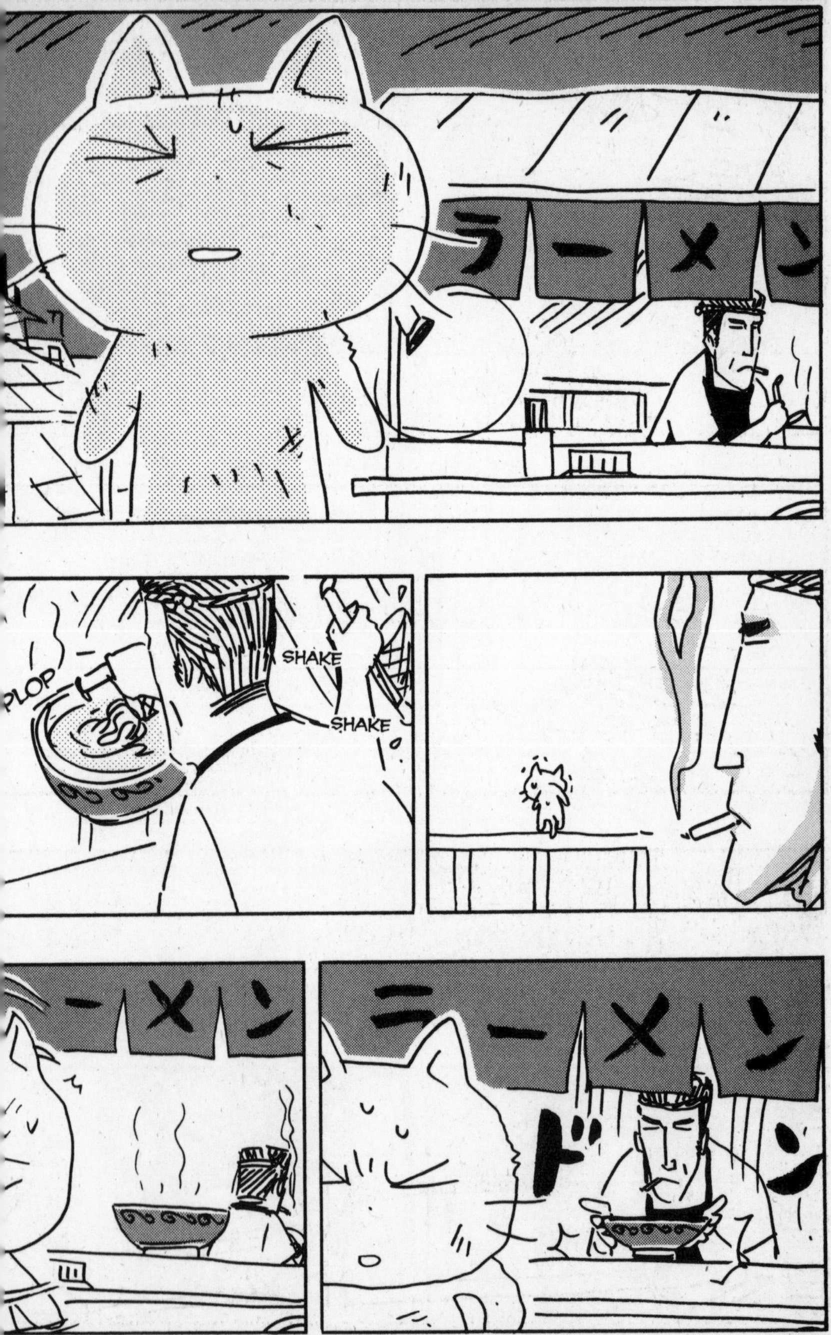
ラーメン
SHAKE
SHAKE
PLOP
ラーメン
ドン
ーメン

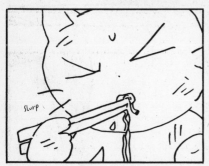

Slurp

ssss

Chomp
Munch
Slurp

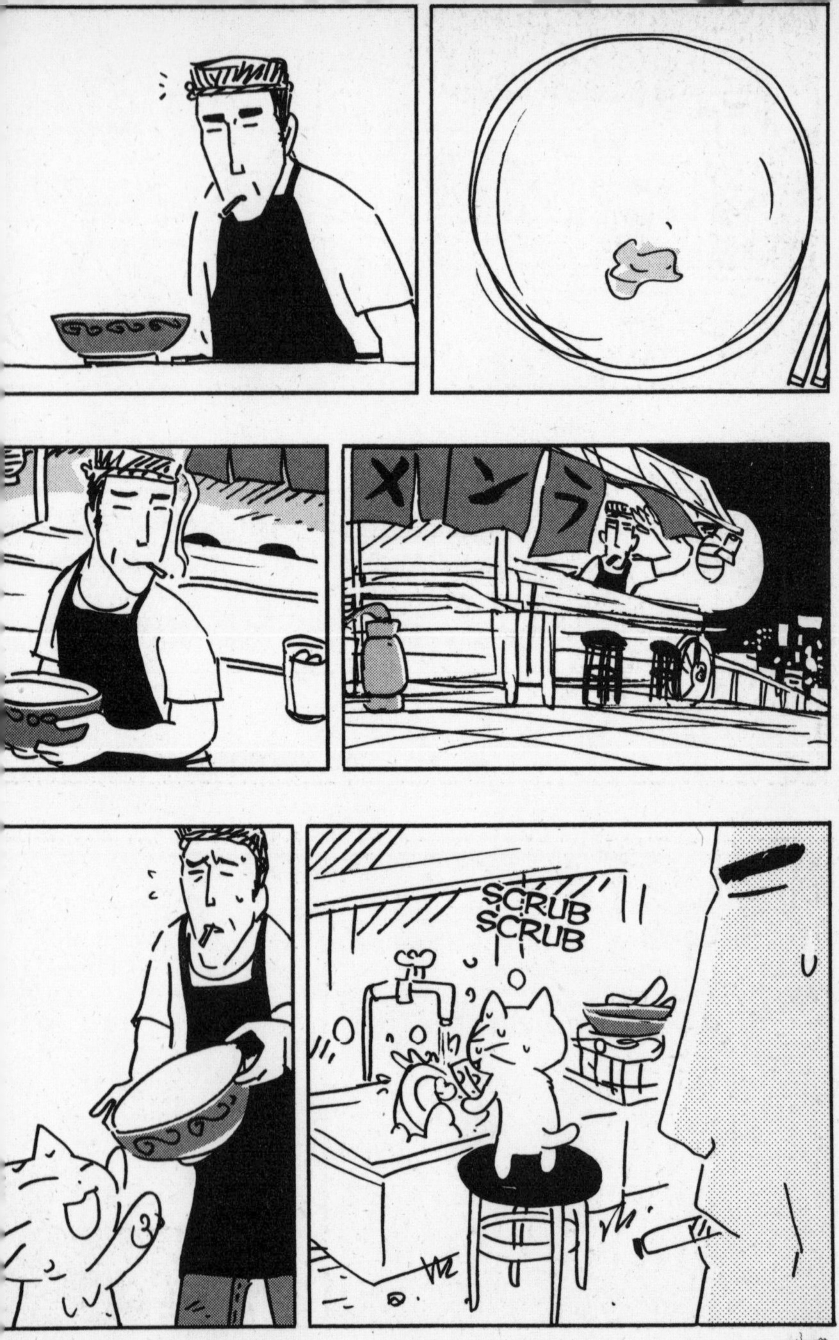
メンラ
SCRUB
SCRUB

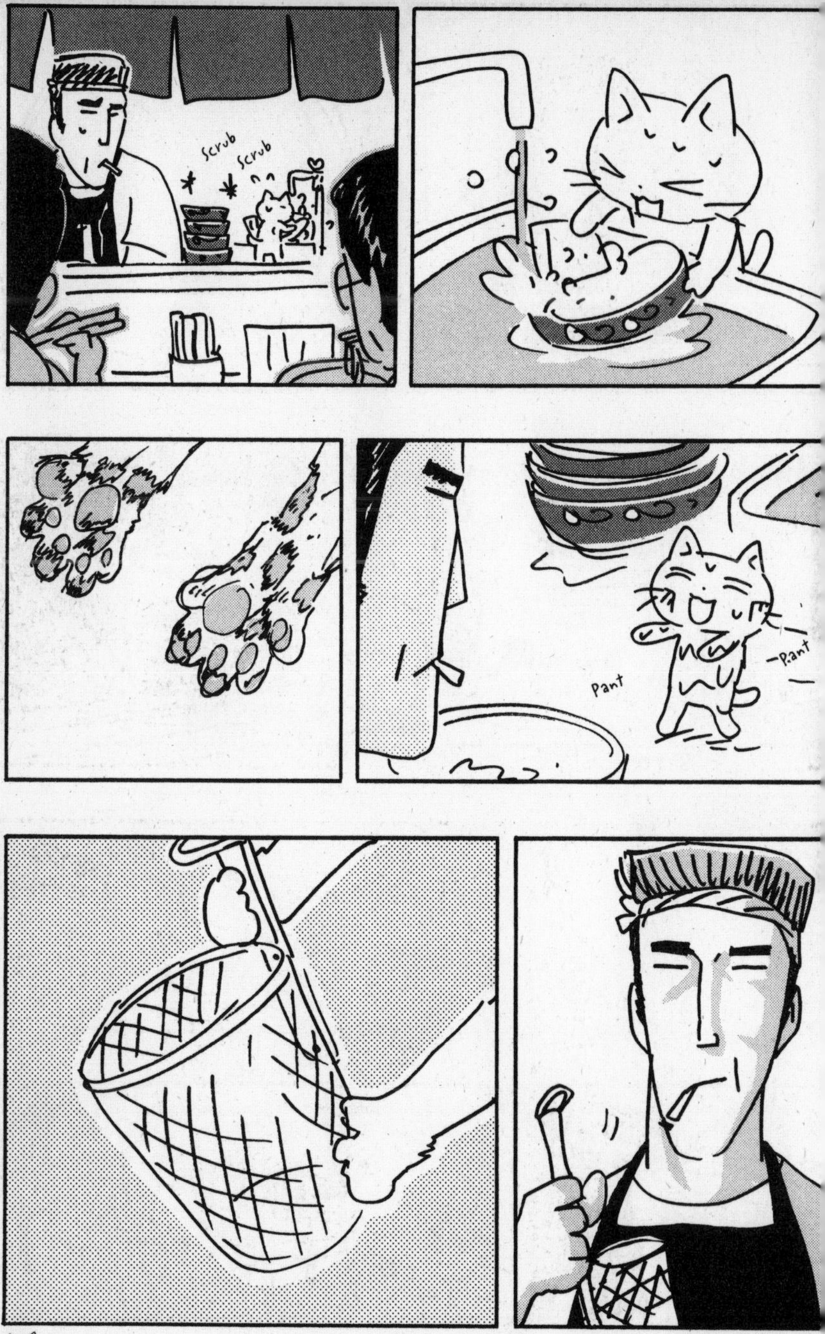
Scrub
Scrub
Pant
Pant

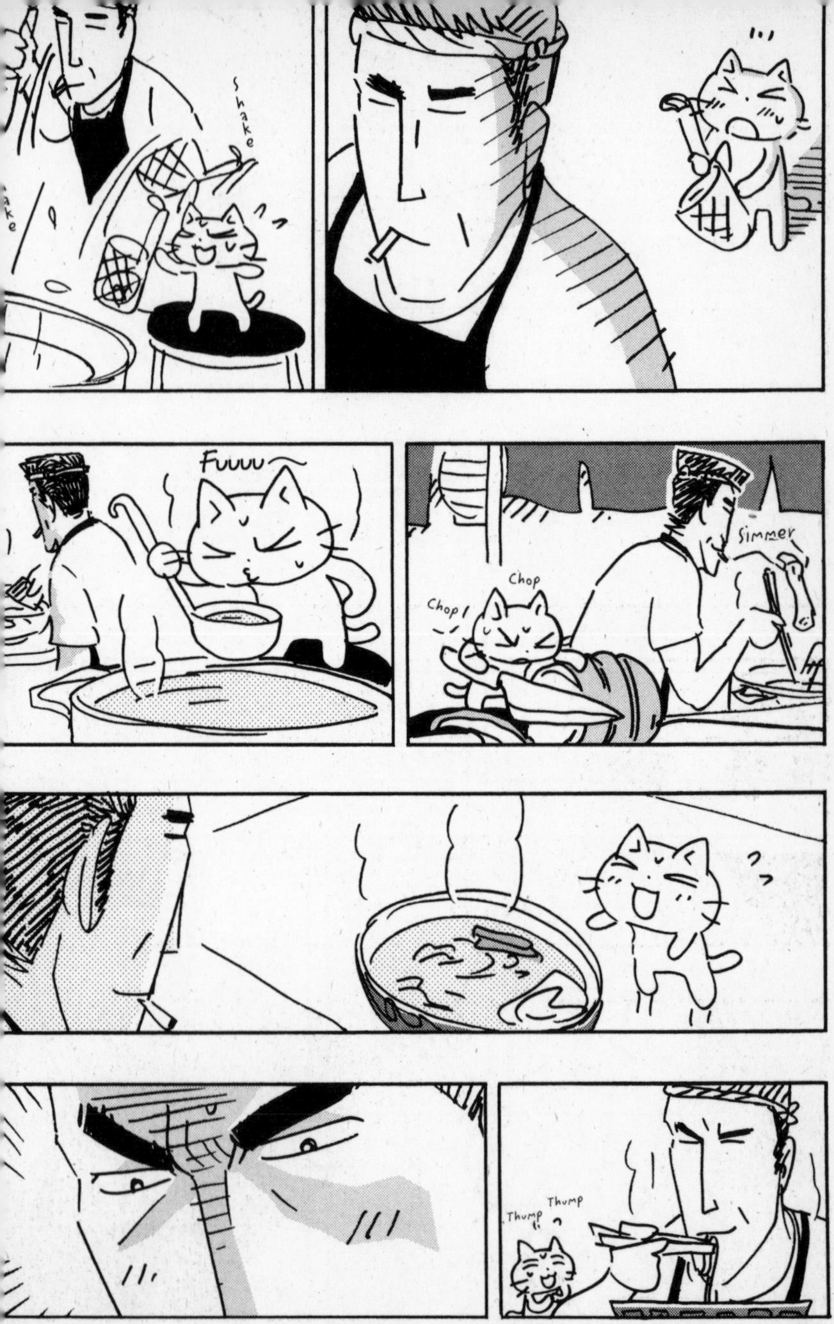

Shake
Fuuuu~
Simmer
Chop
Chop!
Thump
Thump

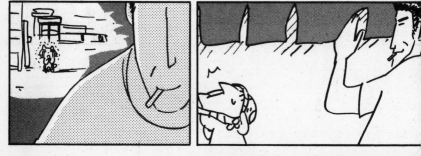

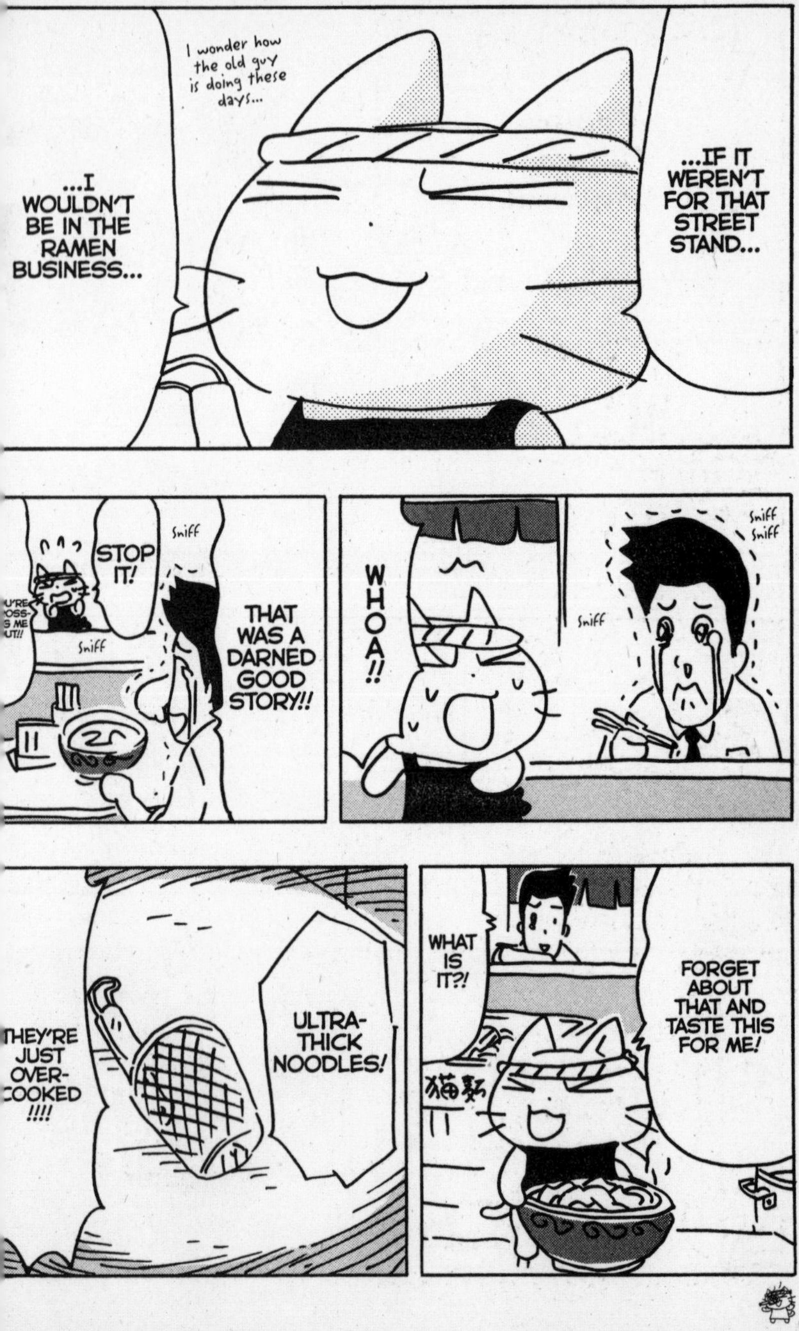
...IF IT WEREN'T FOR THAT STREET STAND...
...I WOULDN'T BE IN THE RAMEN BUSINESS...
I wonder how the old guy is doing these days...
Sniff Sniff
Sniff
WHOA!!
THAT WAS A DARNED GOOD STORY!!
Sniff
STOP IT!
Sniff
FORGET ABOUT THAT AND TASTE THIS FOR ME!
WHAT IS IT?!
ULTRA-THICK NOODLES!
THEY'RE JUST OVER-COOKED !!!!

猫ラーメン

Chapter 7

New Name

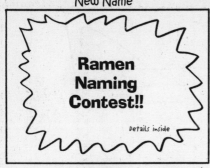

Ramen Naming Contest!!
Details inside
Naming Contest!!
WHAT'S WITH THIS?!
AH! YOU WANNA TRY NAMING THE NEW RAMEN?!
NOT REALLY ...
BUT WHAT HAVE YOU GOT?
HERE, I'LL SHOW YOU!
HERE'S WHAT I'VE GOT SO FAR!
MISO RAAMEN
MISO RAMEEN
MISO RUMEN
MISO RARAA
MISO MENRA
MISO RAA
HUH?!

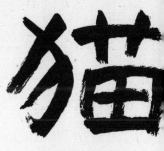

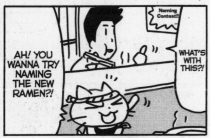

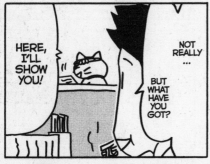

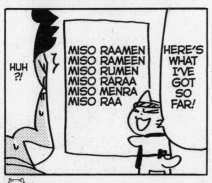

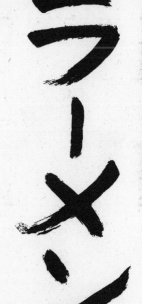

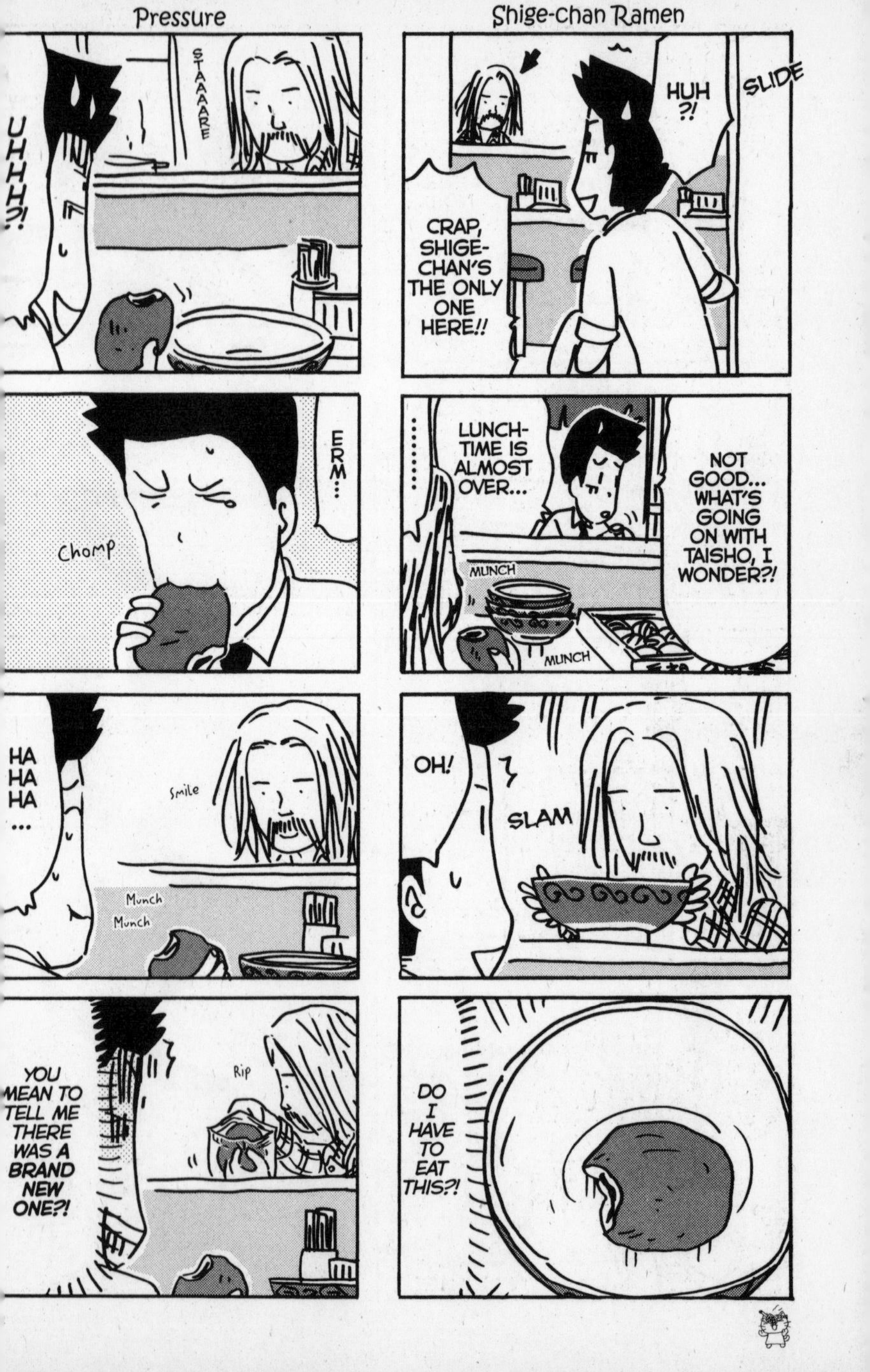
Shige-chan Ramen
HUH ?!
SLIDE
CRAP, SHIGE-CHAN'S THE ONLY ONE HERE!!
LUNCH-TIME IS ALMOST OVER...
NOT GOOD... WHAT'S GOING ON WITH TAISHO, I WONDER?!
MUNCH
MUNCH
OH!
SLAM
DO I HAVE TO EAT THIS?!
Pressure
STAAAARE
UHHHH?!
ERM...
Chomp
HA HA HA ...
Smile
Munch
Munch
YOU MEAN TO TELL ME THERE WAS A BRAND NEW ONE?!
Rip

The IT Age

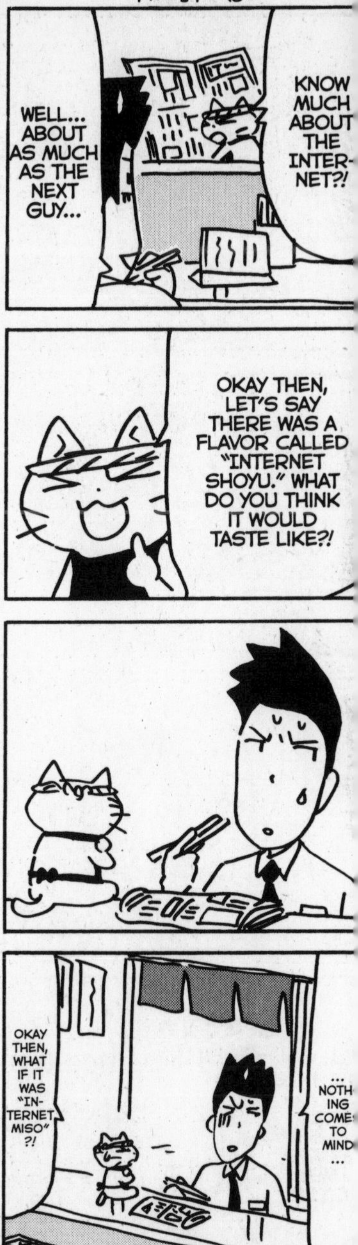

KNOW MUCH ABOUT THE INTERNET?!
WELL... ABOUT AS MUCH AS THE NEXT GUY...
OKAY THEN, LET'S SAY THERE WAS A FLAVOR CALLED "INTERNET SHOYU." WHAT DO YOU THINK IT WOULD TASTE LIKE?!
OKAY THEN, WHAT IF IT WAS "INTERNET MISO"?!
...NOTHING COME TO MIND...

Girlfriend

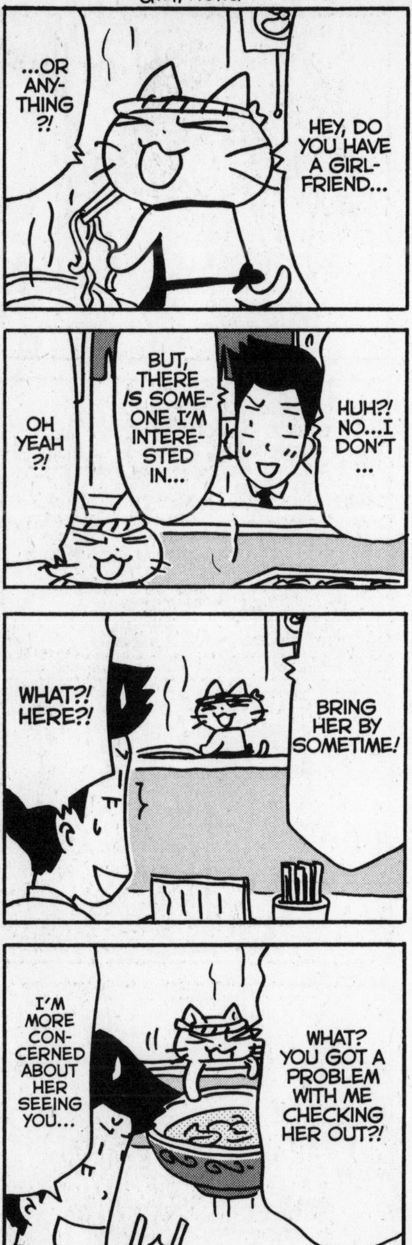

HEY, DO YOU HAVE A GIRLFRIEND...
...OR ANYTHING?!
HUH?! NO...I DON'T ...
BUT, THERE IS SOMEONE I'M INTERESTED IN...
OH YEAH?!
BRING HER BY SOMETIME!
WHAT?! HERE?!
WHAT? YOU GOT A PROBLEM WITH ME CHECKING HER OUT?!
I'M MORE CONCERNED ABOUT HER SEEING YOU...

First Impressions

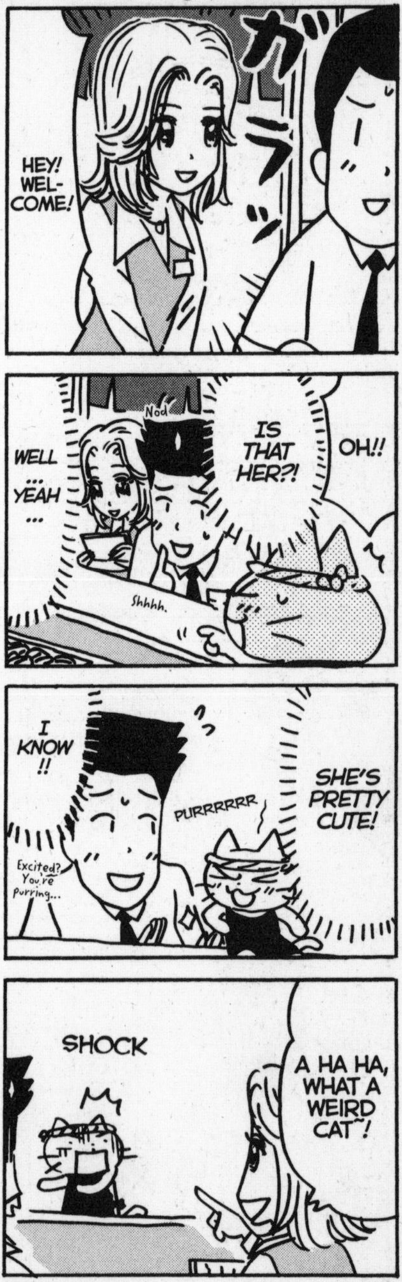
ガラッ
HEY! WEL-COME!
OH!!
IS THAT HER?!
Nod
WELL... YEAH...
Shhhh.
SHE'S PRETTY CUTE!
PURRRRRR
I KNOW!!
Excited? You're purring...
A HA HA, WHAT A WEIRD CAT~!
SHOCK

Order

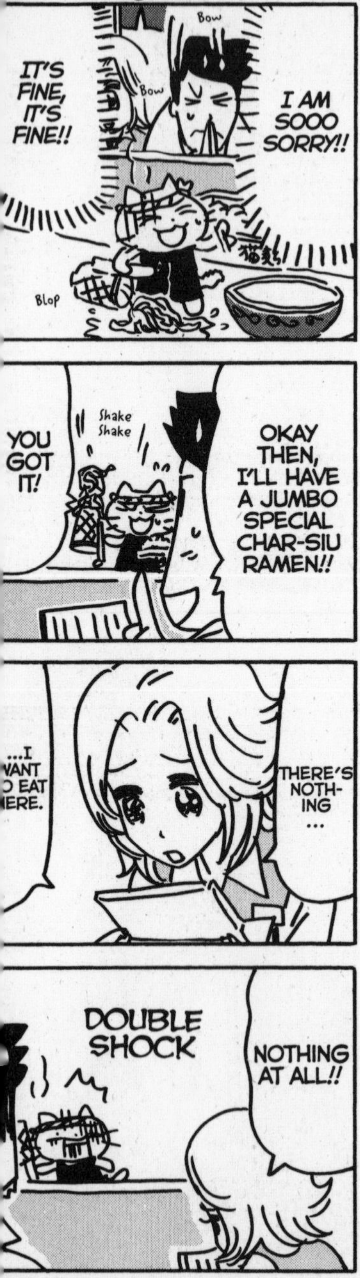
I AM SOOO SORRY!!
Bow
Bow
IT'S FINE, IT'S FINE!!
Blop
OKAY THEN, I'LL HAVE A JUMBO SPECIAL CHAR-SIU RAMEN!!
Shake Shake
YOU GOT IT!
THERE'S NOTH-ING...
...I WANT O EAT ERE.
NOTHING AT ALL!!
DOUBLE SHOCK

Reason

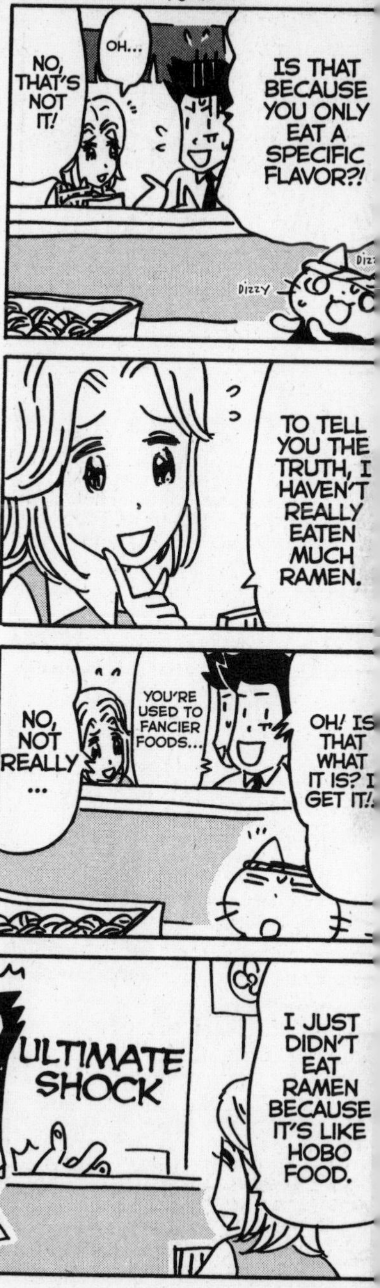
IS THAT BECAUSE YOU ONLY EAT A SPECIFIC FLAVOR?!
OH...
NO, THAT'S NOT IT!
DIZZY
TO TELL YOU THE TRUTH, I HAVEN'T REALLY EATEN MUCH RAMEN.
OH! IS THAT WHAT IT IS? I GET IT!
YOU'RE USED TO FANCIER FOODS...
NO, NOT REALLY ...
I JUST DIDN'T EAT RAMEN BECAUSE IT'S LIKE HOBO FOOD.
ULTIMATE SHOCK

Insert

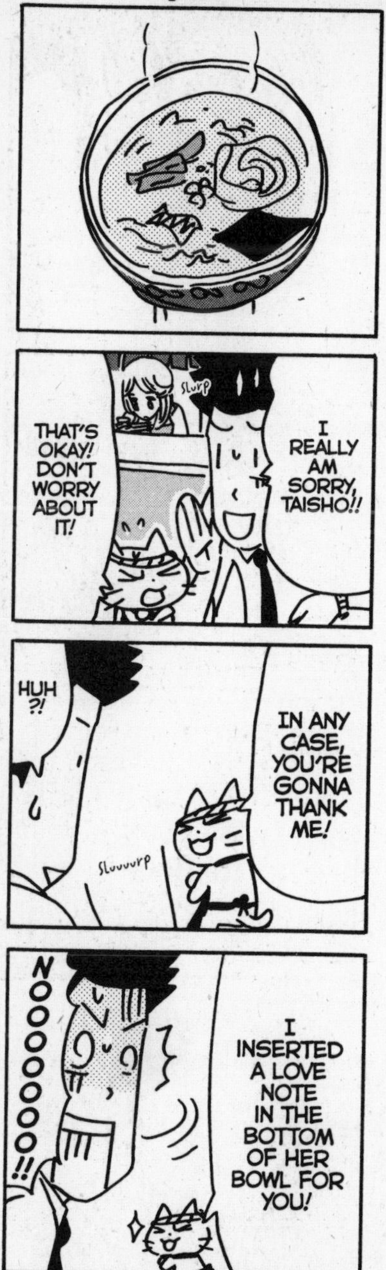
I REALLY AM SORRY, TAISHO!!
SLURP
THAT'S OKAY! DON'T WORRY ABOUT IT!
IN ANY CASE, YOU'RE GONNA THANK ME!
SLUUUURP
HUH ?!
I INSERTED A LOVE NOTE IN THE BOTTOM OF HER BOWL FOR YOU!
NOOOOOOOOO!!

Message

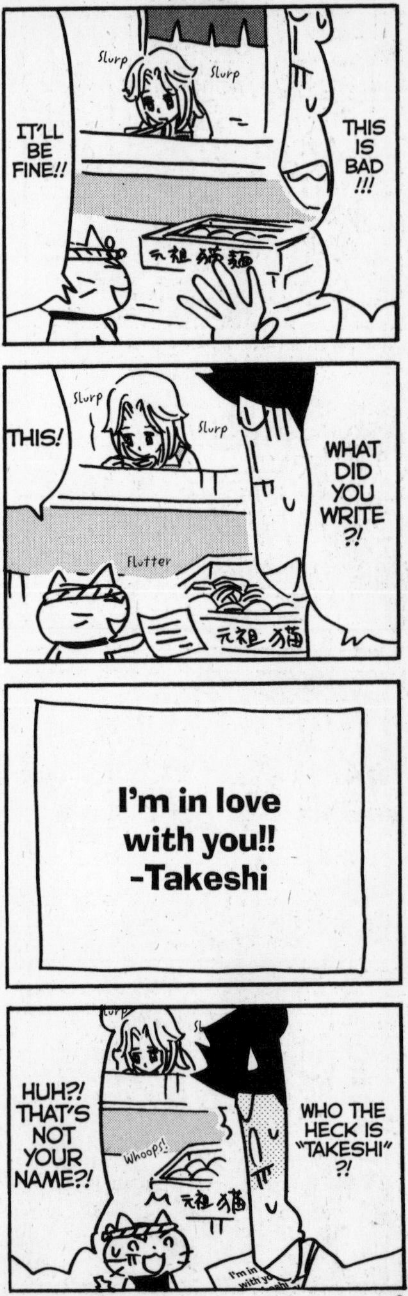
Slurp
Slurp
THIS IS BAD!!!
IT'LL BE FINE!!
元祖 猫
Slurp
Slurp
WHAT DID YOU WRITE?!
THIS!
Flutter
元祖 猫
I'm in love with you!! -Takeshi
WHO THE HECK IS "TAKESHI"?!
HUH?! THAT'S NOT YOUR NAME?!
Whoops!
元祖 猫

Message: Second Try

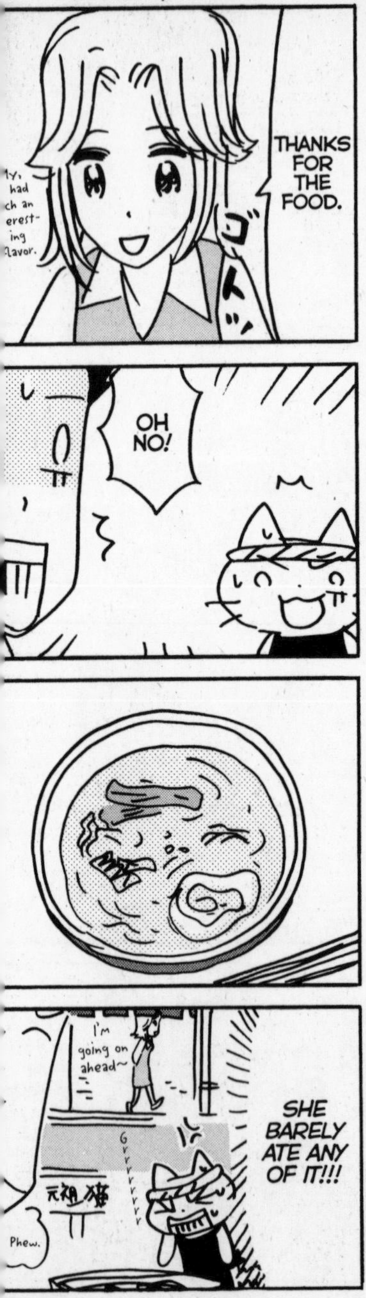
THANKS FOR THE FOOD.
ゴトッ
OH NO!
I'm going on ahead~
SHE BARELY ATE ANY OF IT!!!
Grrrrrrrr
元祖 猫
Phew.

So Cute!!

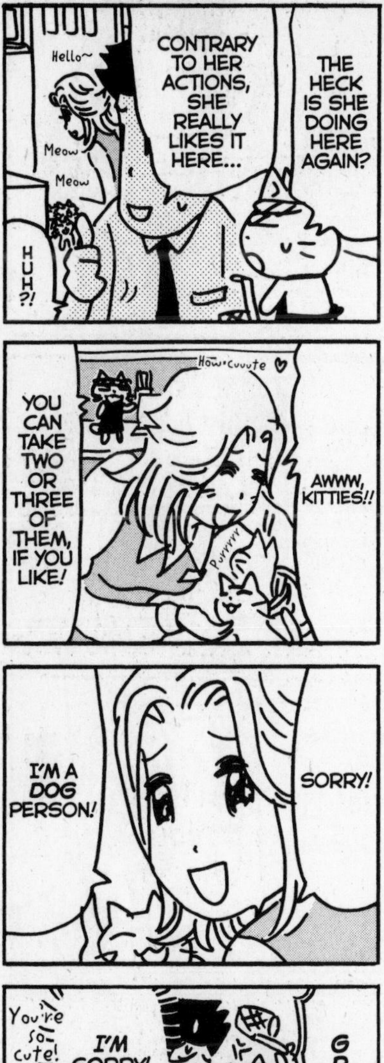
THE HECK IS SHE DOING HERE AGAIN?
CONTRARY TO HER ACTIONS, SHE REALLY LIKES IT HERE...
Hello~
Meow
Meow
HUH?!
How cuuute ♡
AWWW, KITTIES!!
YOU CAN TAKE TWO OR THREE OF THEM, IF YOU LIKE!
Purrrrr
SORRY!
I'M A *DOG* PERSON!
GRRRRRR!!
I'M SORRY! I'M SORRY!!
You're so cute!
Purrrr

Job Opening

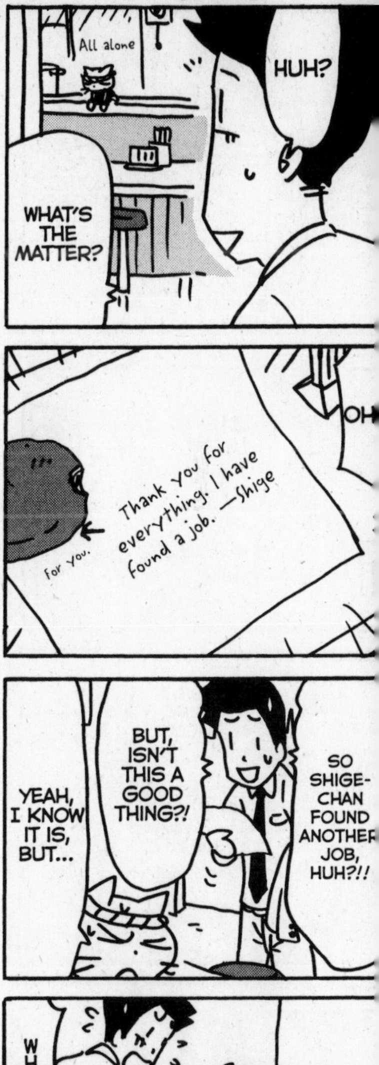
HUH?
All alone
WHAT'S THE MATTER?
OH
Thank you for everything. I have found a job. —Shige
For you.
SO SHIGE-CHAN FOUND ANOTHER JOB, HUH?!!
BUT, ISN'T THIS A GOOD THING?!
YEAH, I KNOW IT IS, BUT...
...HE LEFT ALL MY LITTLE BROTHERS BEHIND...
WHOA?!
Meow
Meow
Meow
Meow

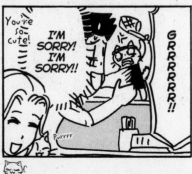

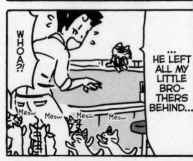

Pasta

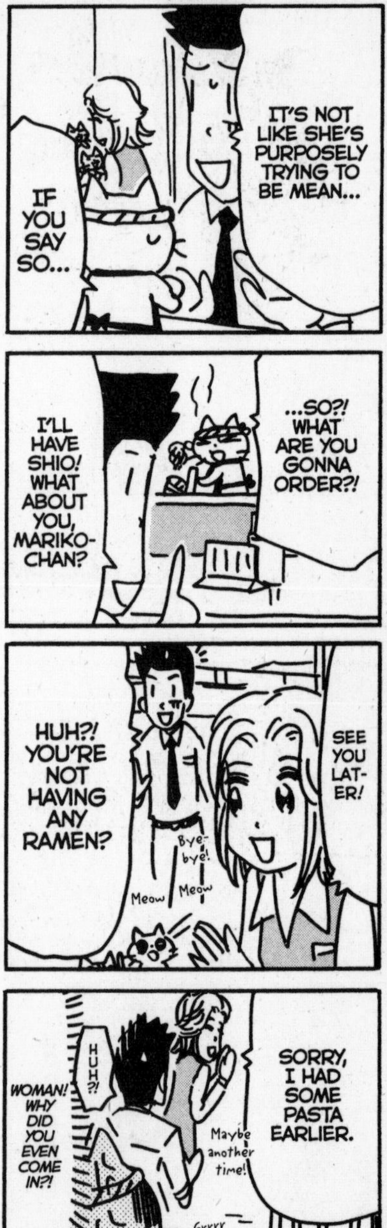

IT'S NOT LIKE SHE'S PURPOSELY TRYING TO BE MEAN...
IF YOU SAY SO...
...SO?! WHAT ARE YOU GONNA ORDER?!
I'LL HAVE SHIO! WHAT ABOUT YOU, MARIKO-CHAN?
SEE YOU LAT-ER!
HUH?! YOU'RE NOT HAVING ANY RAMEN?
Bye-bye!
Meow
Meow
SORRY, I HAD SOME PASTA EARLIER.
Maybe another time!
HUH?!
WOMAN! WHY DID YOU EVEN COME IN?!
Grrrr

Milk

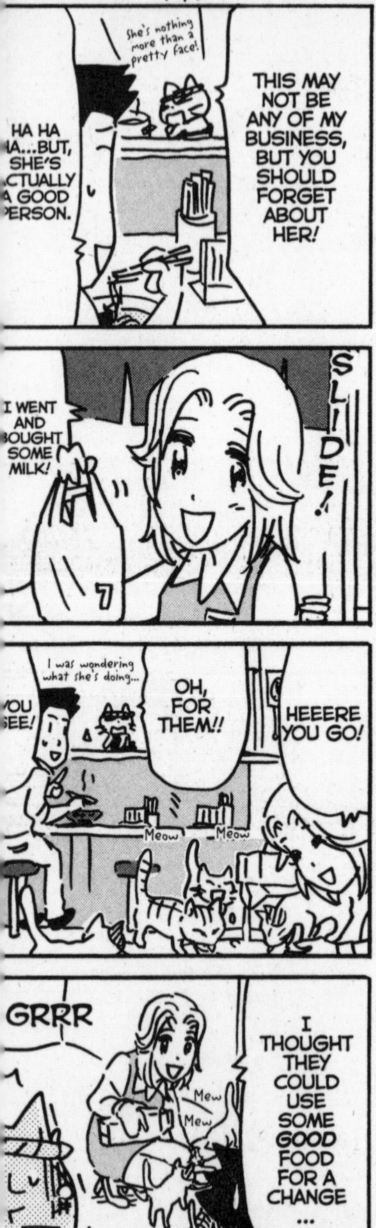

THIS MAY NOT BE ANY OF MY BUSINESS, BUT YOU SHOULD FORGET ABOUT HER!
She's nothing more than a pretty face!
HA HA A...BUT, SHE'S CTUALLY A GOOD ERSON.
SLIDE!
I WENT AND OUGHT SOME MILK!
HEEERE YOU GO!
OH, FOR THEM!!
I was wondering what she's doing...
OU SEE!
Meow
Meow
I THOUGHT THEY COULD USE SOME GOOD FOOD FOR A CHANGE...
Mew
Mew
GRRR

猫ラーメン

Short Comic Special

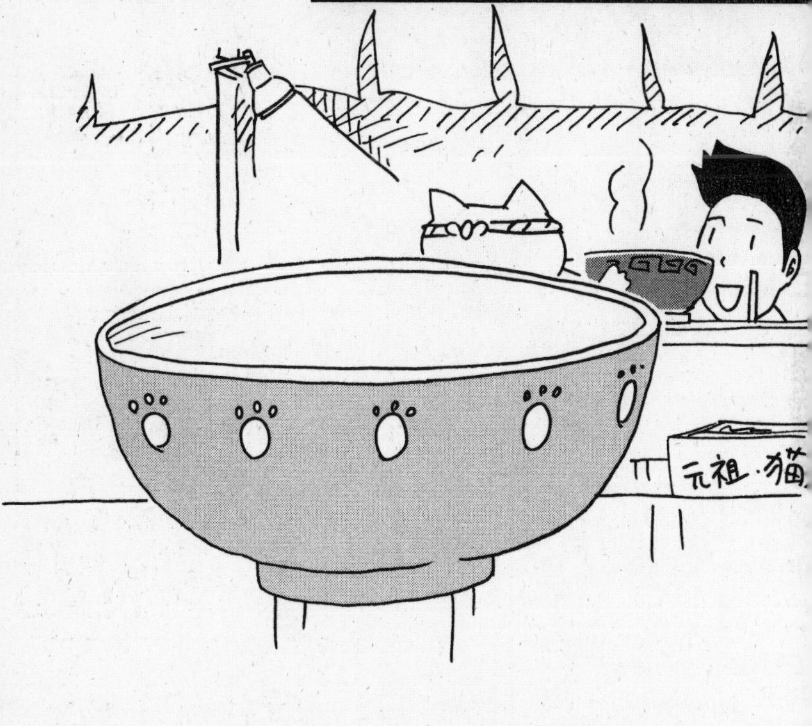
元祖・猫

The Bowl of Friendship

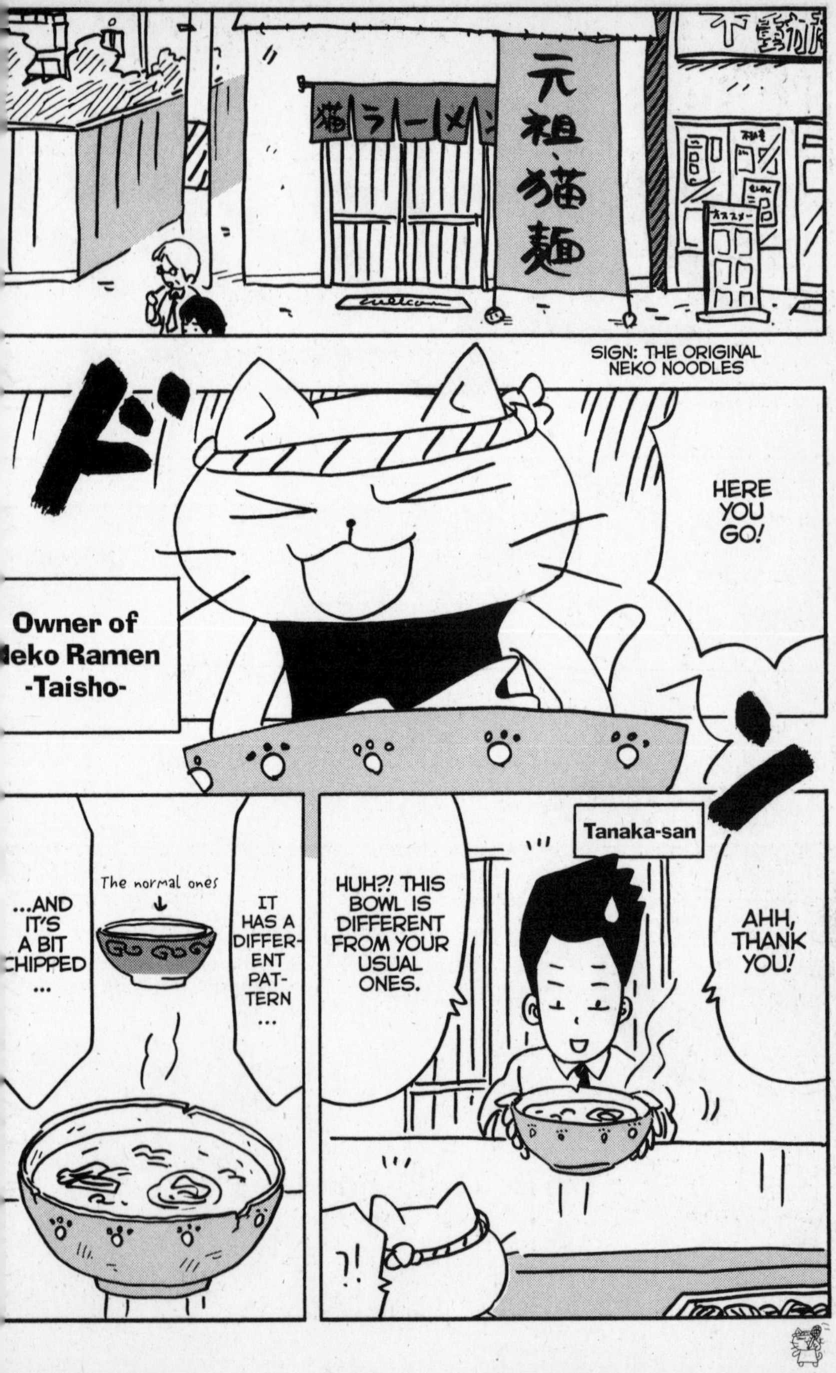
猫ラーメン
元祖、猫麺
オススメ
SIGN: THE ORIGINAL NEKO NOODLES
ド
HERE YOU GO!
Owner of
eko Ramen
-Taisho-
Tanaka-san
AHH, THANK YOU!
HUH?! THIS BOWL IS DIFFERENT FROM YOUR USUAL ONES.
IT HAS A DIFFER-ENT PAT-TERN ...
The normal ones
...AND IT'S A BIT HIPPED ...
?!

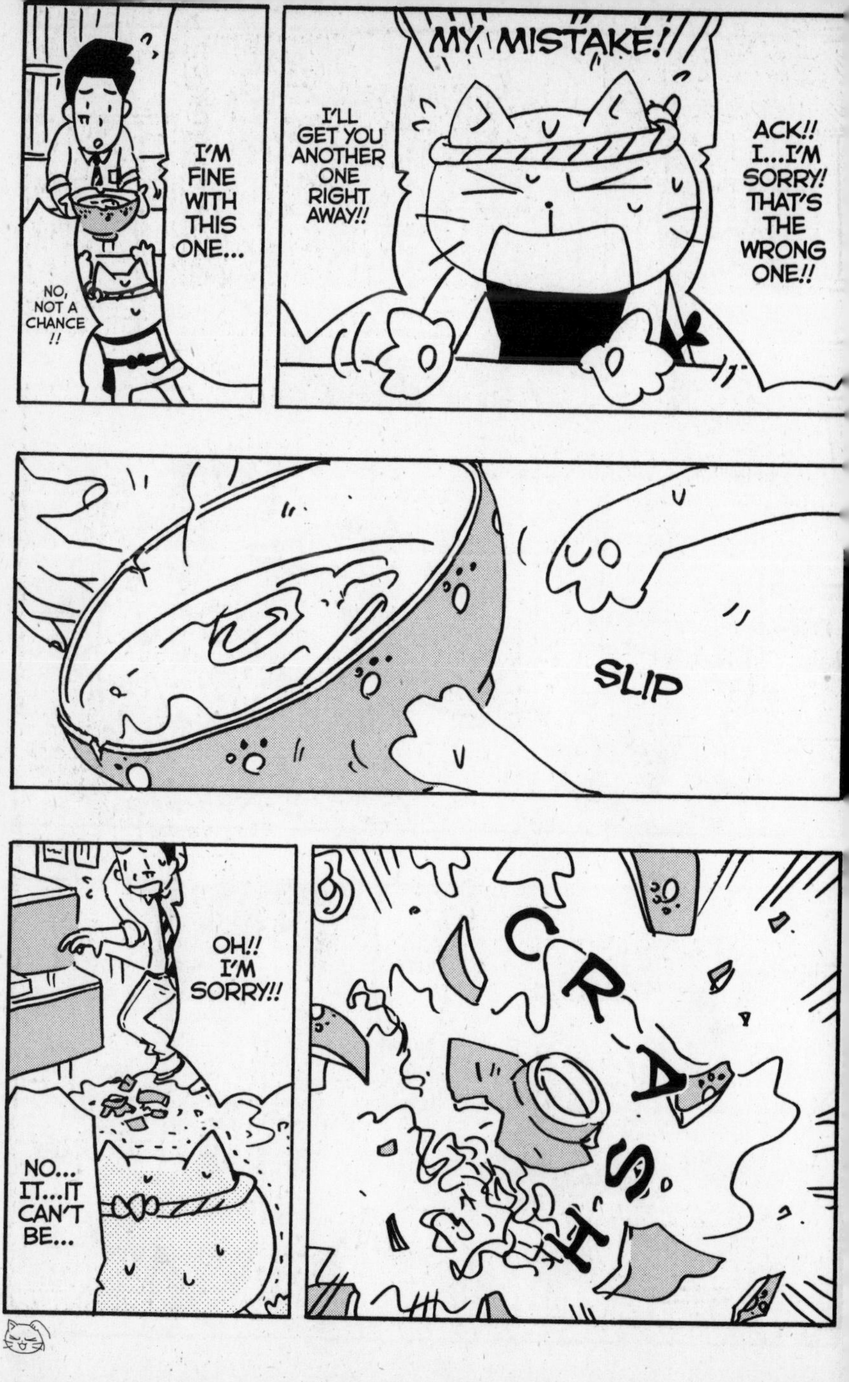
I'M FINE WITH THIS ONE...
NO, NOT A CHANCE!!
MY MISTAKE!!
I'LL GET YOU ANOTHER ONE RIGHT AWAY!!
ACK!! I...I'M SORRY! THAT'S THE WRONG ONE!!
SLIP
OH!! I'M SORRY!!
NO... IT...IT CAN'T BE...
CRASH

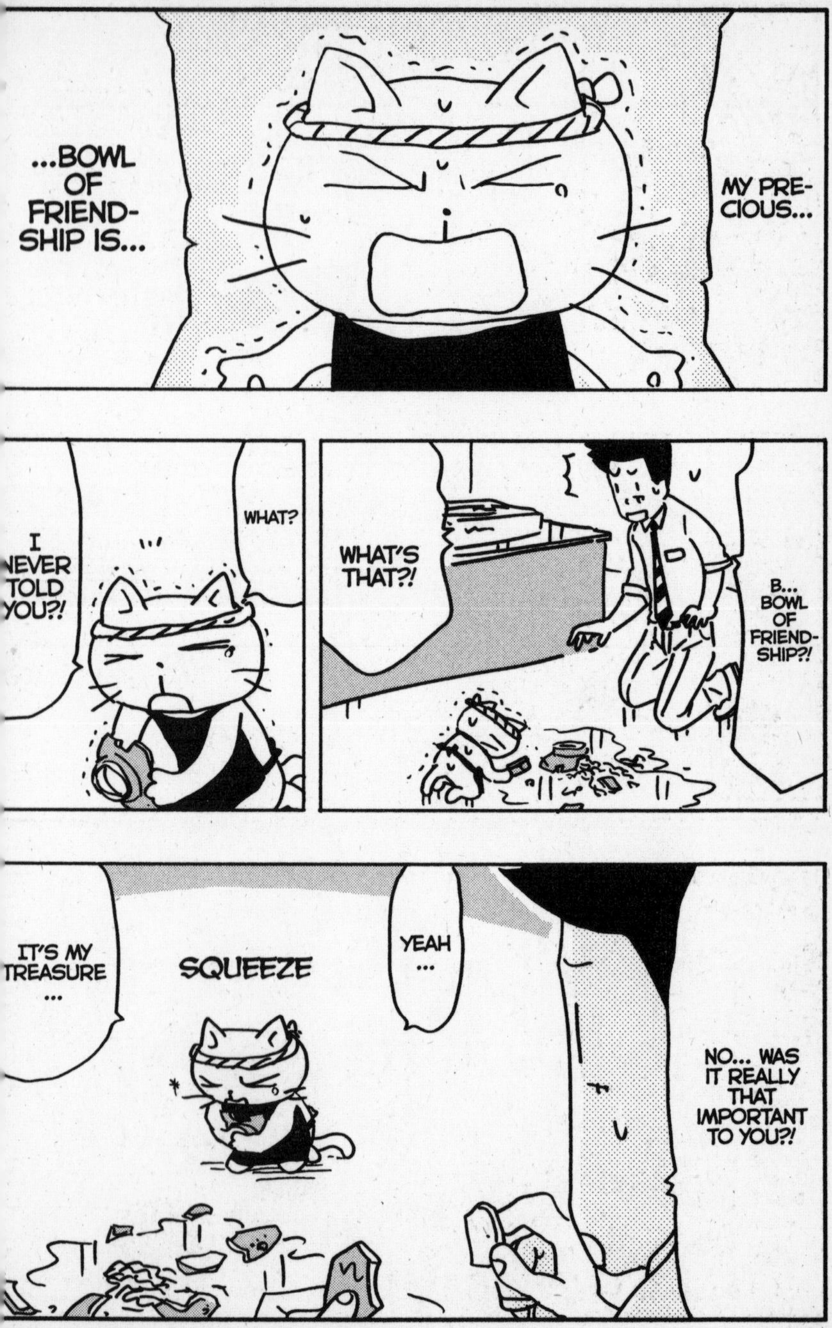
MY PRE-CIOUS...
...BOWL OF FRIEND-SHIP IS...
B... BOWL OF FRIEND-SHIP?!
WHAT'S THAT?!
WHAT?
I NEVER TOLD YOU?!
NO... WAS IT REALLY THAT IMPORTANT TO YOU?!
YEAH ...
SQUEEZE
IT'S MY TREASURE ...

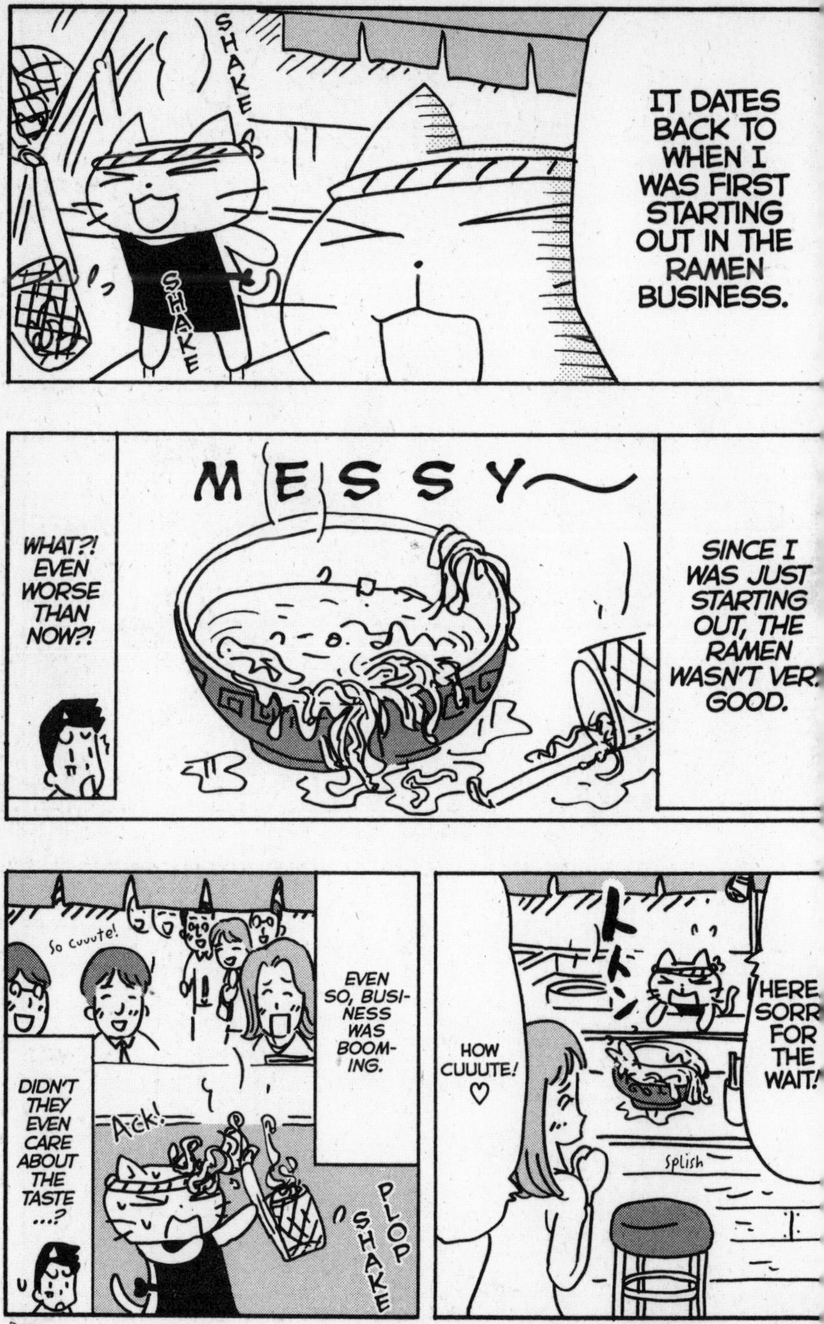
IT DATES BACK TO WHEN I WAS FIRST STARTING OUT IN THE RAMEN BUSINESS.
SHAKE
SHAKE
SINCE I WAS JUST STARTING OUT, THE RAMEN WASN'T VER
GOOD.
MESSY~
WHAT?! EVEN WORSE THAN NOW?!
HERE
SORR
FOR THE WAIT!
HOW CUUUTE! ♡
Splish
EVEN SO, BUSINESS WAS BOOMING.
So cuuute!
Ack!
PLOP
SHAKE
DIDN'T THEY EVEN CARE ABOUT THE TASTE ...?

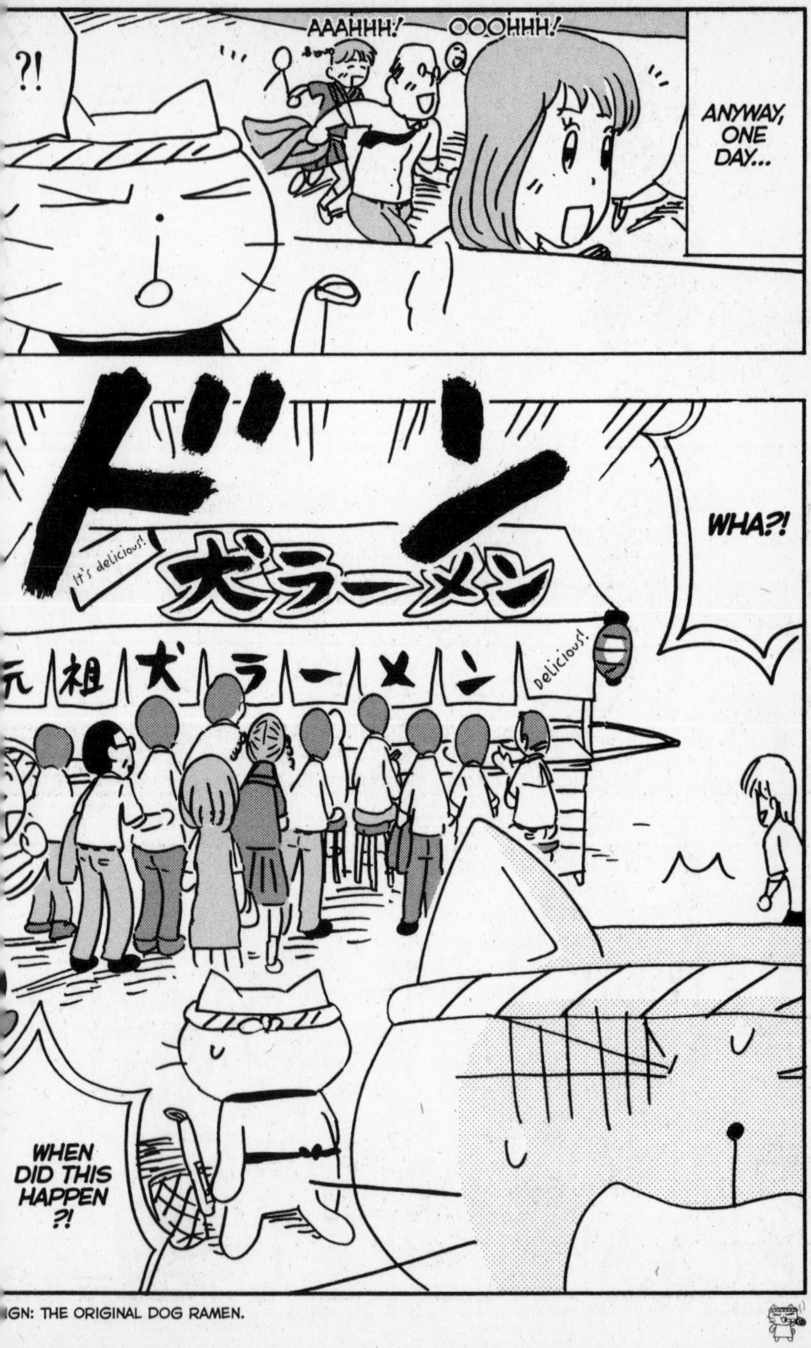
ANYWAY, ONE DAY...
OOOHHH!
AAAHHH!
?!
ドーン
犬ラーメン
It's delicious!
元祖犬ラーメン
Delicious!
WHA?!
WHEN DID THIS HAPPEN ?!

IGN: THE ORIGINAL DOG RAMEN.

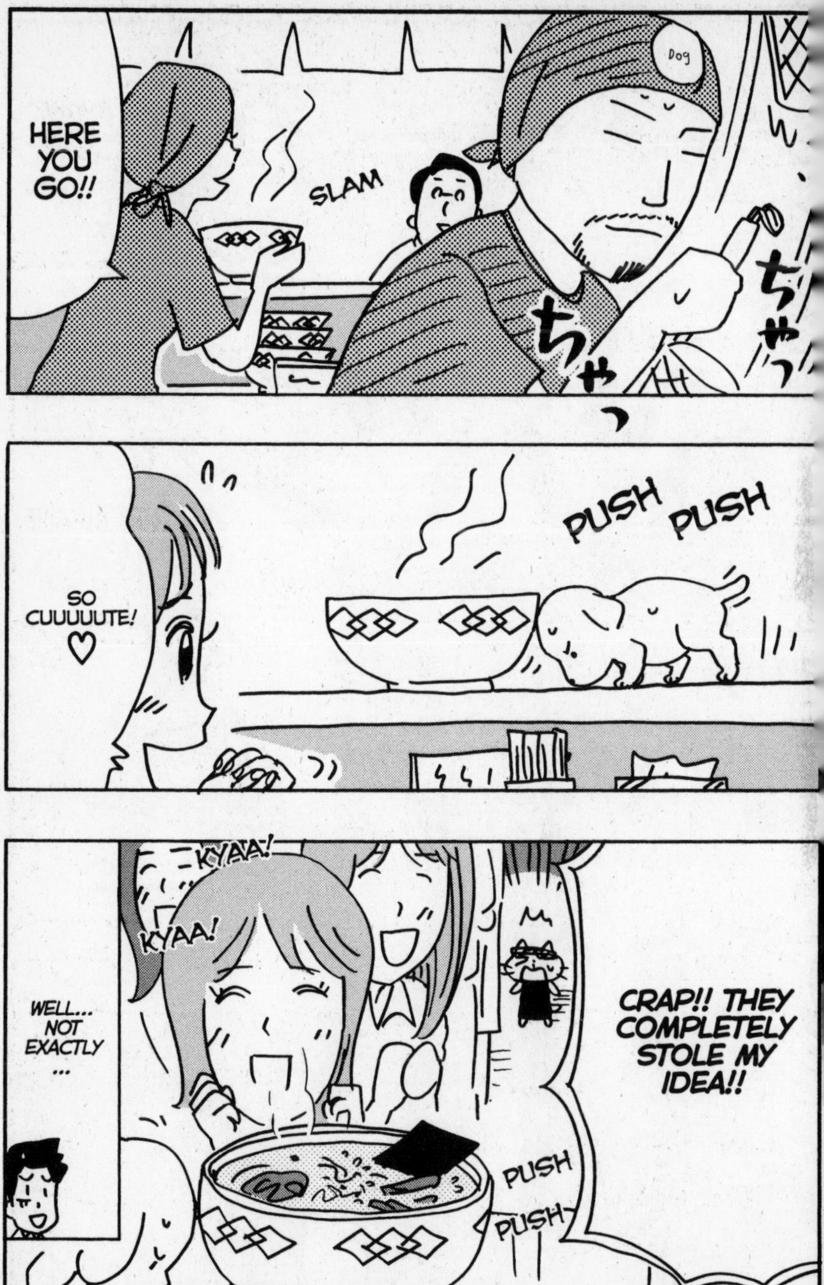
HERE YOU GO!!
SLAM
Dog
ちゃっ
ちゃっ
SO CUUUUUTE! ♥
PUSH
PUSH
KYAA!
KYAA!
WELL... NOT EXACTLY ...
CRAP!! THEY COMPLETELY STOLE MY IDEA!!
PUSH
PUSH

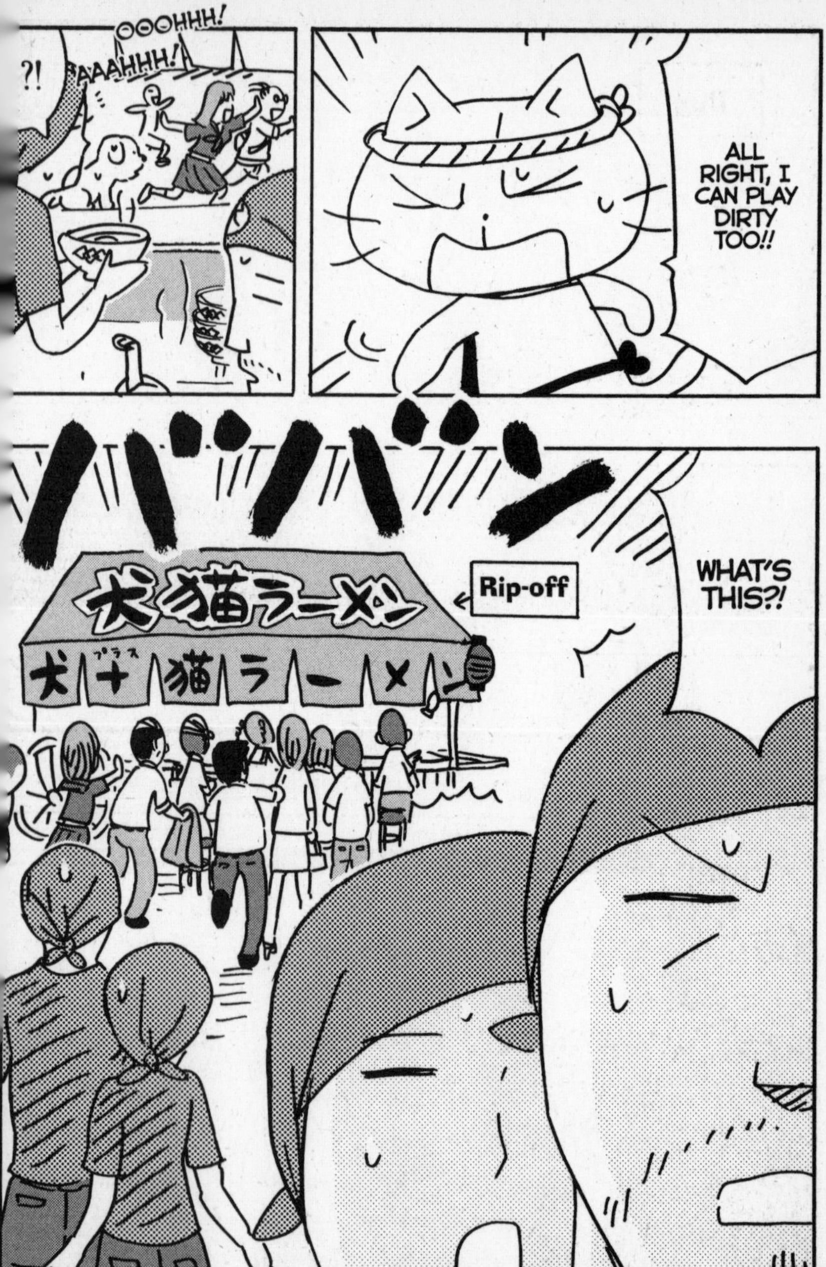
OOOHHH!
AAAAHHH!
?!
ALL RIGHT, I CAN PLAY DIRTY TOO!!
バンバン
犬猫ラーメン
Rip-off
犬+猫ラーメン
WHAT'S THIS?!

SIGN: DOG + NEKO RAMEN

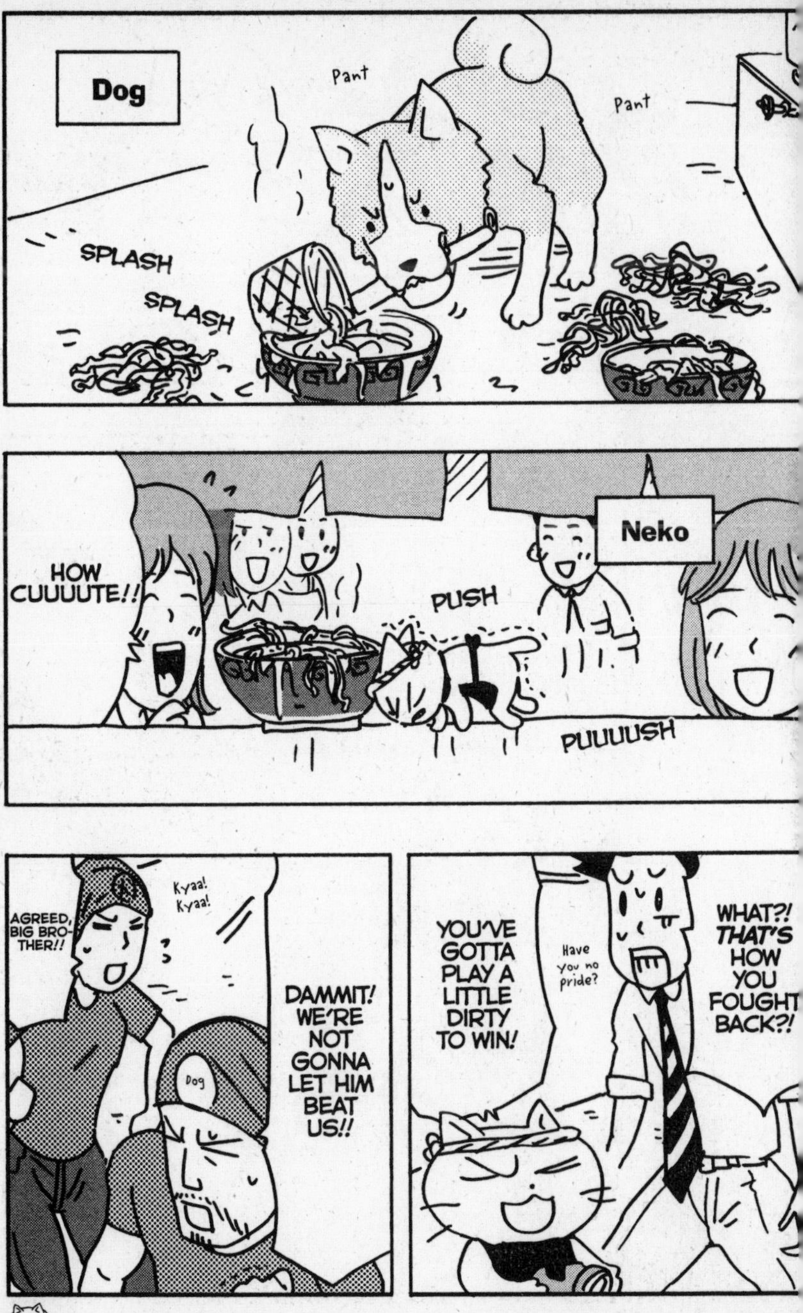

Dog
Pant
Pant
SPLASH
SPLASH
HOW CUUUUTE!!
PUSH
Neko
PUUUUSH
AGREED, BIG BROTHER!!
Kyaa! Kyaa!
DAMMIT! WE'RE NOT GONNA LET HIM BEAT US!!
Dog
YOU'VE GOTTA PLAY A LITTLE DIRTY TO WIN!
Have you no pride?
WHAT?! THAT'S HOW YOU FOUGHT BACK?!

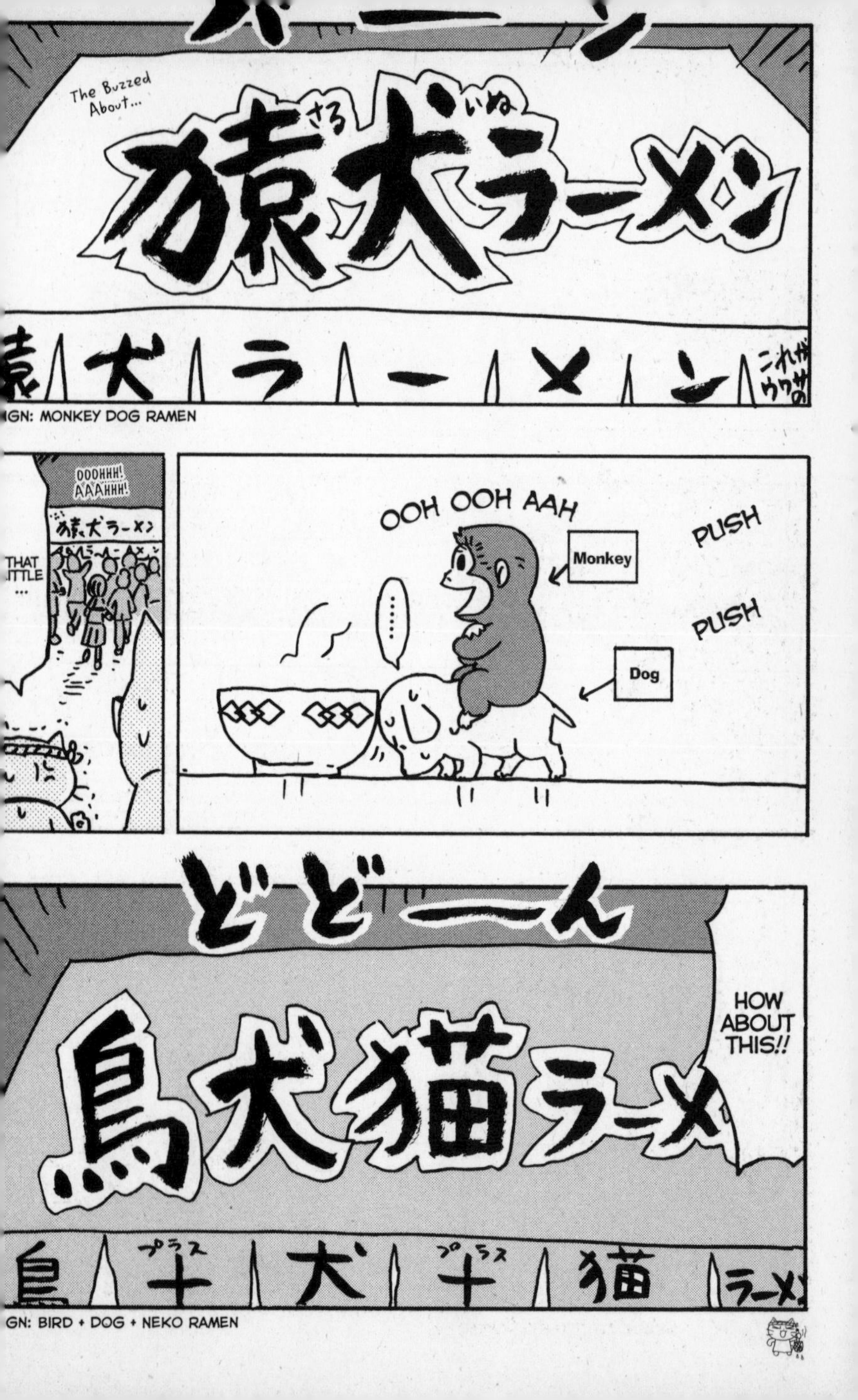

The Buzzed About...
猿犬ラーメン
猿犬ラーメン
これがウワサの
IGN: MONKEY DOG RAMEN
OOH OOH AAH
PUSH
PUSH
Monkey
Dog
……
OOOHHH! AAAHHH!
猿犬ラーメン
THAT ITTLE ...
どどーーん
HOW ABOUT THIS!!
鳥犬猫ラーメ
鳥+犬+猫ラーメ
GN: BIRD + DOG + NEKO RAMEN

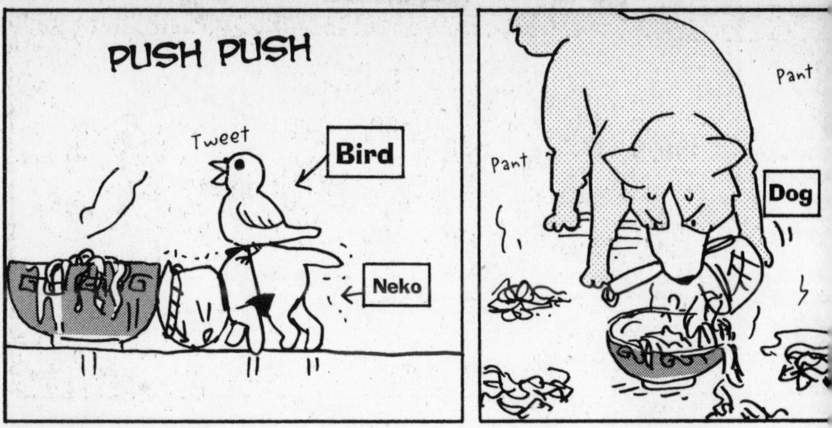
Pant
Pant
Dog
PUSH PUSH
Tweet
Bird
Neko

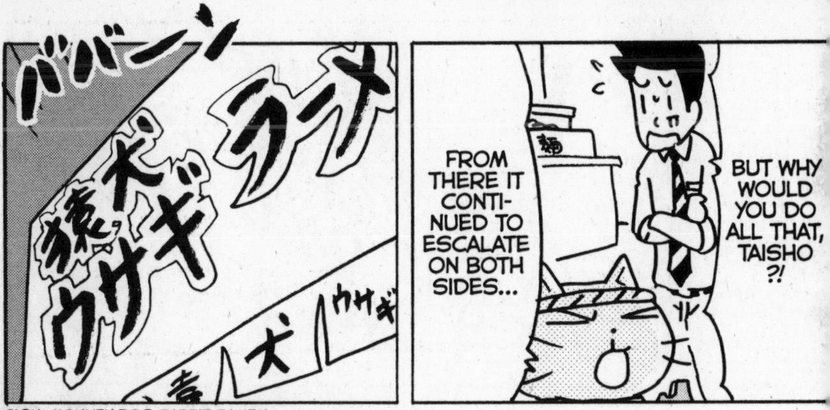
BUT WHY WOULD YOU DO ALL THAT, TAISHO ?!
FROM THERE IT CONTI-NUED TO ESCALATE ON BOTH SIDES...
バババーン
猿犬ウサギラーメン

SIGN: MONKEY DOG RABBIT RAMEN

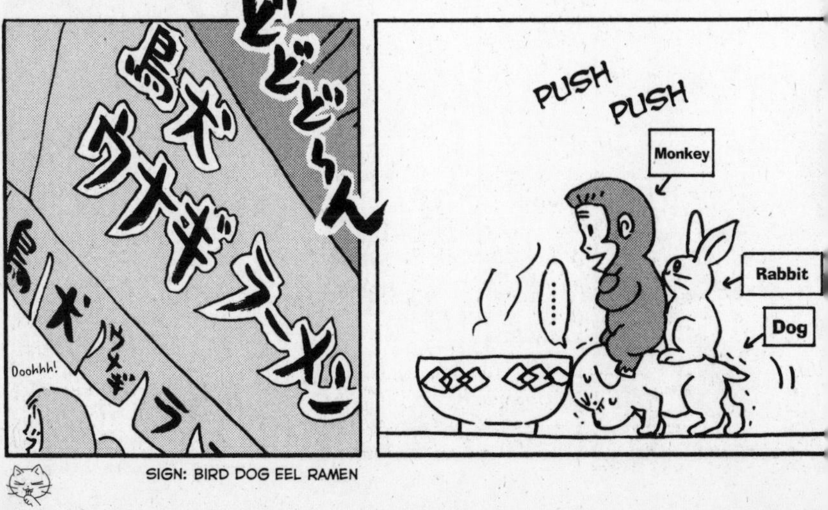
PUSH PUSH
Monkey
Rabbit
Dog
……
どどど～ん
鳥犬ウナギラーメン
Doohhh!

SIGN: BIRD DOG EEL RAMEN

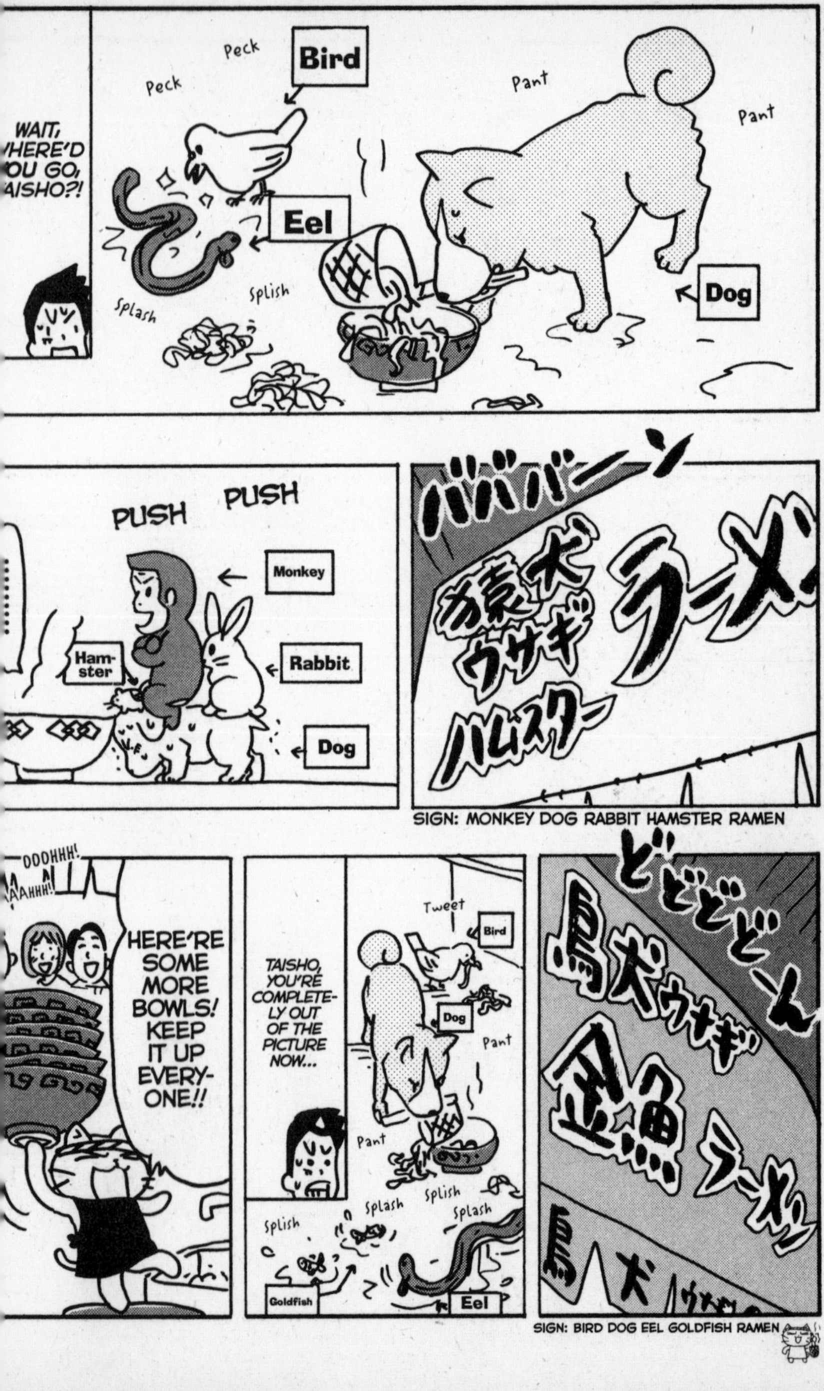
Peck
Peck
Bird
Pant
Pant
Eel
Dog
Splish
Splash
WAIT, HERE'D OU GO, AISHO?!
ババーン
猿犬ウサギハムスターラーメン
SIGN: MONKEY DOG RABBIT HAMSTER RAMEN
PUSH
PUSH
Monkey
Rabbit
Ham-ster
Dog
どどどどーん
鳥犬ウナギ金魚ラーメン
鳥 犬 ウナギ
SIGN: BIRD DOG EEL GOLDFISH RAMEN
Tweet
Bird
Dog
Pant
Pant
TAISHO, YOU'RE COMPLETE-LY OUT OF THE PICTURE NOW...
Splish
Splash
Splish
Splash
Goldfish
Eel
OOOHHH!
AAHHH!
HERE'RE SOME MORE BOWLS! KEEP IT UP EVERY-ONE!!

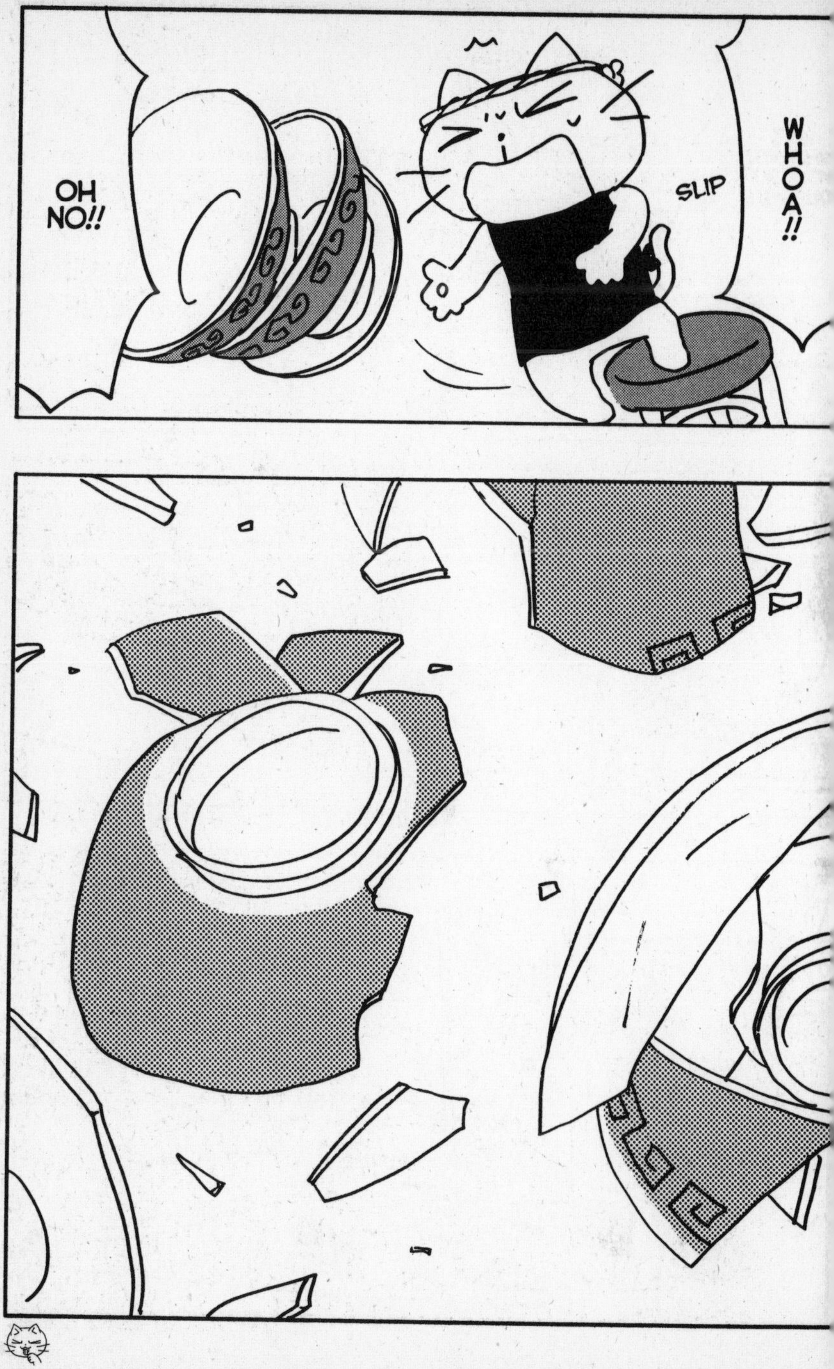
WHOA!!
SLIP
OH NO!!

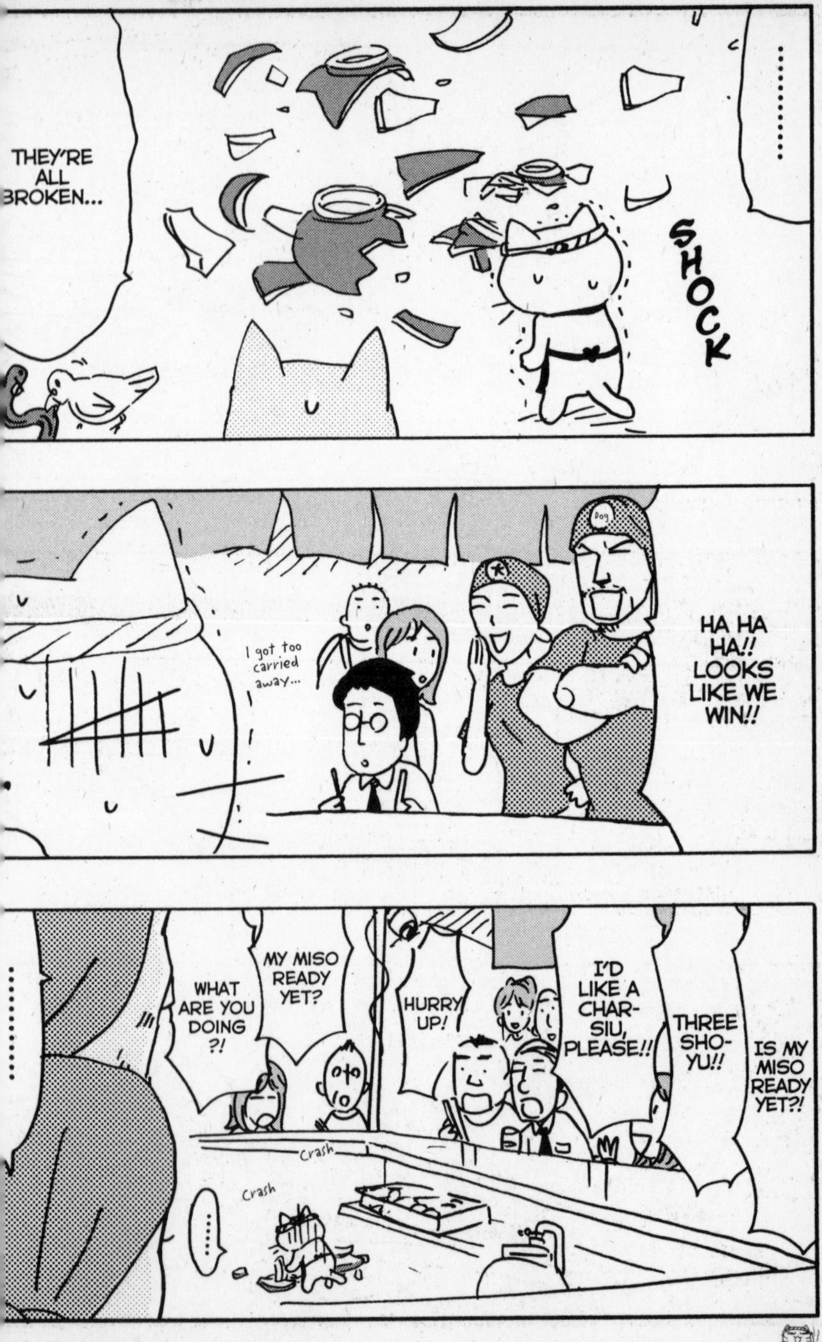
......
SHOCK
THEY'RE ALL BROKEN...
HA HA HA!! LOOKS LIKE WE WIN!!
I got too carried away...
IS MY MISO READY YET?!
THREE SHO-YU!!
I'D LIKE A CHAR-SIU, PLEASE!!
HURRY UP!
MY MISO READY YET?
WHAT ARE YOU DOING ?!
Crash
Crash
......
......

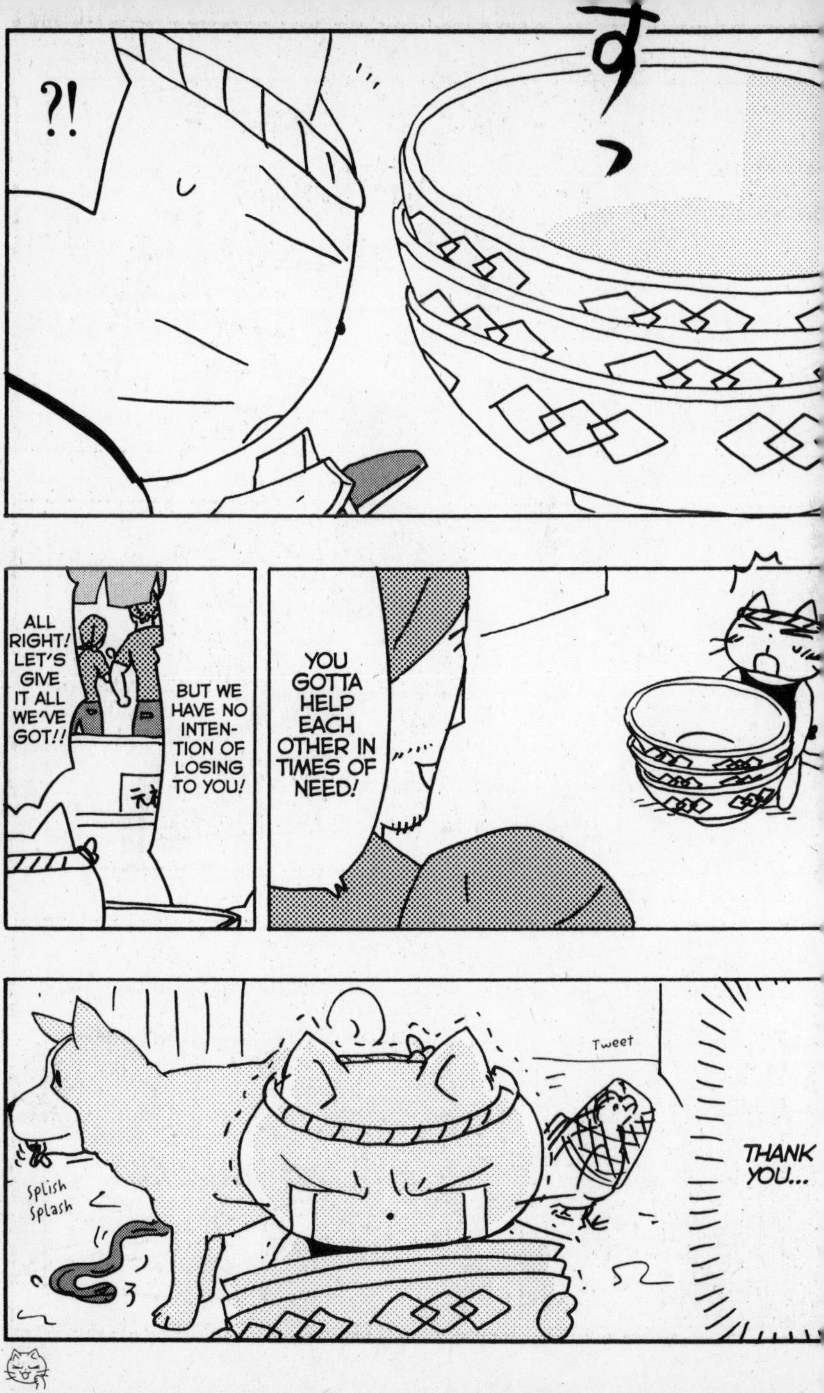
すっ
?!
YOU GOTTA HELP EACH OTHER IN TIMES OF NEED!
BUT WE HAVE NO INTENTION OF LOSING TO YOU!
ALL RIGHT! LET'S GIVE IT ALL WE'VE GOT!!
THANK YOU...
Tweet
Splish Splash

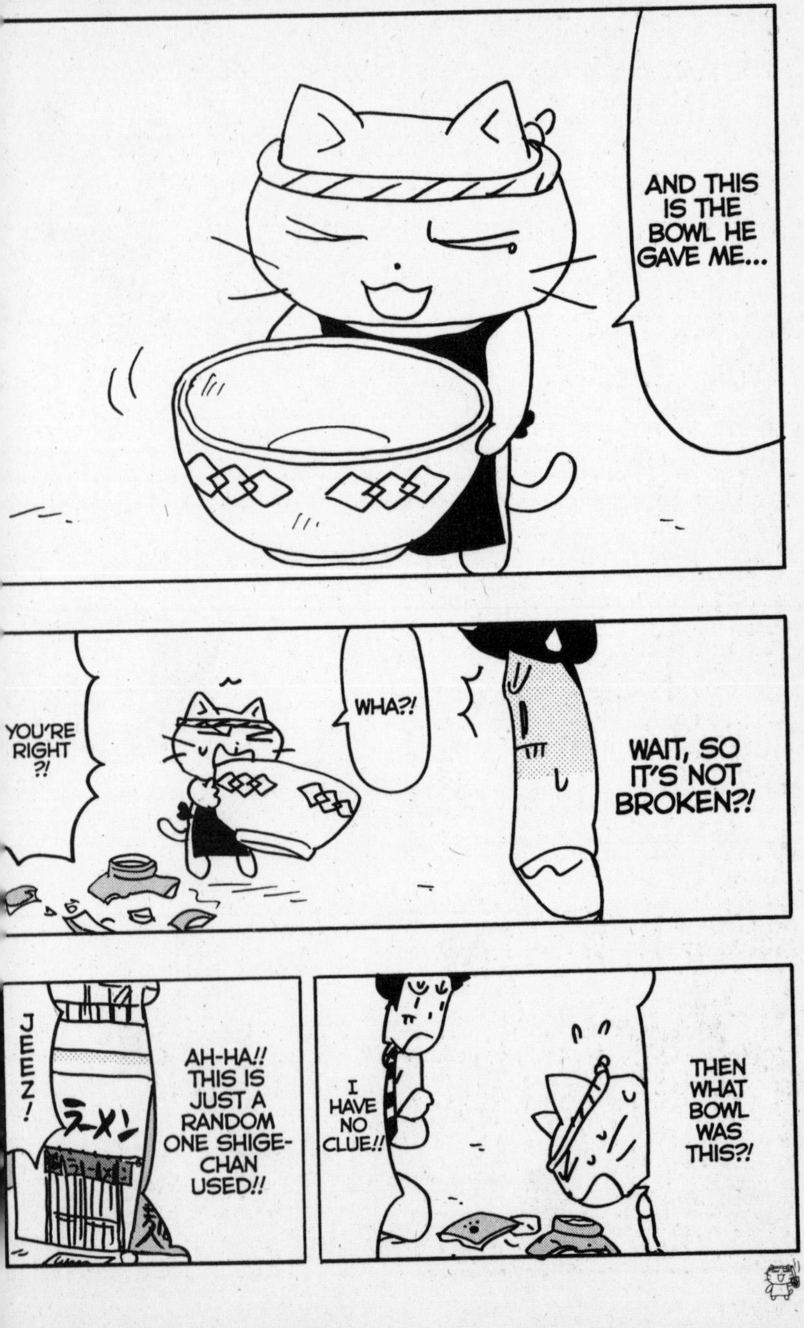
AND THIS IS THE BOWL HE GAVE ME...
WAIT, SO IT'S NOT BROKEN?!
WHA?!
YOU'RE RIGHT ?!
THEN WHAT BOWL WAS THIS?!
I HAVE NO CLUE!!
AH-HA!! THIS IS JUST A RANDOM ONE SHIGE-CHAN USED!!
JEEZ!
ラーメン

Popular Menu

Shop's "Top 10 Most Popular" Menu
#1 Shoyu
#2 Miso
Shop's "Top 10 Most Popular" Menu
#1 Shoyu
#2 Miso
#3 Shio
#4 Char-siu Noodles
#5
#6
#7
#8
HUH?! WHAT ABOUT THE REST?!
WELL, I'M UNDECIDED.
I CAN'T DECIDE WHICH ONES I LIKE BEST...
...SO I'M NOT SURE ABOUT THE REST.
What should come next...?
YOU'RE DECIDING?!

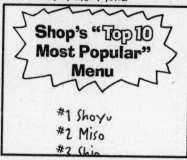

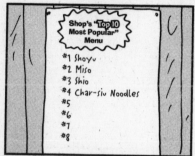

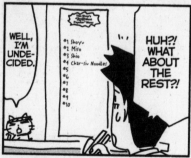

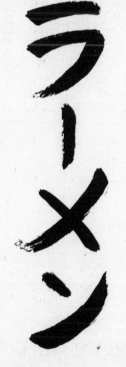

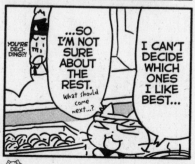

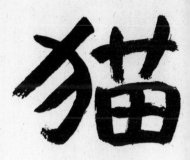

猫ラーメン

Chapter 8

A Quick Drag

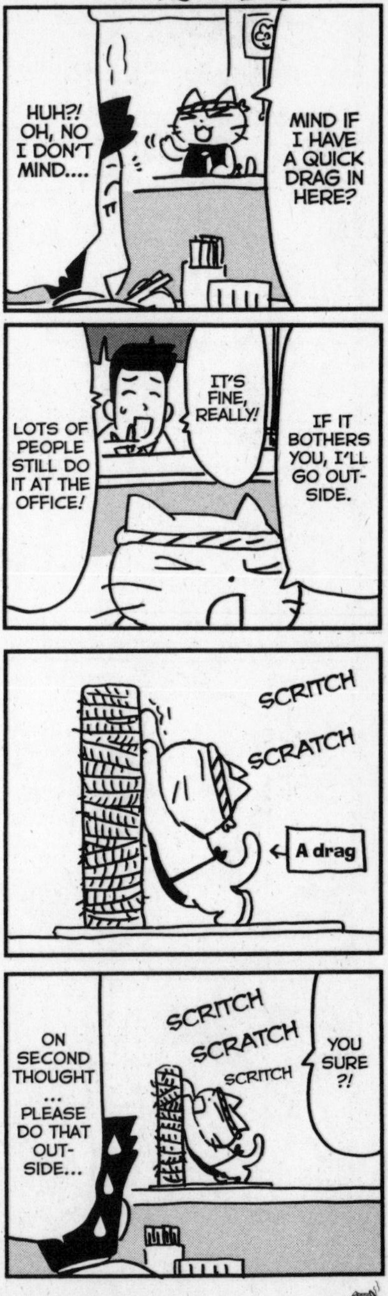
MIND IF I HAVE A QUICK DRAG IN HERE?
HUH?! OH, NO I DON'T MIND....
IF IT BOTHERS YOU, I'LL GO OUTSIDE.
IT'S FINE, REALLY!
LOTS OF PEOPLE STILL DO IT AT THE OFFICE!
SCRITCH
SCRATCH
A drag
YOU SURE?!
SCRITCH
SCRATCH
SCRITCH
ON SECOND THOUGHT ... PLEASE DO THAT OUTSIDE...

Splitting a Table

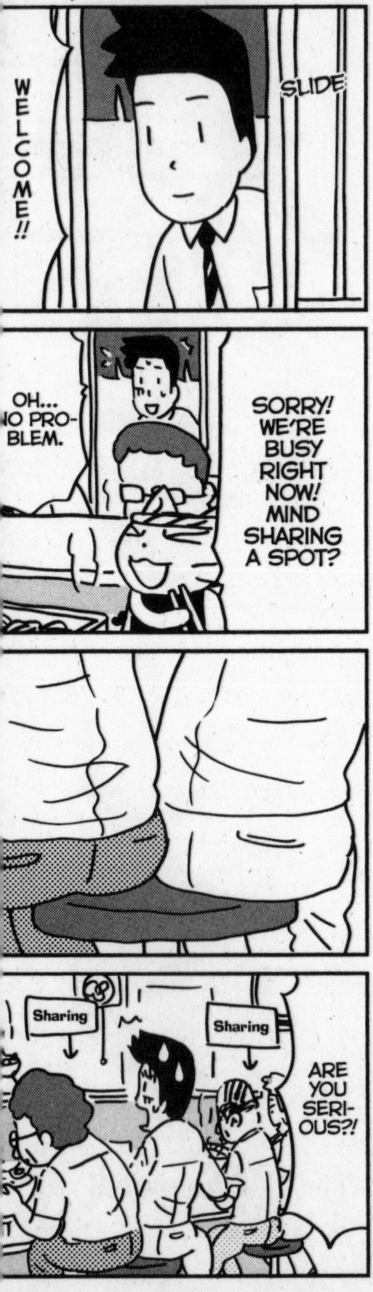
SLIDE
WELCOME!!
SORRY! WE'RE BUSY RIGHT NOW! MIND SHARING A SPOT?
OH... NO PROBLEM.
ARE YOU SERIOUS?!
Sharing
Sharing

Cards

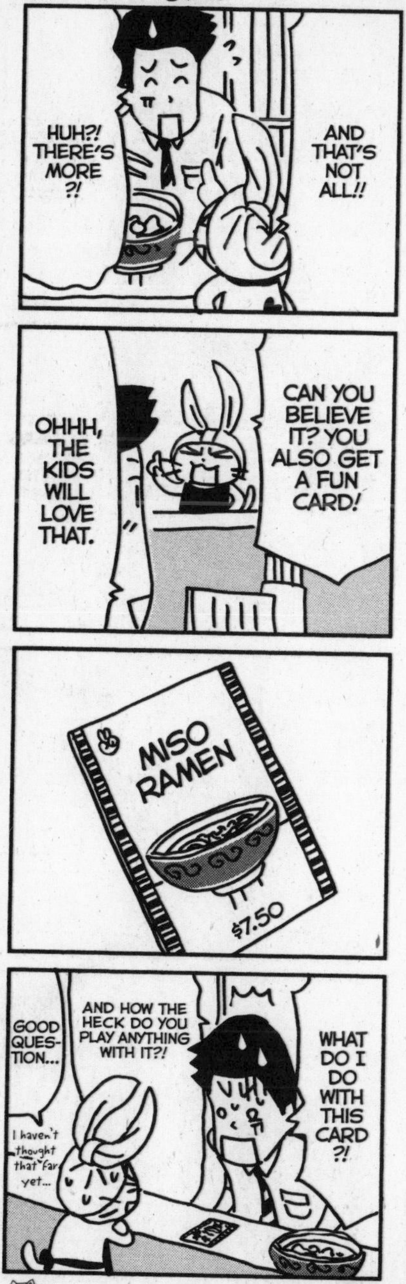
AND THAT'S NOT ALL!!
HUH?! THERE'S MORE ?!
CAN YOU BELIEVE IT? YOU ALSO GET A FUN CARD!
OHHH, THE KIDS WILL LOVE THAT.
MISO RAMEN
$7.50
WHAT DO I DO WITH THIS CARD ?!
AND HOW THE HECK DO YOU PLAY ANYTHING WITH IT?!
GOOD QUES-TION...
I haven't thought that far yet...

Intensity

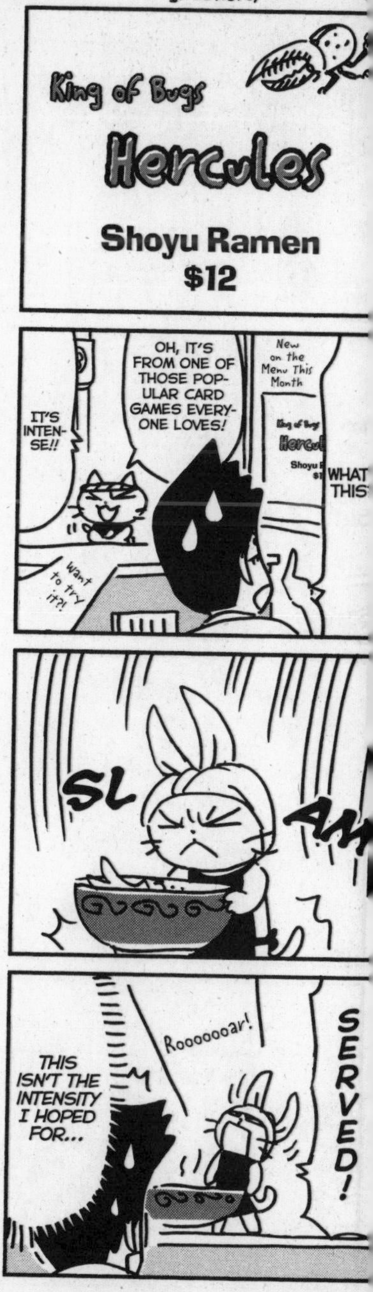
King of Bugs
Hercules
Shoyu Ramen
$12
New on the Menu This Month
OH, IT'S FROM ONE OF THOSE POP-ULAR CARD GAMES EVERY-ONE LOVES!
IT'S INTEN-SE!!
WHAT
THIS
Want to try it?!
SL
SERVED!
Roooooar!
THIS ISN'T THE INTENSITY I HOPED FOR...

Standing

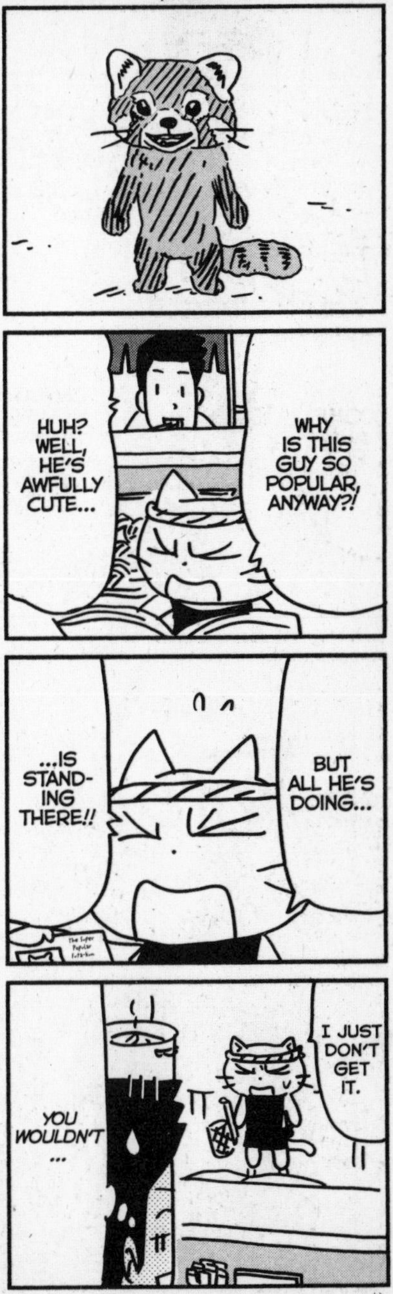
WHY IS THIS GUY SO POPULAR, ANYWAY?!
HUH? WELL, HE'S AWFULLY CUTE...
BUT ALL HE'S DOING...
...IS STANDING THERE!!
I JUST DON'T GET IT.
YOU WOULDN'T ...

Not Standing

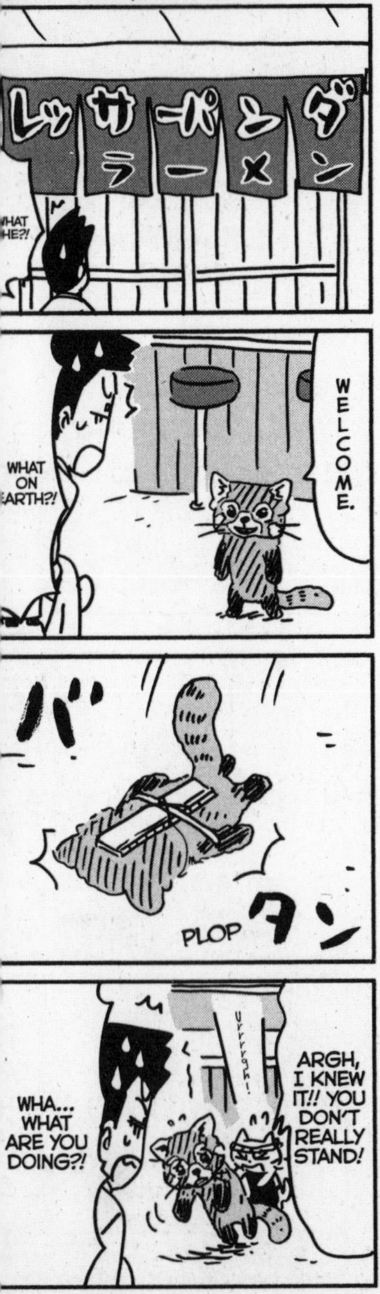
レッサーパンダ
ラーメン
WELCOME.
WHAT ON
ARTH?!
バ
PLOP タン
ARGH, I KNEW IT!! YOU DON'T REALLY STAND!
WHA... WHAT ARE YOU DOING?!

Mascot

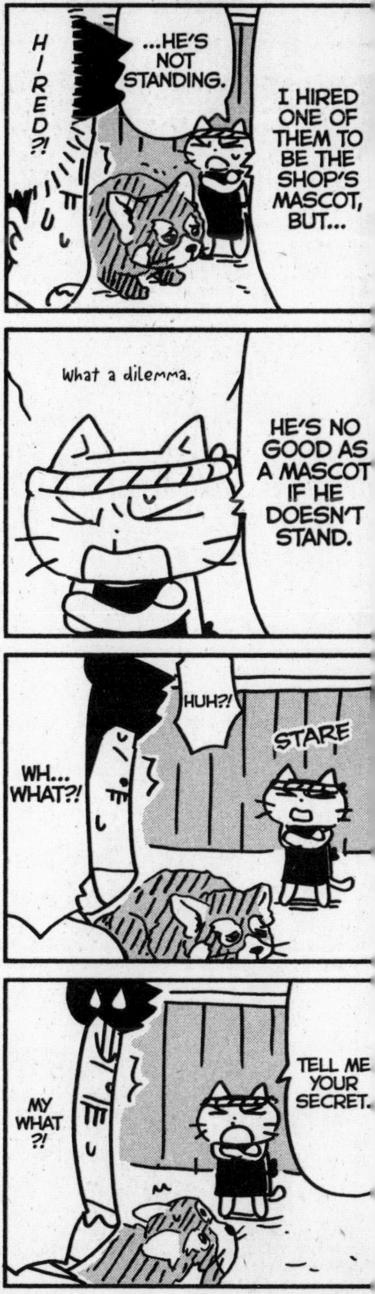
I HIRED ONE OF THEM TO BE THE SHOP'S MASCOT, BUT...
...HE'S NOT STANDING.
HIRED?!
HE'S NO GOOD AS A MASCOT IF HE DOESN'T STAND.
What a dilemma.
STARE
HUH?!
WH... WHAT?!
TELL ME YOUR SECRET.
MY WHAT?!

Training

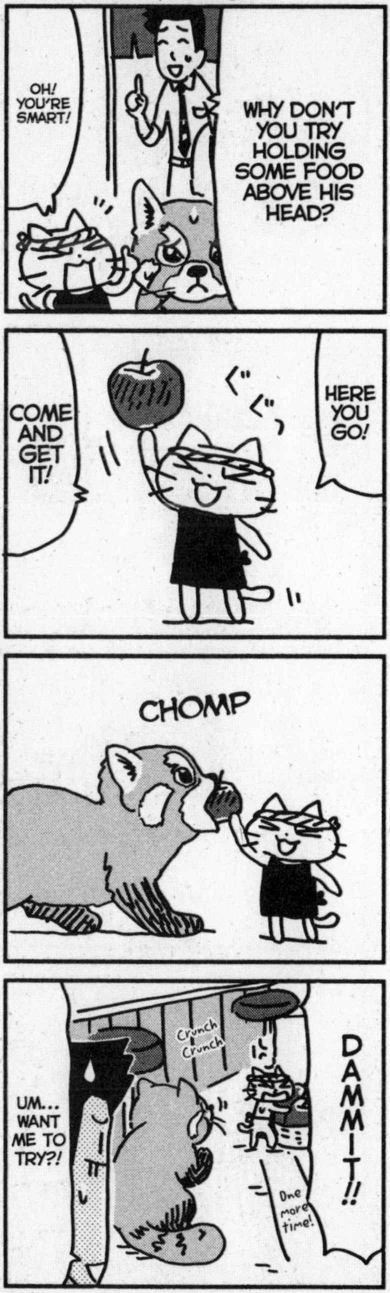
WHY DON'T YOU TRY HOLDING SOME FOOD ABOVE HIS HEAD?
OH! YOU'RE SMART!
HERE YOU GO!
COME AND GET IT!
CHOMP
DAMMIT!!
One more time!
Crunch Crunch
UM... WANT ME TO TRY?!

A Little More

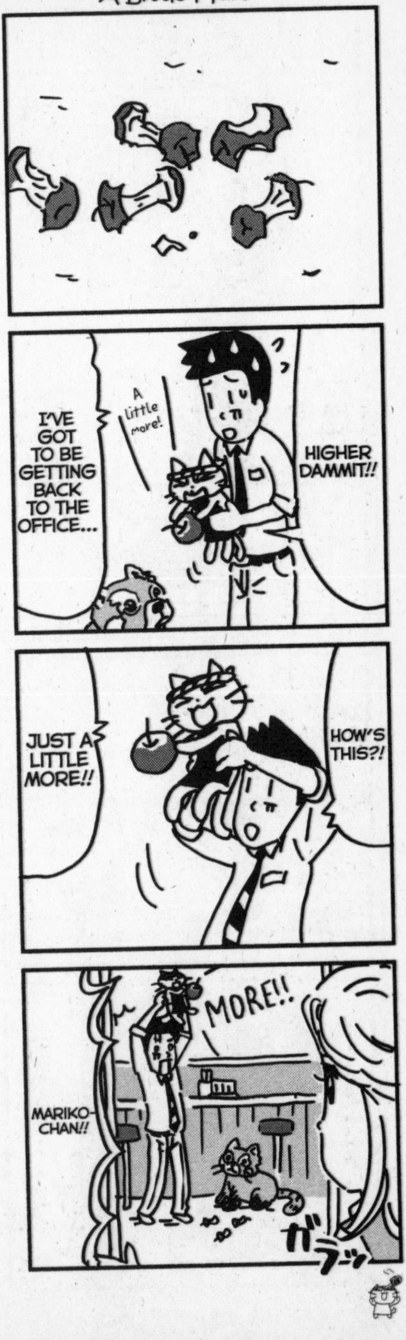
HIGHER DAMMIT!!
A little more!
I'VE GOT TO BE GETTING BACK TO THE OFFICE...
HOW'S THIS?!
JUST A LITTLE MORE!!
MORE!!
MARIKO-CHAN!!
ガラッ

You Can Do It

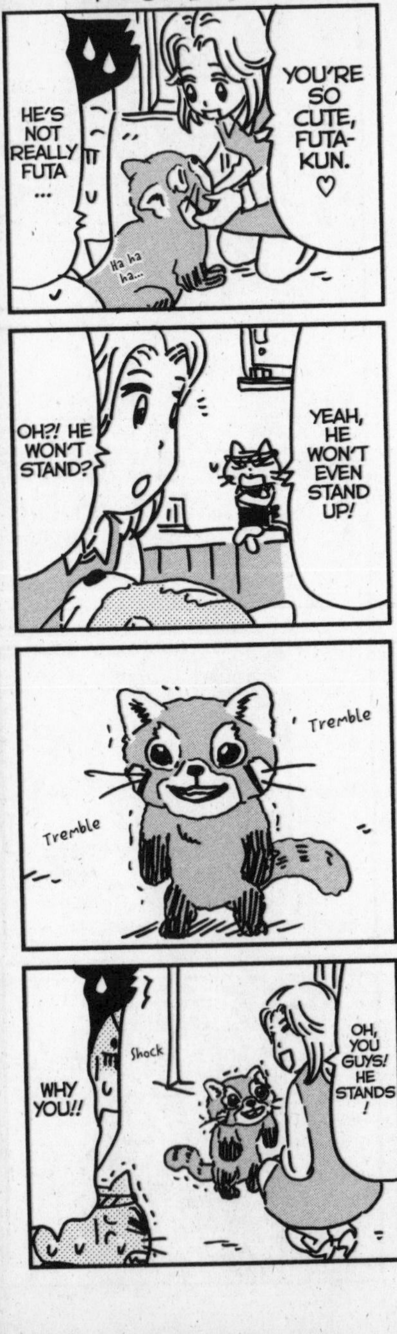
YOU'RE SO CUTE, FUTA-KUN. ♡
HE'S NOT REALLY FUTA...
Ha ha ha...
YEAH, HE WON'T EVEN STAND UP!
OH?! HE WON'T STAND?
Tremble
Tremble
OH, YOU GUYS! HE STANDS!
Shock
WHY YOU!!

How to Make It

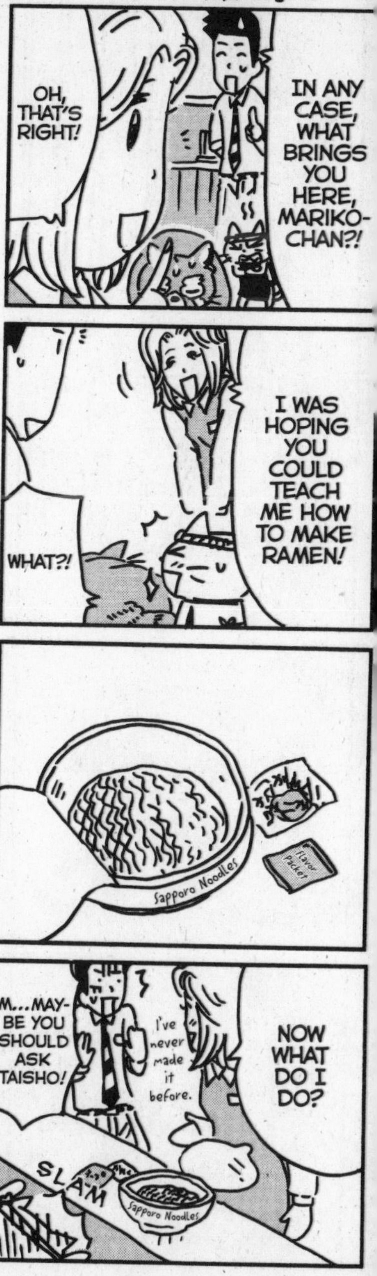
IN ANY CASE, WHAT BRINGS YOU HERE, MARIKO-CHAN?!
OH, THAT'S RIGHT!
I WAS HOPING YOU COULD TEACH ME HOW TO MAKE RAMEN!
WHAT?!
Sapporo Noodles
Flavor Packet
NOW WHAT DO I DO?
I've never made it before.
M...MAY-BE YOU SHOULD ASK TAISHO!
SLAM
Sapporo Noodles

Thanks

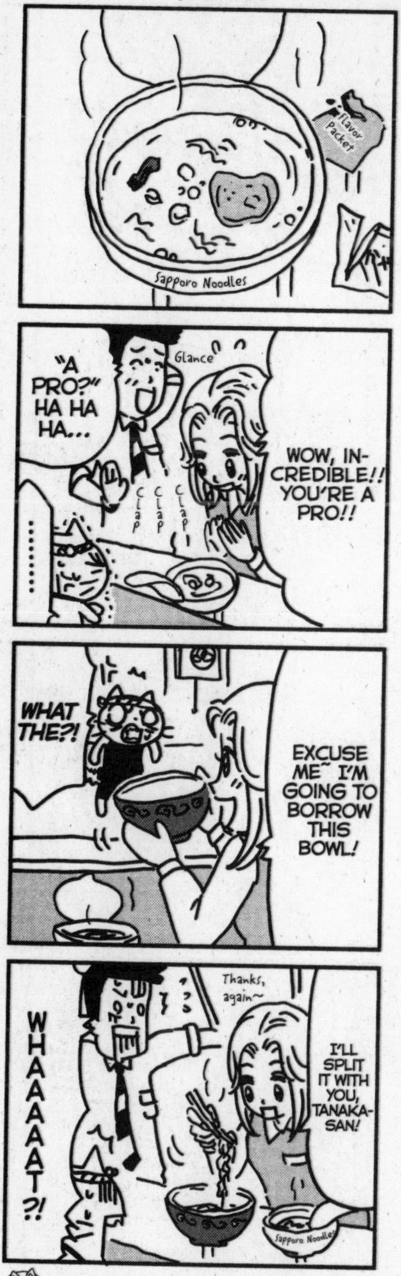
Flavor Packet
Sapporo Noodles
WOW, IN-CREDIBLE!! YOU'RE A PRO!!
Glance
"A PRO?" HA HA HA...
Clap Clap Clap
....
EXCUSE ME~ I'M GOING TO BORROW THIS BOWL!
WHAT THE?!
I'LL SPLIT IT WITH YOU, TANAKA-SAN!
Thanks, again~
WHAAAAAT?!
Sapporo Noodles

Diet

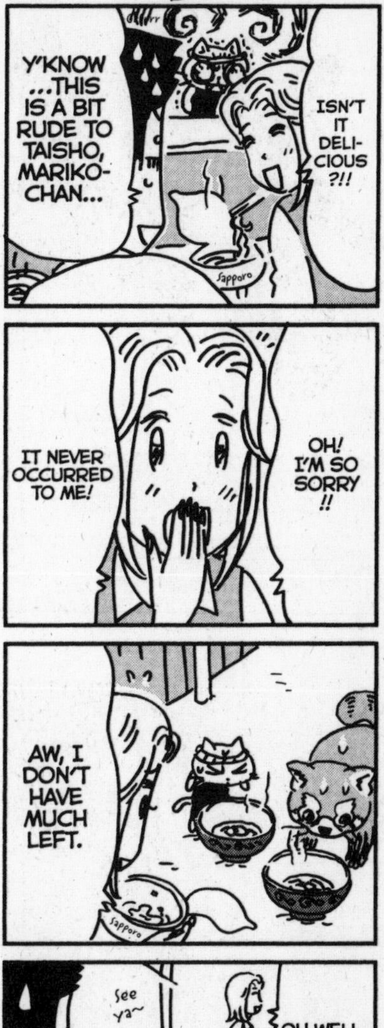
Y'KNOW ...THIS IS A BIT RUDE TO TAISHO, MARIKO-CHAN...
ISN'T IT DELI-CIOUS ?!!
Sapporo
OH! I'M SO SORRY !!
IT NEVER OCCURRED TO ME!
AW, I DON'T HAVE MUCH LEFT.
Sapporo
See ya~
OH WELL, I'M ON A DIET ANYWAY, SO I'LL MANAGE !!
....

Returning

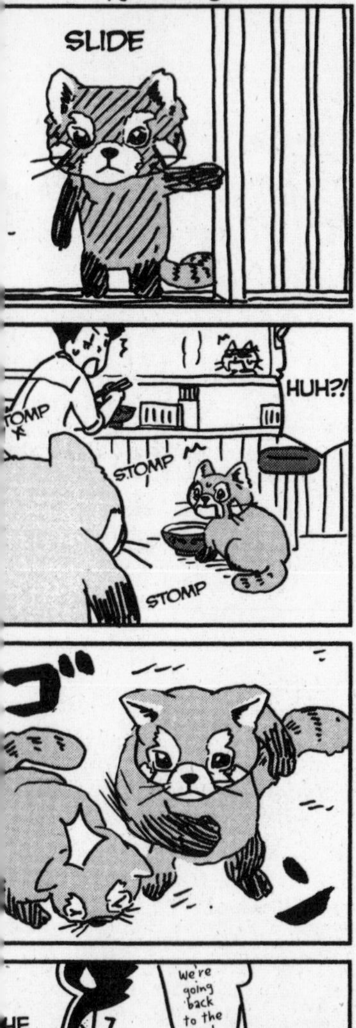
SLIDE
HUH?!
STOMP
STOMP
STOMP
We're going back to the zoo!
Sorry, dear.
DO YOU KNOW HOW LATE IT IS?!!

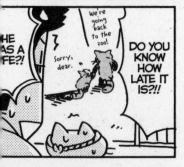

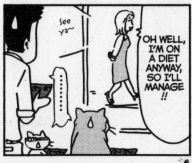

猫ラーメン

Short Comic Special

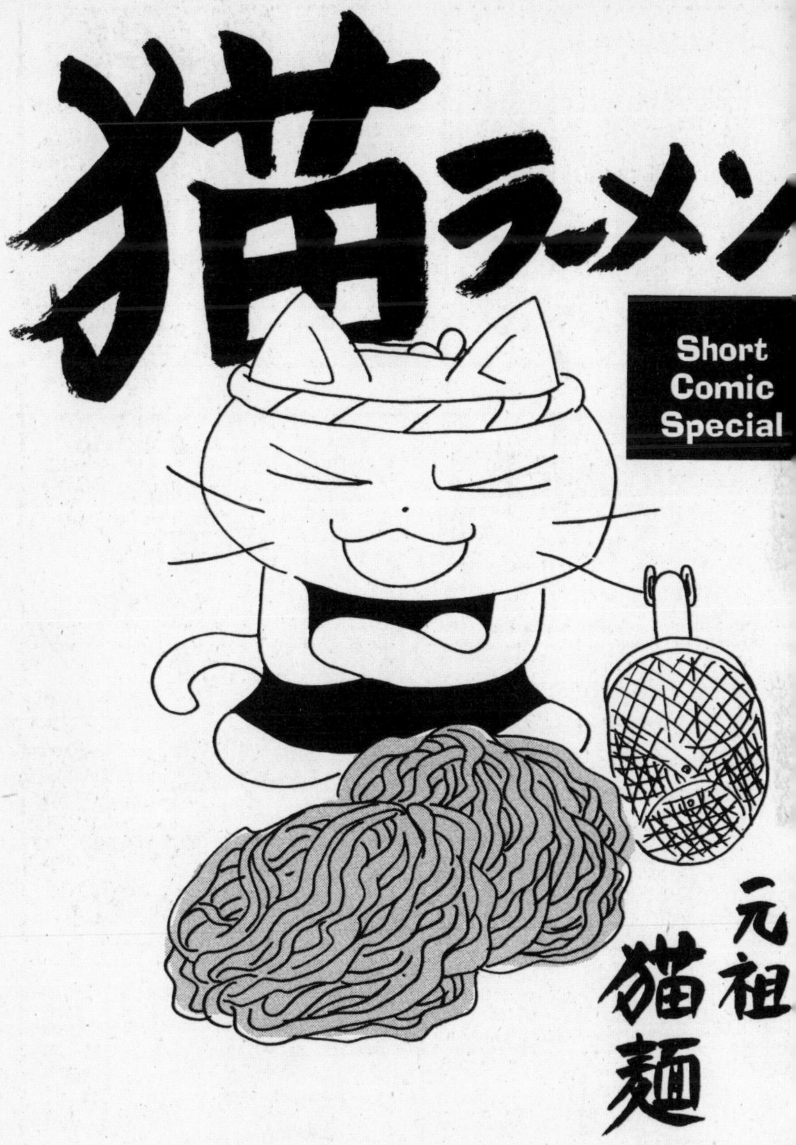

元祖猫麺

The Secret of Neko Noodles

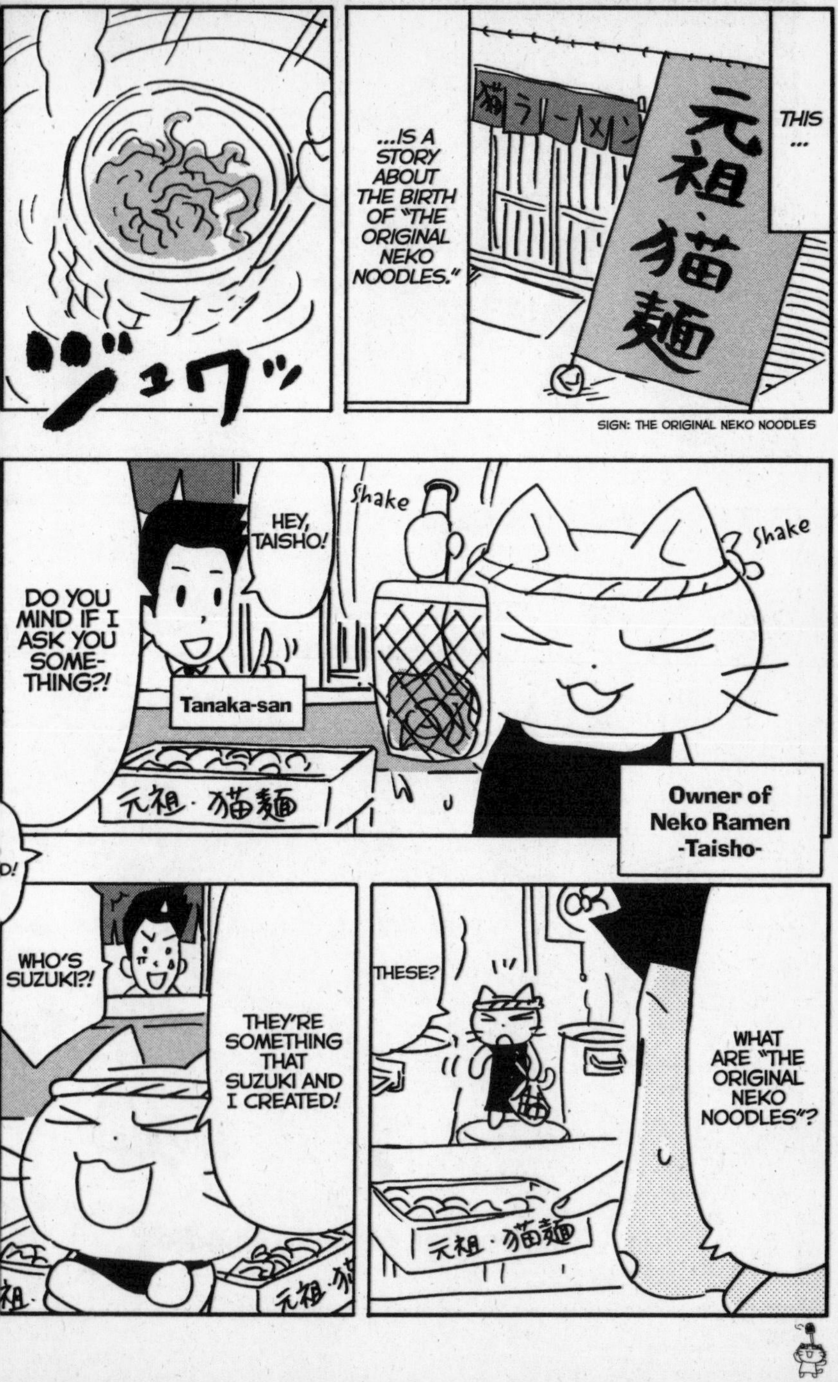
THIS ...
...IS A STORY ABOUT THE BIRTH OF "THE ORIGINAL NEKO NOODLES."
元祖・猫麺
ジュワッ
SIGN: THE ORIGINAL NEKO NOODLES
Shake
Shake
HEY, TAISHO!
DO YOU MIND IF I ASK YOU SOME-THING?!
Tanaka-san
元祖・猫麺
Owner of Neko Ramen -Taisho-
WHAT ARE "THE ORIGINAL NEKO NOODLES"?
THESE?
元祖・猫麺
THEY'RE SOMETHING THAT SUZUKI AND I CREATED!
WHO'S SUZUKI?!

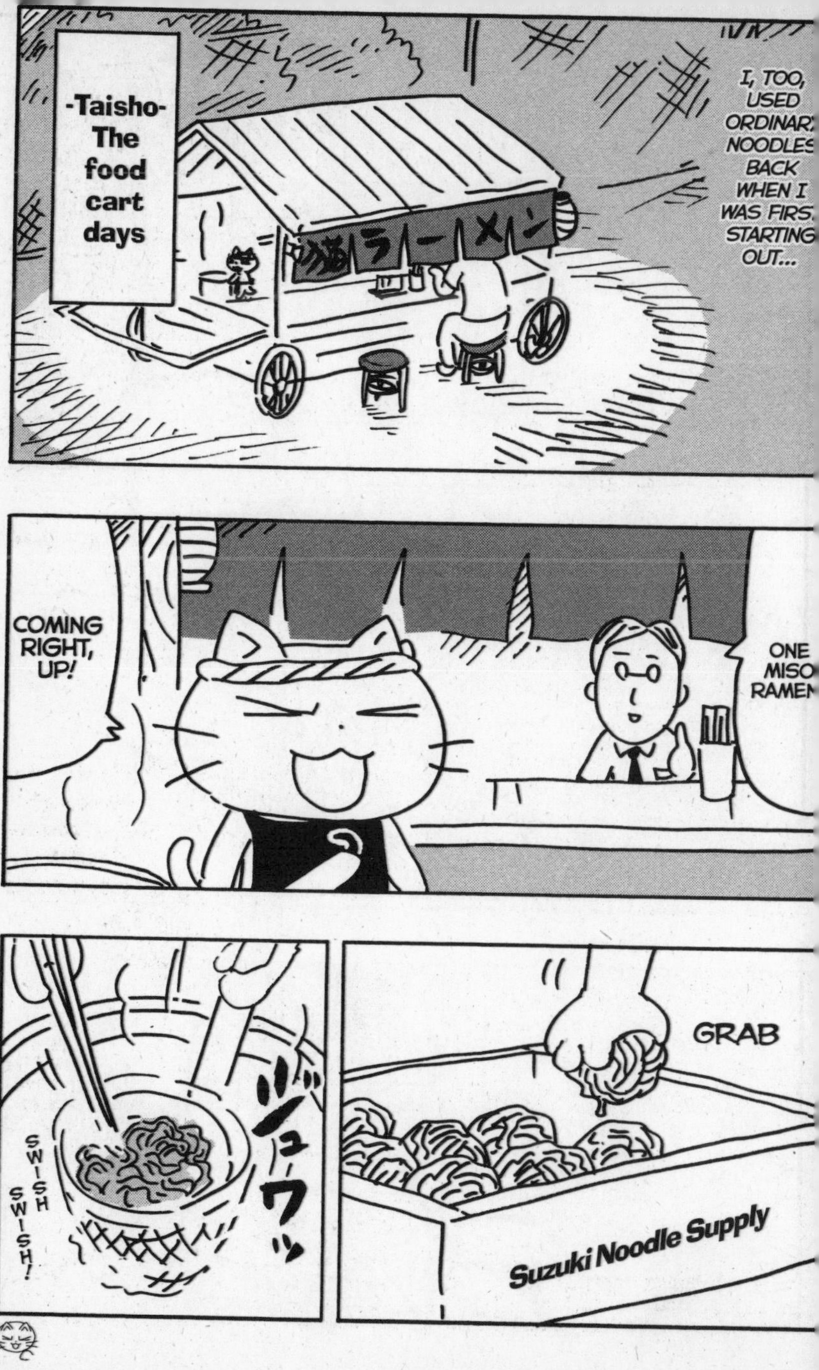
-Taisho- The food cart days
I, TOO, USED ORDINAR NOODLES BACK WHEN I WAS FIRS STARTING OUT...
ラーメン
ONE MISO RAMEN
COMING RIGHT, UP!
GRAB
Suzuki Noodle Supply
ジューワッ
SWISH SWISH!

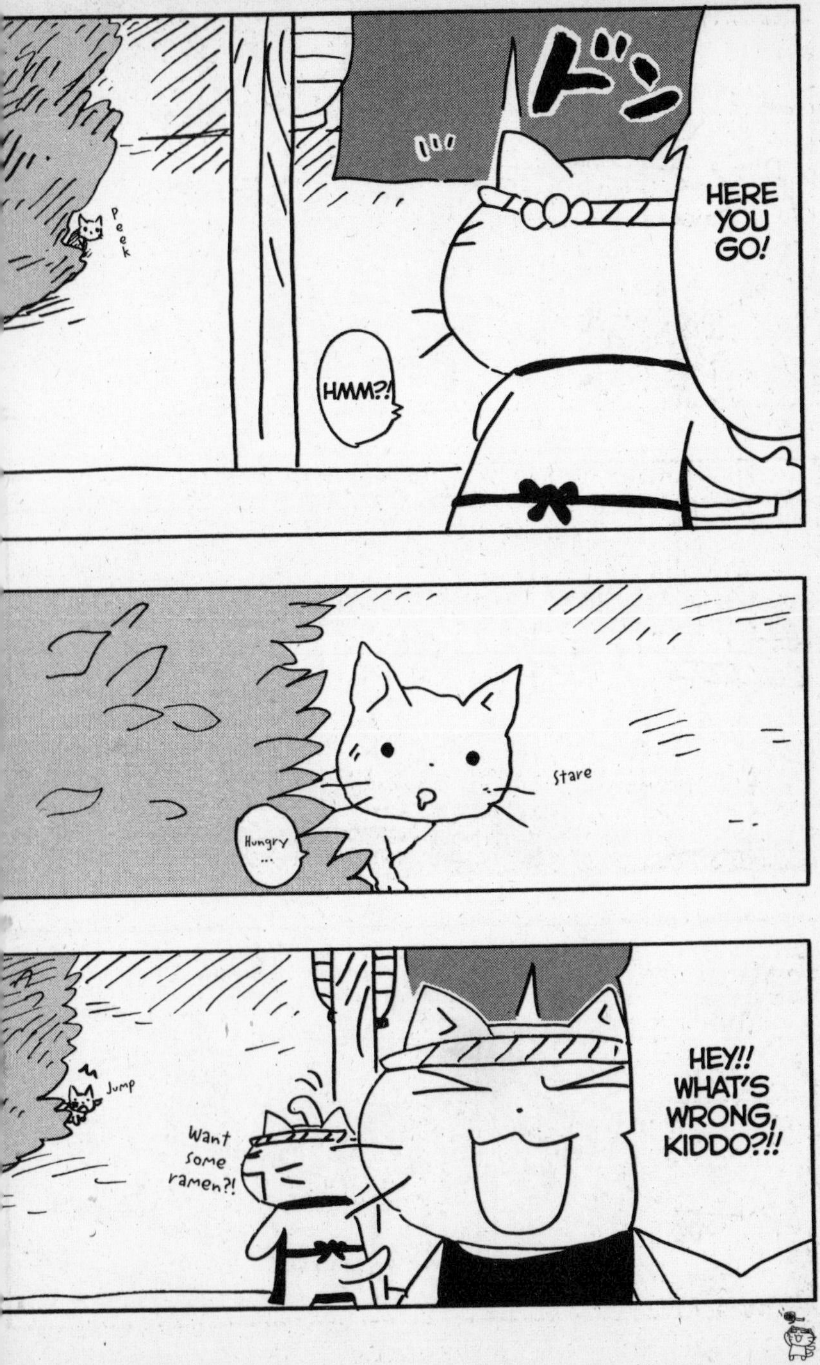
ドン
HERE YOU GO!
HMM?!
Peek
Stare
Hungry ...
HEY!! WHAT'S WRONG, KIDDO?!!
Want some ramen?!
Jump

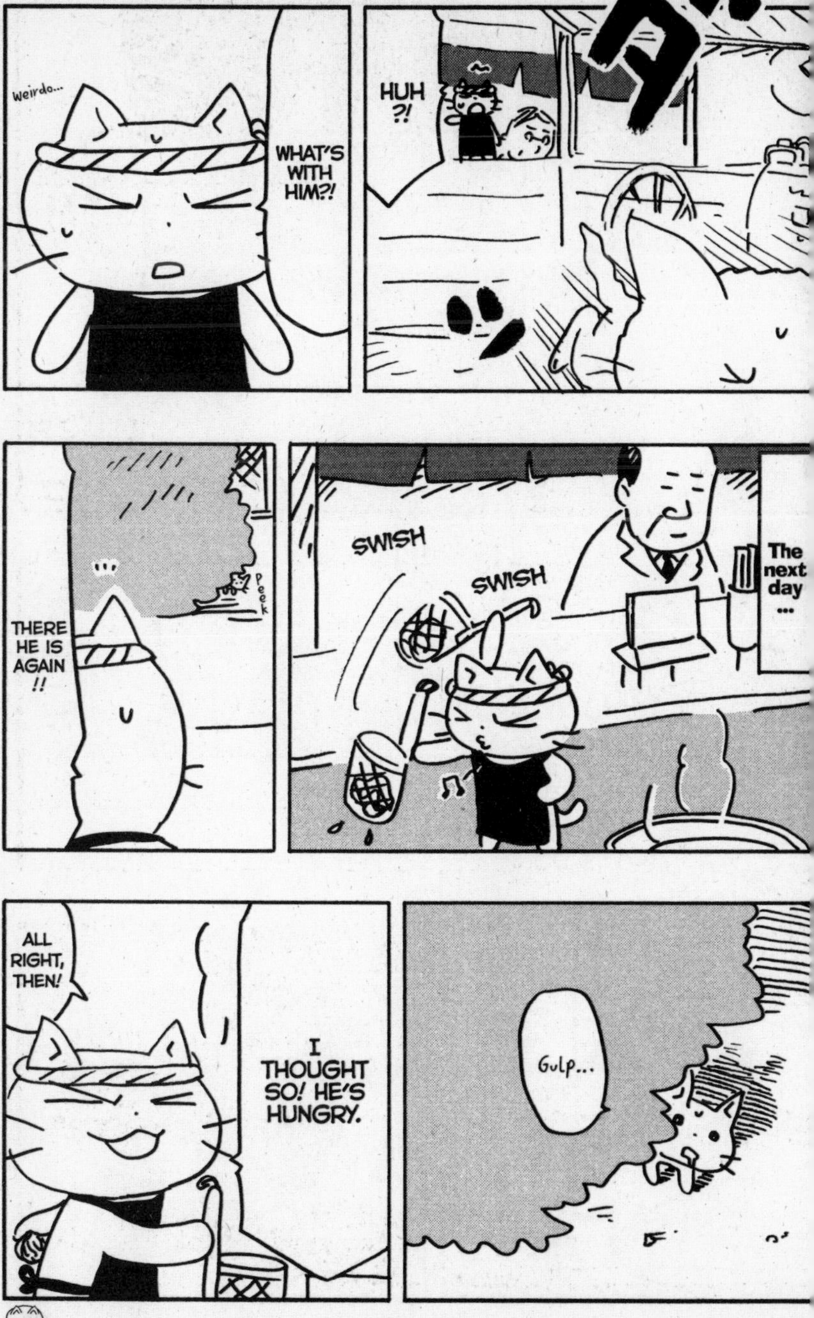

ダ
HUH ?!
WHAT'S WITH HIM?!
Weirdo...
The next day...
SWISH
SWISH
Peek
THERE HE IS AGAIN !!
Gulp...
I THOUGHT SO! HE'S HUNGRY.
ALL RIGHT, THEN!

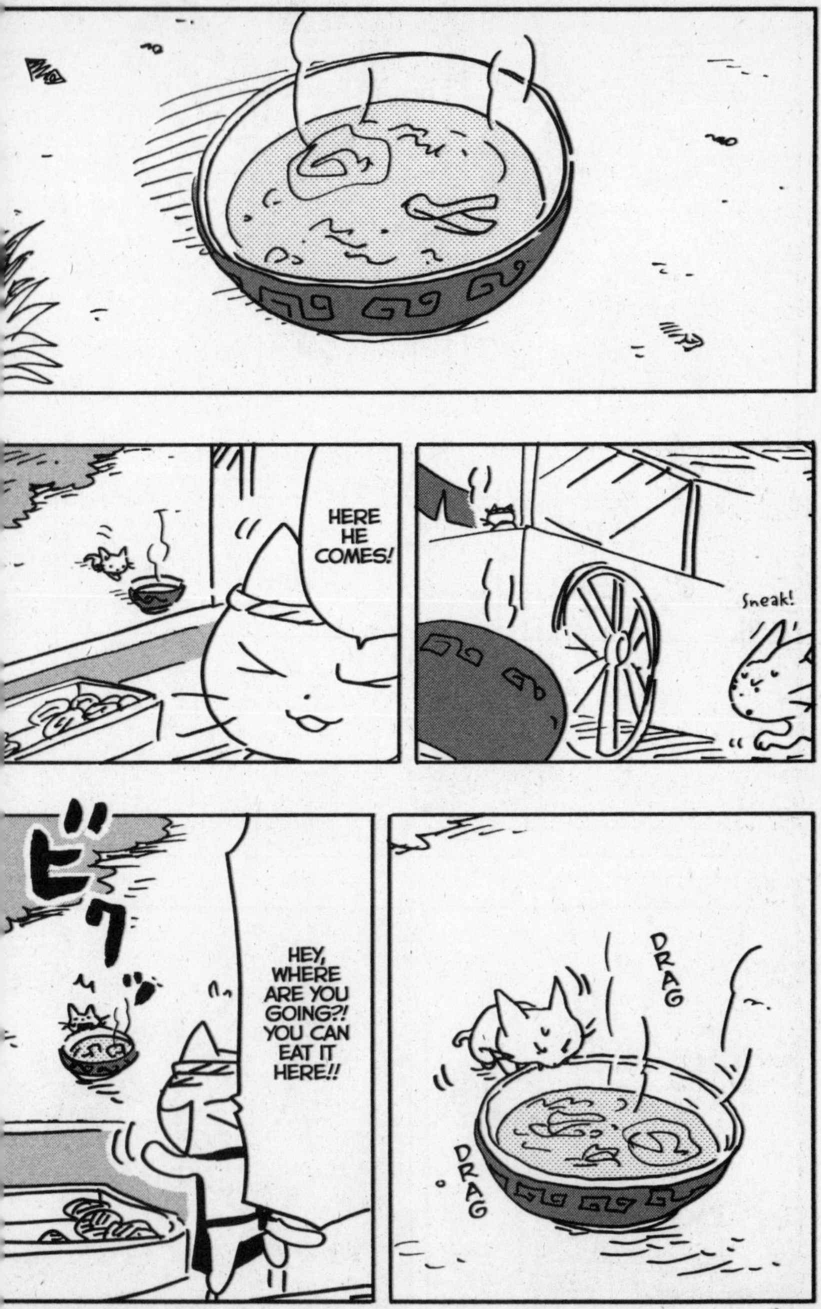
HERE HE COMES!
Sneak!
ビク
HEY, WHERE ARE YOU GOING?! YOU CAN EAT IT HERE!!
DRAG
DRAG

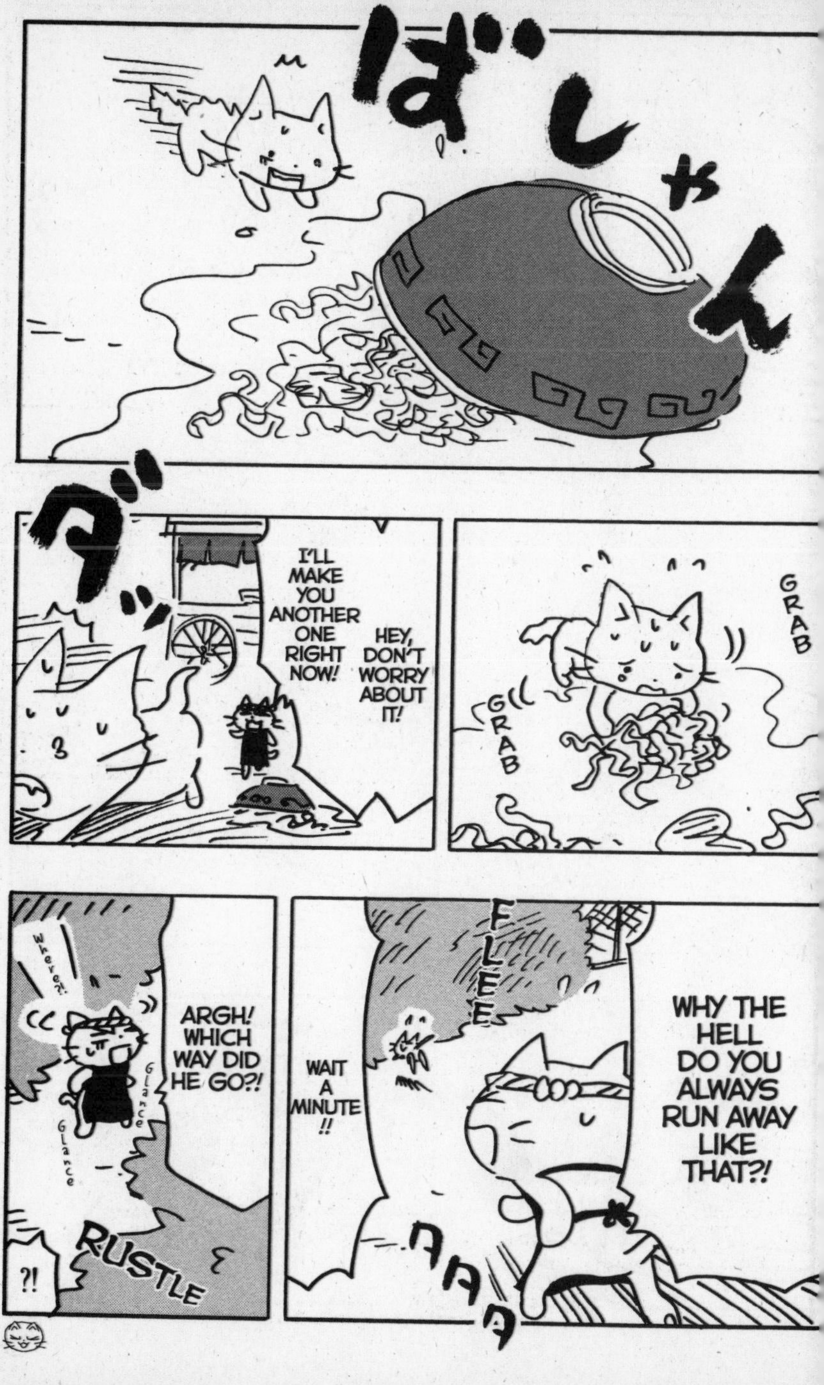

ばしゃん
GRAB
GRAB
HEY, DON'T WORRY ABOUT IT!
I'LL MAKE YOU ANOTHER ONE RIGHT NOW!
ダッ
WHY THE HELL DO YOU ALWAYS RUN AWAY LIKE THAT?!
FLEE
WAIT A MINUTE!!
ARGH! WHICH WAY DID HE GO?!
Where?!
Glance
Glance
RUSTLE
?!

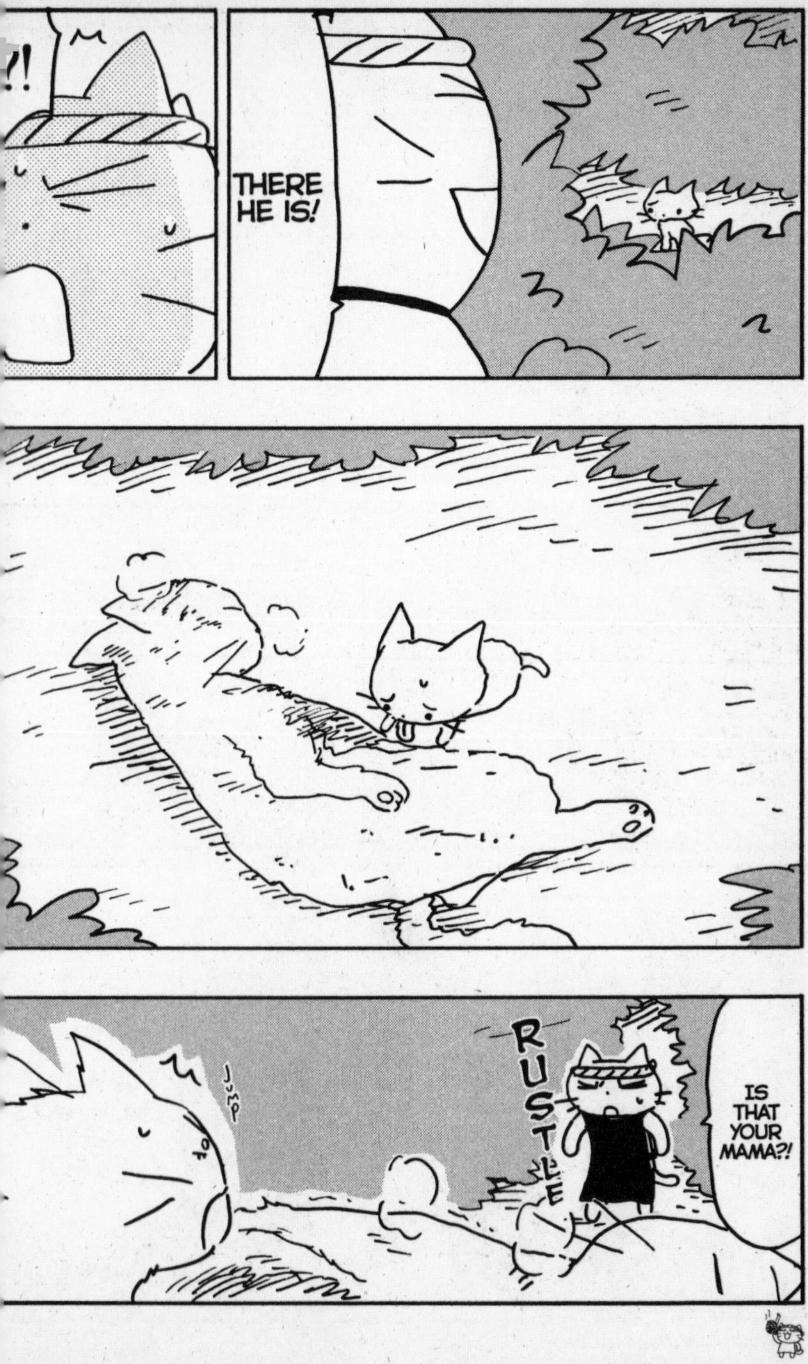
?!
THERE HE IS!
JUMP
RUSTLE
IS THAT YOUR MAMA?!

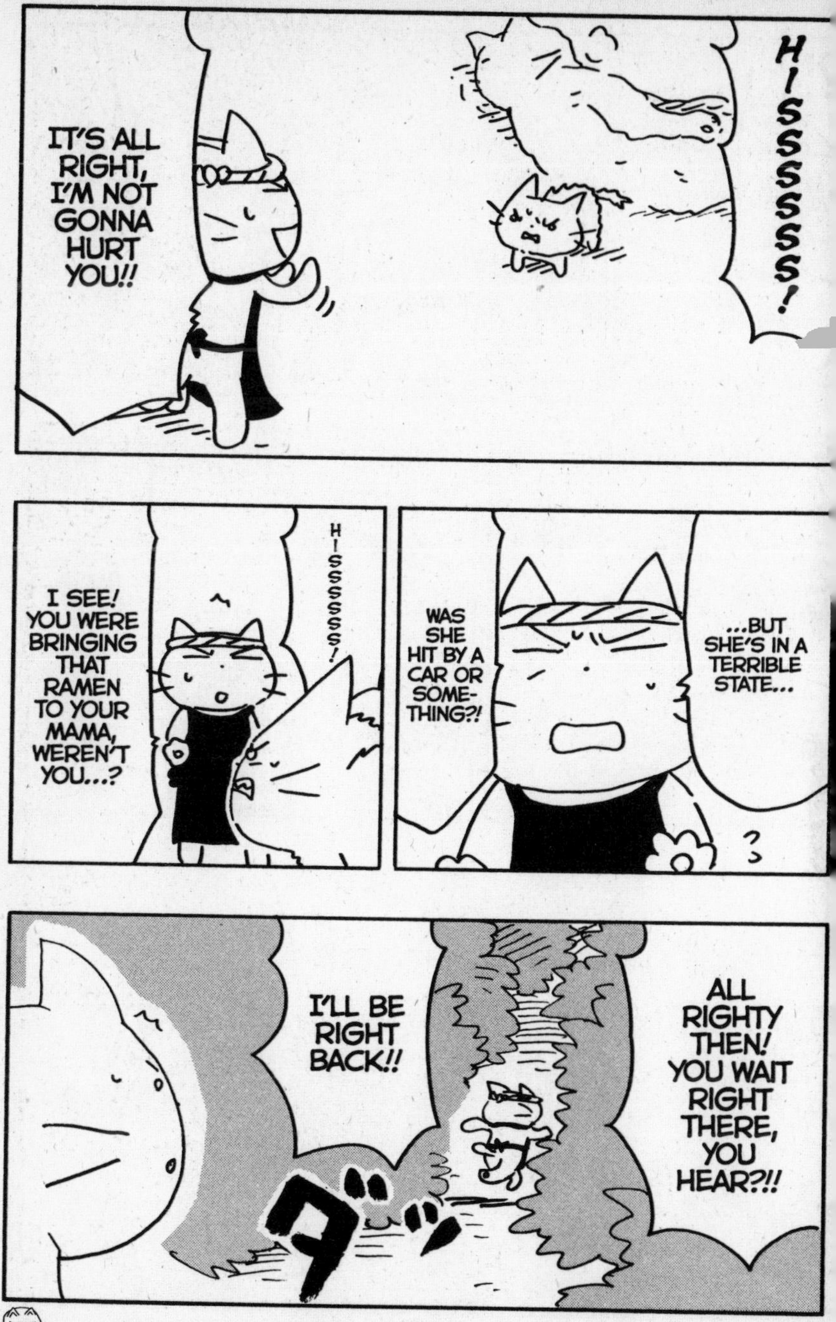
HISSSSSS!
IT'S ALL RIGHT, I'M NOT GONNA HURT YOU!!
...BUT SHE'S IN A TERRIBLE STATE...
WAS SHE HIT BY A CAR OR SOME-THING?!
HISSSSSS!
I SEE! YOU WERE BRINGING THAT RAMEN TO YOUR MAMA, WEREN'T YOU...?
ALL RIGHTY THEN! YOU WAIT RIGHT THERE, YOU HEAR?!!
I'LL BE RIGHT BACK!!
ダッ

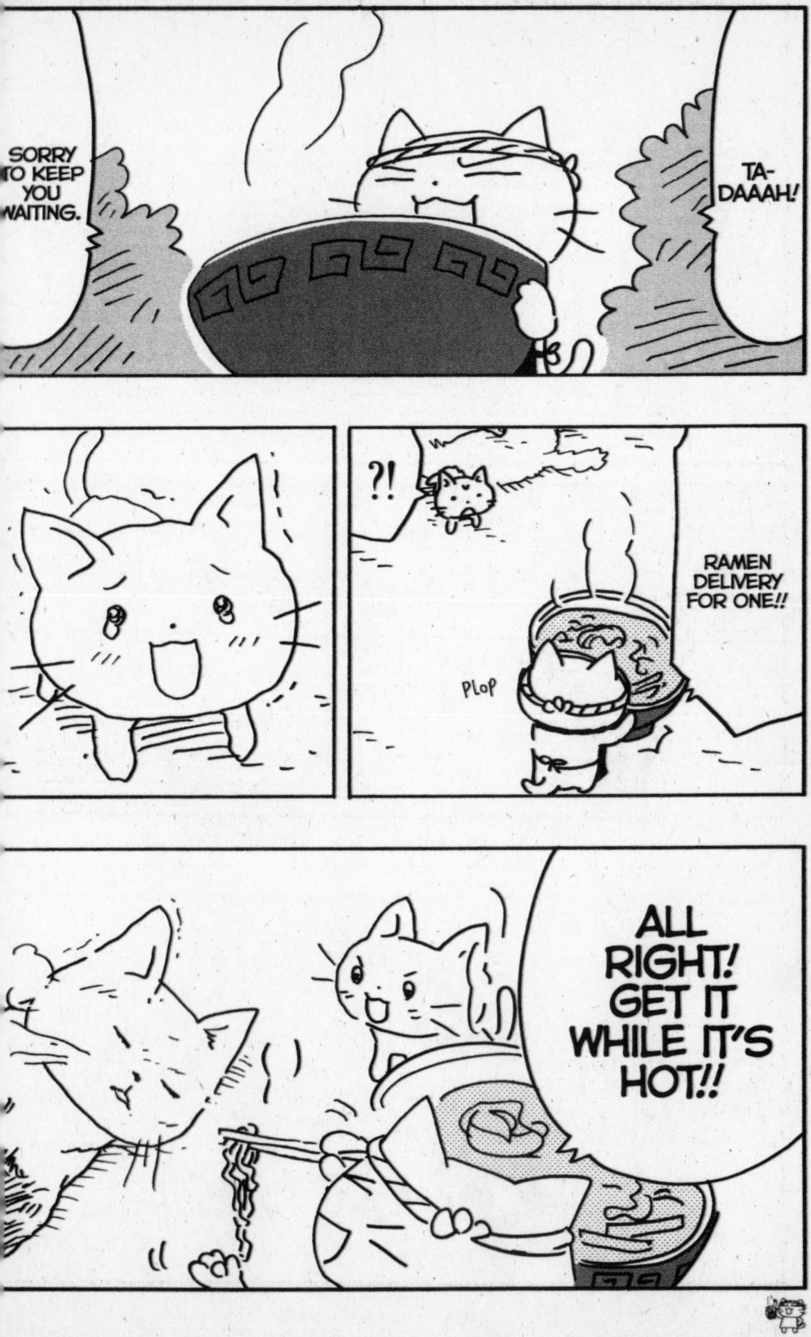
TA-DAAAH!
SORRY TO KEEP YOU WAITING.
?!
RAMEN DELIVERY FOR ONE!!
PLOP
ALL RIGHT! GET IT WHILE IT'S HOT!!

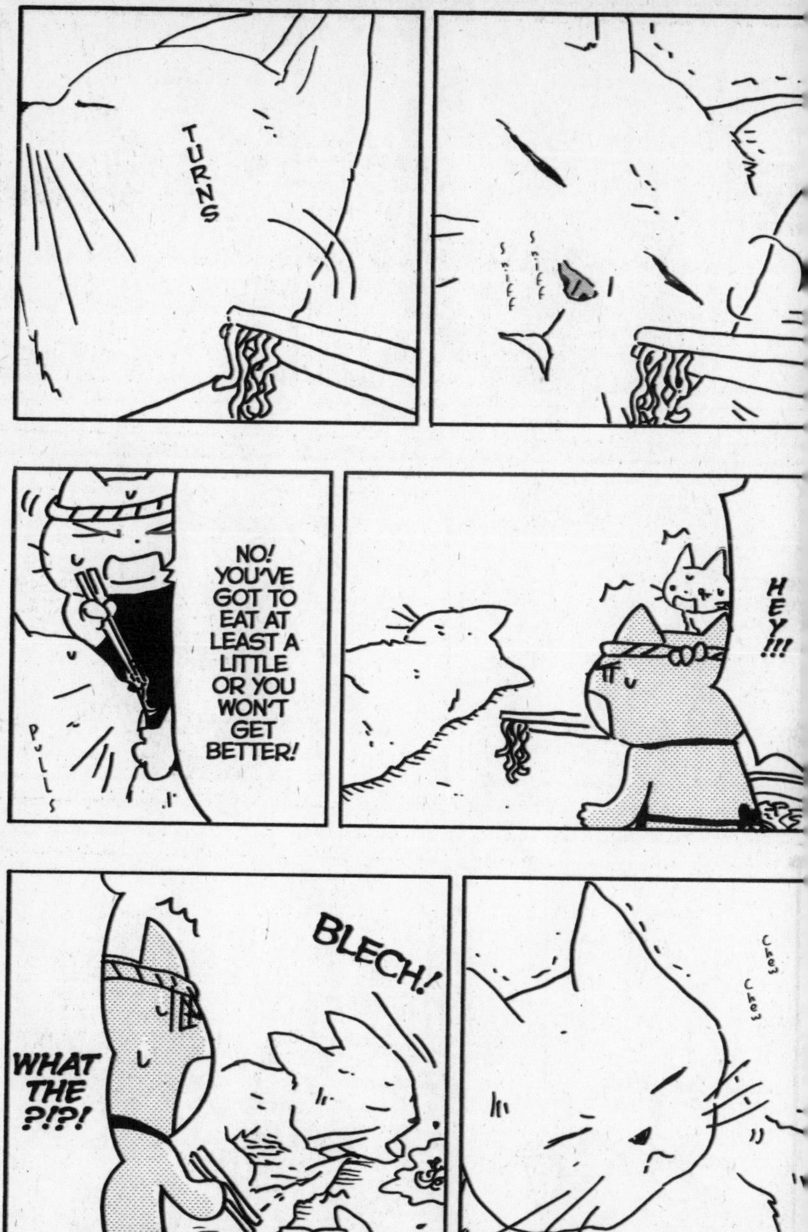
sniff
sniff
TURNS
HEY!!!
NO! YOU'VE GOT TO EAT AT LEAST A LITTLE OR YOU WON'T GET BETTER!
PULLS
chew
chew
BLECH!
WHAT THE ?!?!

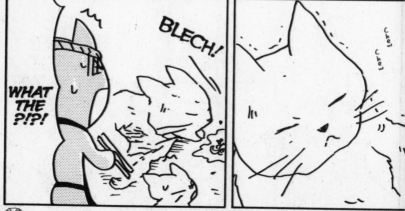

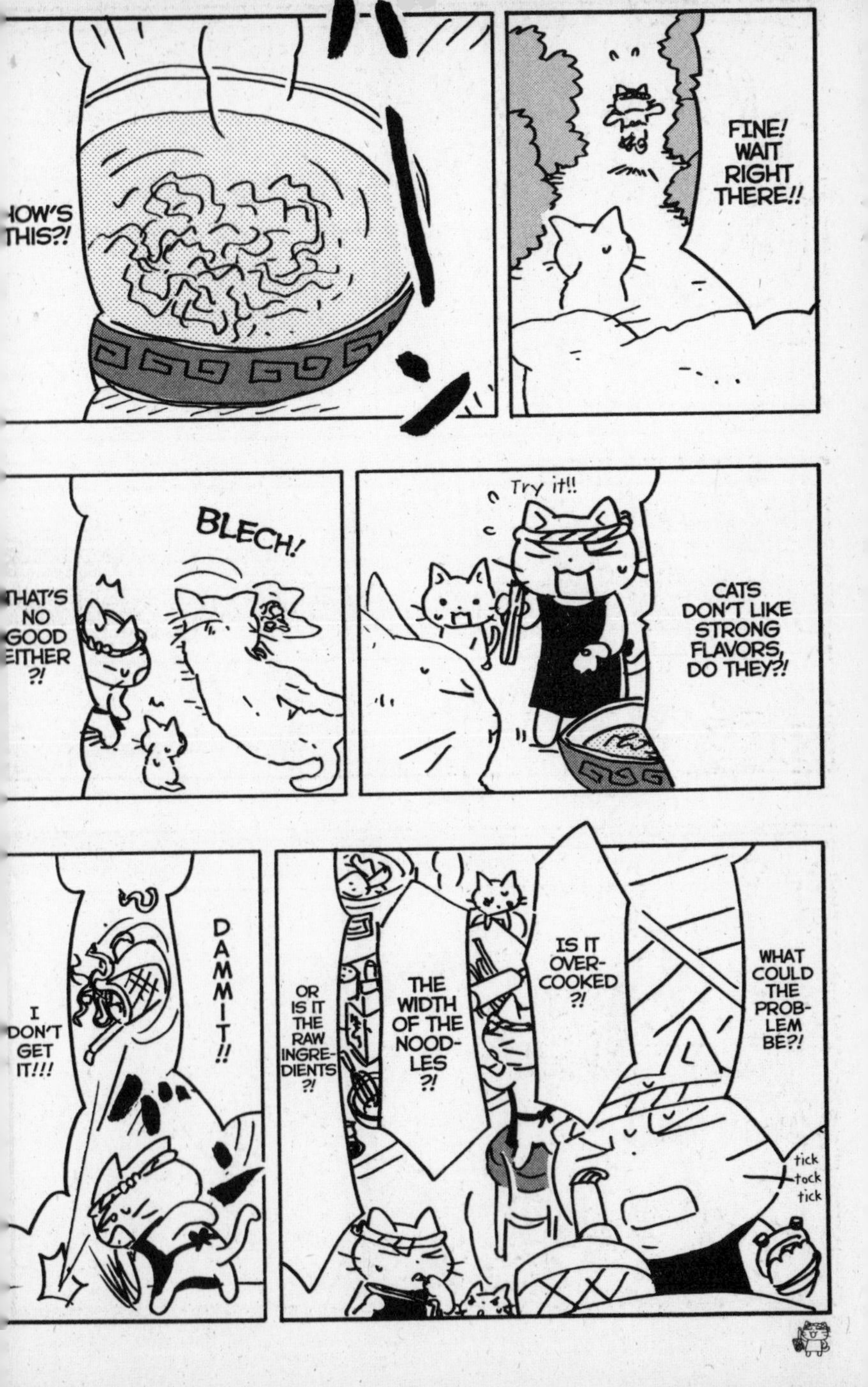

FINE! WAIT RIGHT THERE!!
HOW'S THIS?!
Try it!!
CATS DON'T LIKE STRONG FLAVORS, DO THEY?!
BLECH!
THAT'S NO GOOD EITHER?!
WHAT COULD THE PROB-LEM BE?!
IS IT OVER-COOKED?!
THE WIDTH OF THE NOOD-LES?!
OR IS IT THE RAW INGRE-DIENTS?!
tick tock tick
DAMMIT!!
I DON'T GET IT!!!

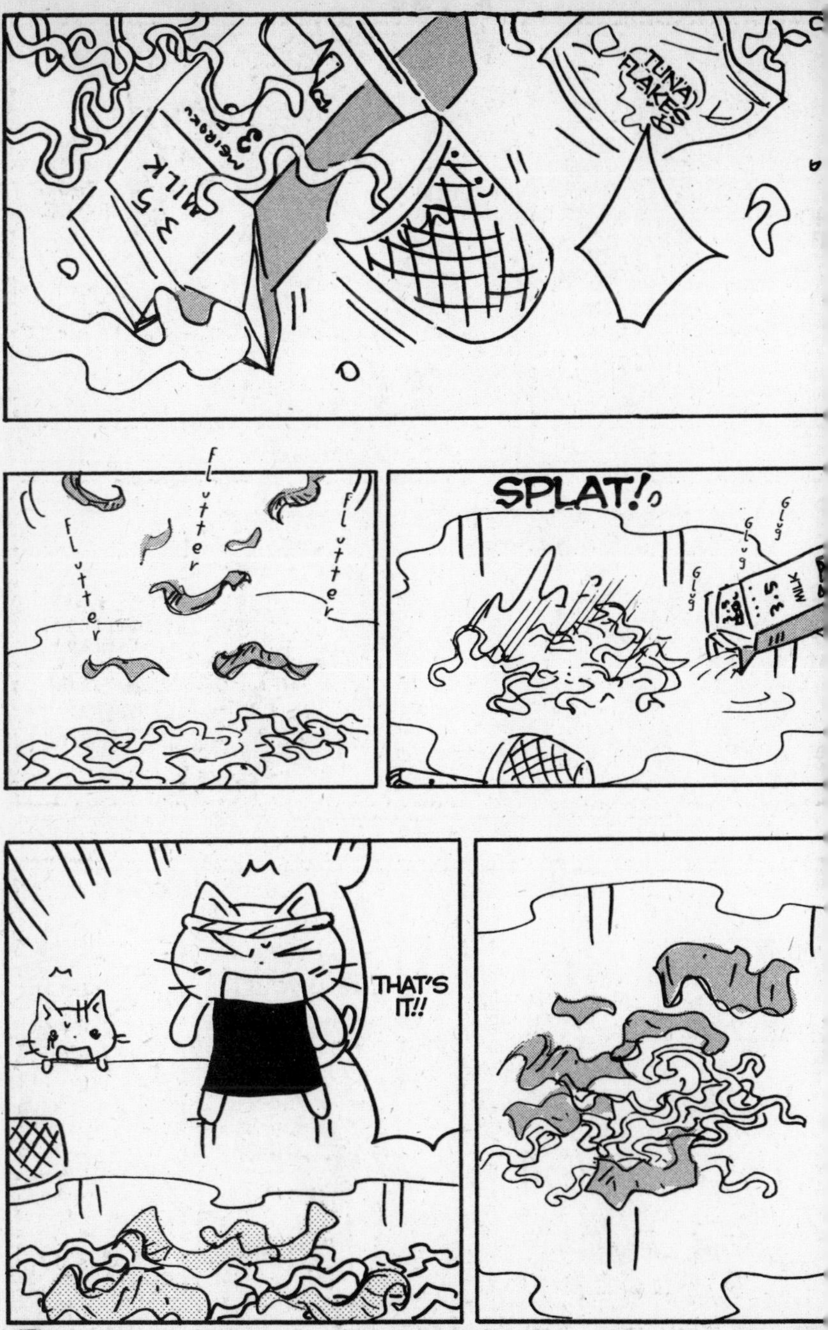

TUNA FLAKES
MILK
3.5
SPLAT!
Glug
Glug
Glug
3.5
MILK
flutter
flutter
flutter
THAT'S IT!!

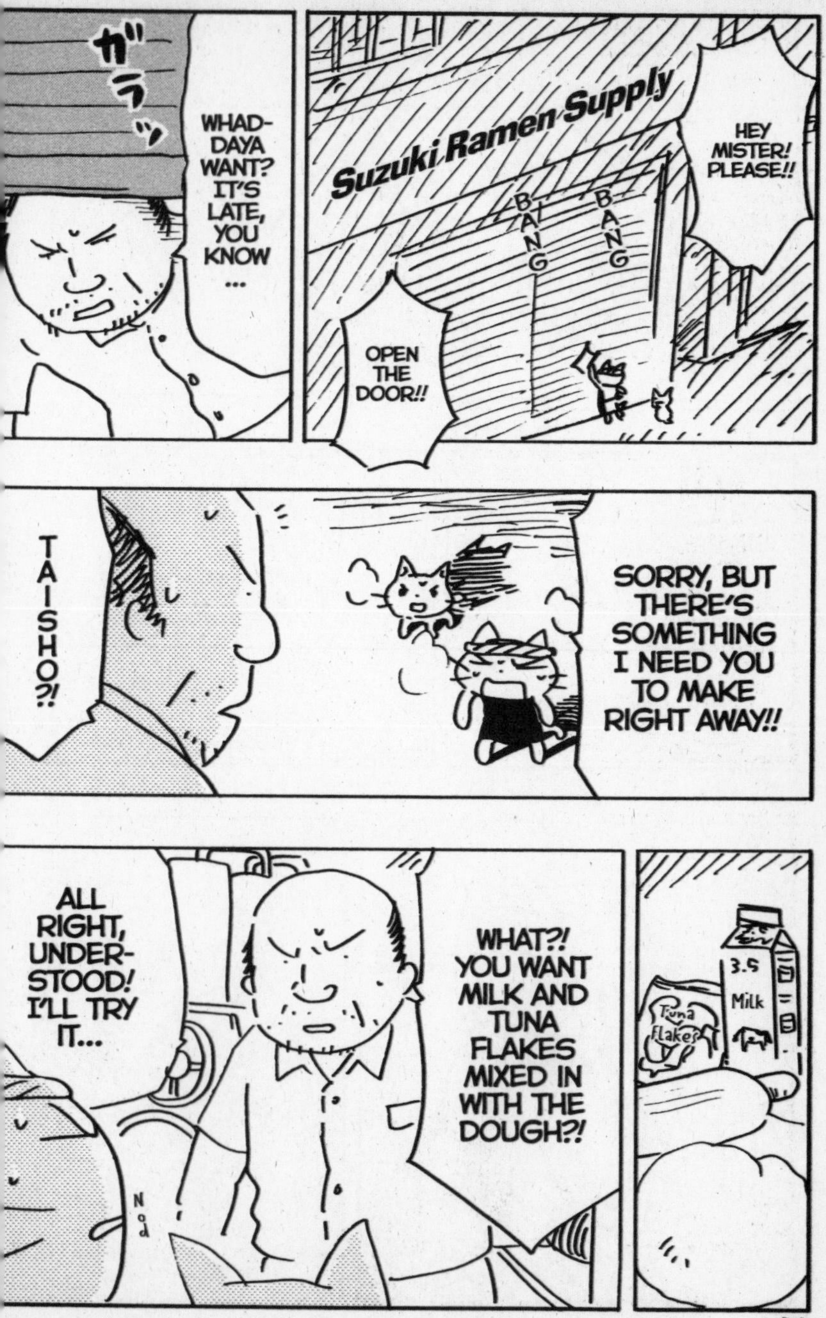Suzuki Ramen Supply
HEY MISTER! PLEASE!!
BANG BANG
OPEN THE DOOR!!
ガラッ
WHADDAYA WANT? IT'S LATE, YOU KNOW ...
SORRY, BUT THERE'S SOMETHING I NEED YOU TO MAKE RIGHT AWAY!!
TAISHO?!
3.5
Milk
Tuna Flakes
WHAT?! YOU WANT MILK AND TUNA FLAKES MIXED IN WITH THE DOUGH?!
ALL RIGHT, UNDERSTOOD! I'LL TRY IT...
Nod

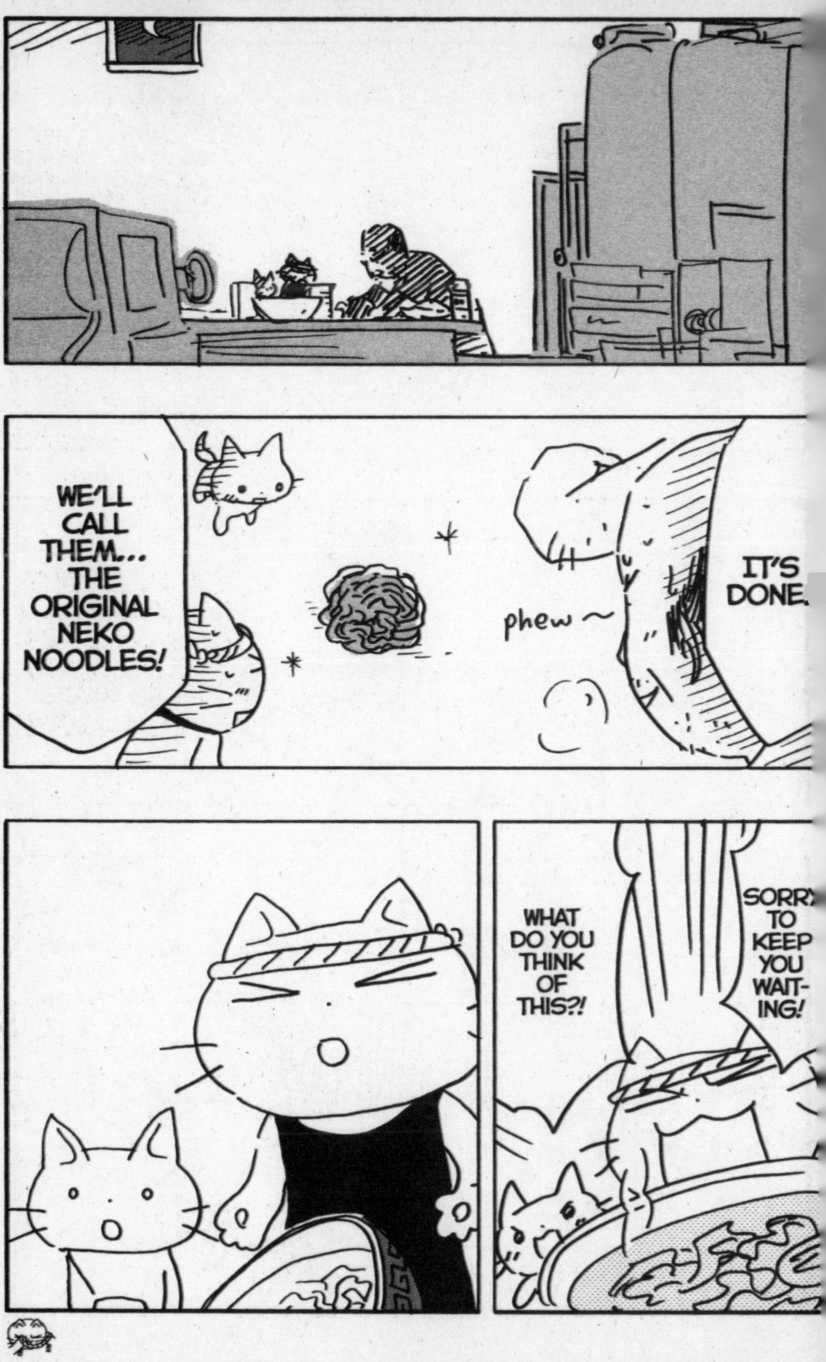
IT'S DONE.
phew~
WE'LL CALL THEM... THE ORIGINAL NEKO NOODLES!
SORRY TO KEEP YOU WAIT-ING!
WHAT DO YOU THINK OF THIS?!

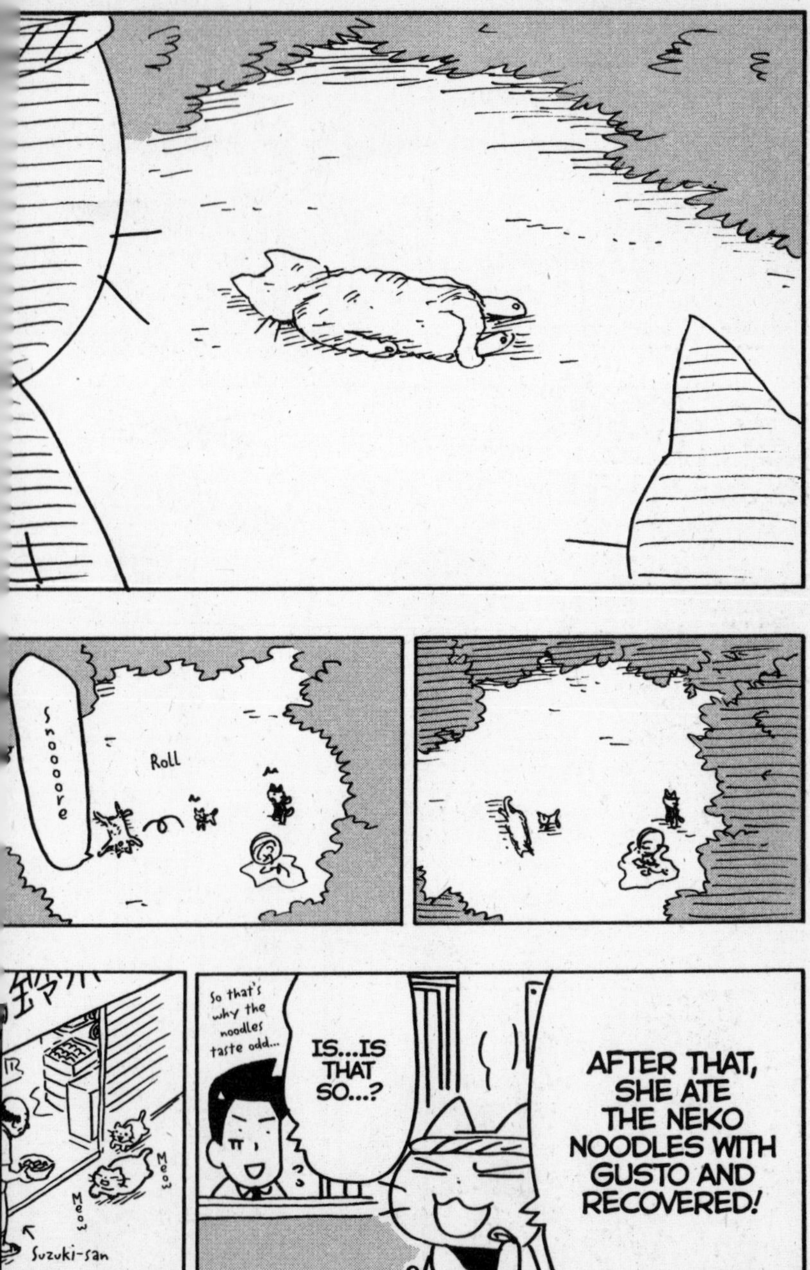
Snoooore
Roll
So that's why the noodles taste odd...
IS...IS THAT SO...?
AFTER THAT, SHE ATE THE NEKO NOODLES WITH GUSTO AND RECOVERED!
Meow
Meow
Suzuki-san

猫ラーメン

Chapter 9

Time

Neko Ramen Deluxe
Now Serving
Gyoza
$3 per order
GYOZA PLEASE!
THEY TAKE SOME TIME. IS THAT ALL RIGHT?
SURE!
Neko Ramen Gyoza
IT TAKES SOME TIME...
...to pick the hair out.
UGGHHHHH?!

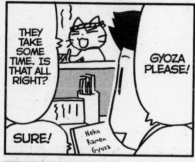

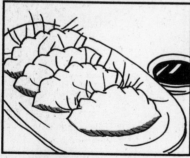

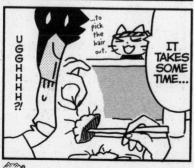

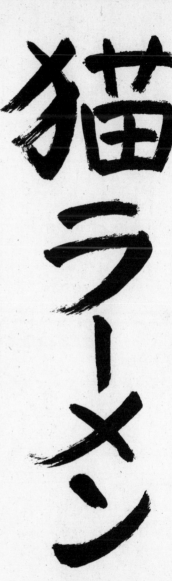

Prototype

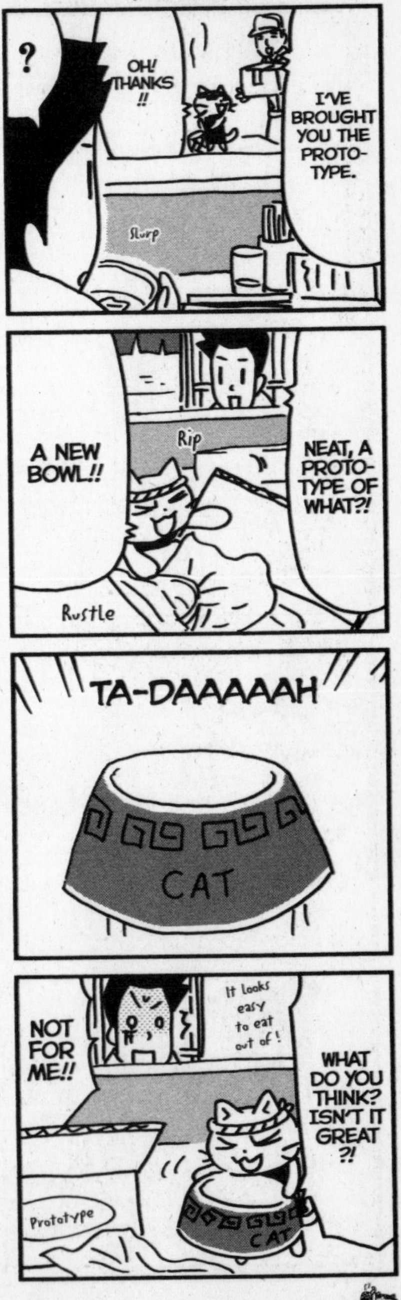
I'VE BROUGHT YOU THE PROTO-TYPE.
OH! THANKS!!
?
Slurp
NEAT, A PROTO-TYPE OF WHAT?!
Rip
A NEW BOWL!!
Rustle
TA-DAAAAAH
CAT
WHAT DO YOU THINK? ISN'T IT GREAT?!
It looks easy to eat out of!
NOT FOR ME!!
Prototype
CAT

Overdid It

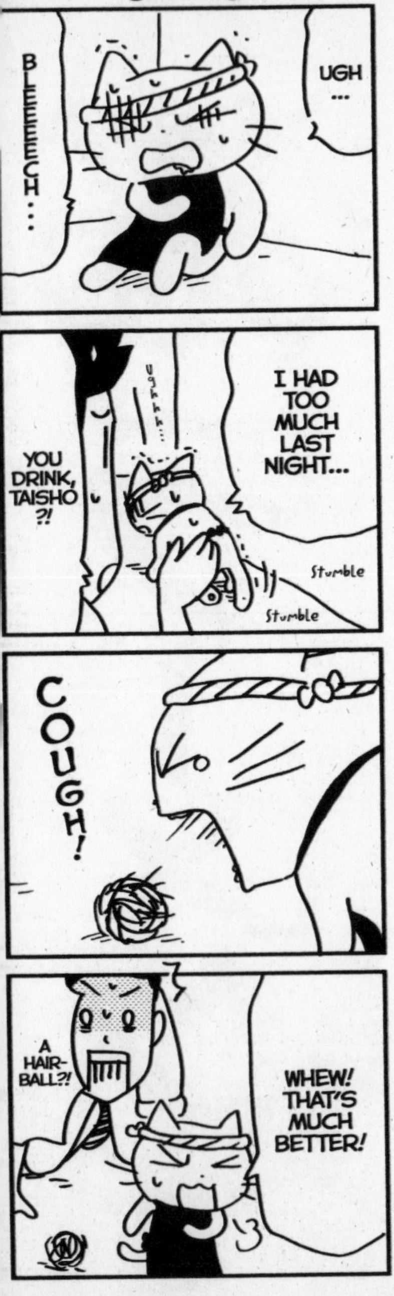
UGH ...
BLEEEECH...
I HAD TOO MUCH LAST NIGHT...
Ughhh...
YOU DRINK, TAISHO?!
Stumble
Stumble
COUGH!
WHEW! THAT'S MUCH BETTER!
A HAIR-BALL?!

Zero Calories

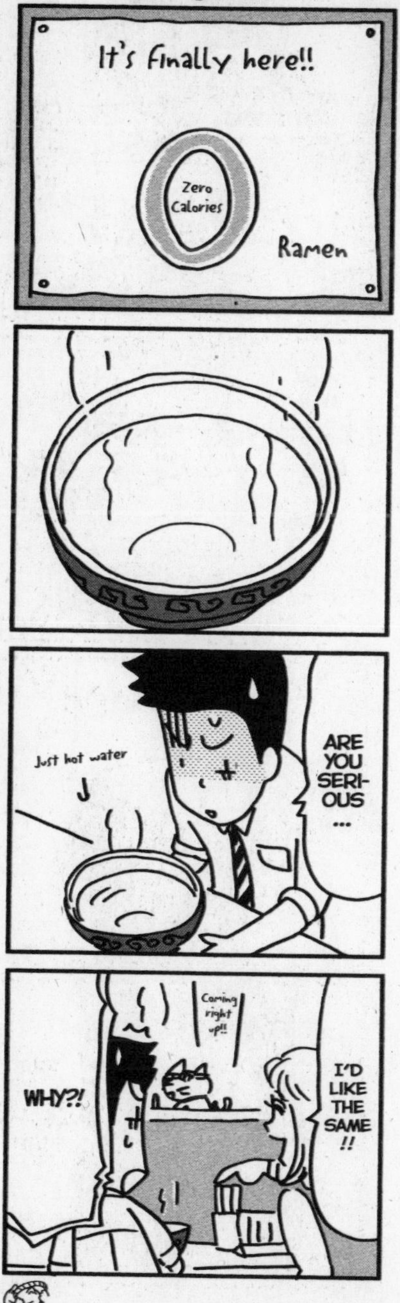

It's finally here!!
0
Zero Calories
Ramen
Just hot water
ARE YOU SERIOUS...
I'D LIKE THE SAME!!
Coming right up!!
WHY?!

½

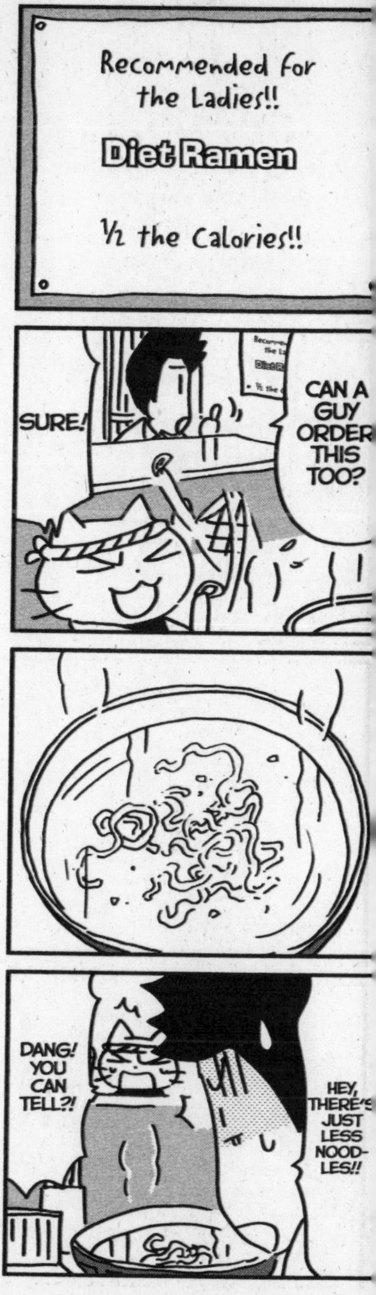

Recommended for the Ladies!!
Diet Ramen
½ the Calories!!
CAN A GUY ORDER THIS TOO?
SURE!
HEY, THERE'S JUST LESS NOOD-LES!!
DANG! YOU CAN TELL?!

What's That?

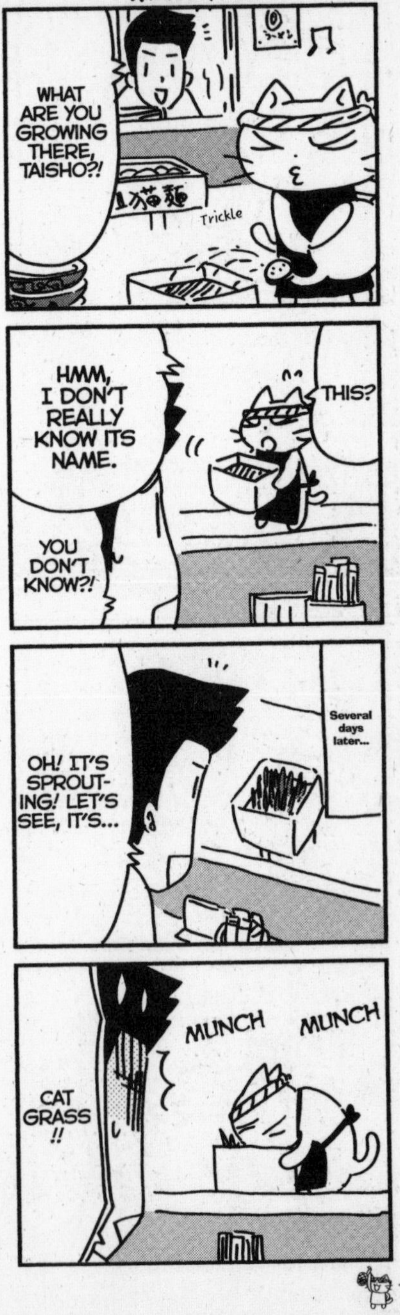
WHAT ARE YOU GROWING THERE, TAISHO?!
Trickle
THIS?
HMM, I DON'T REALLY KNOW ITS NAME.
YOU DON'T KNOW?!
Several days later...
OH! IT'S SPROUT-ING! LET'S SEE, IT'S...
CAT GRASS!!
MUNCH MUNCH

Part-Time Pay

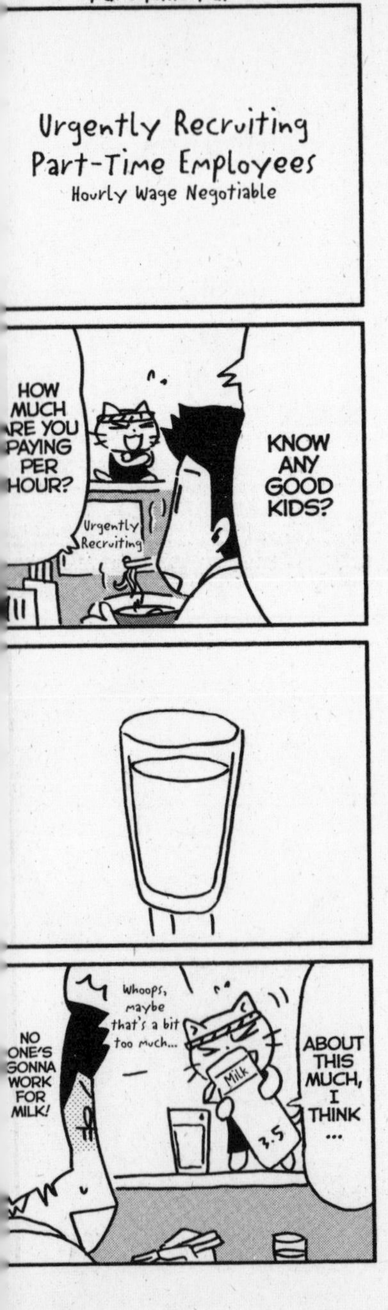
Urgently Recruiting Part-Time Employees
Hourly Wage Negotiable
KNOW ANY GOOD KIDS?
HOW MUCH ARE YOU PAYING PER HOUR?
Urgently Recruiting
ABOUT THIS MUCH, I THINK ...
Whoops, maybe that's a bit too much...
Milk
3.5
NO ONE'S GONNA WORK FOR MILK!

Toku-san

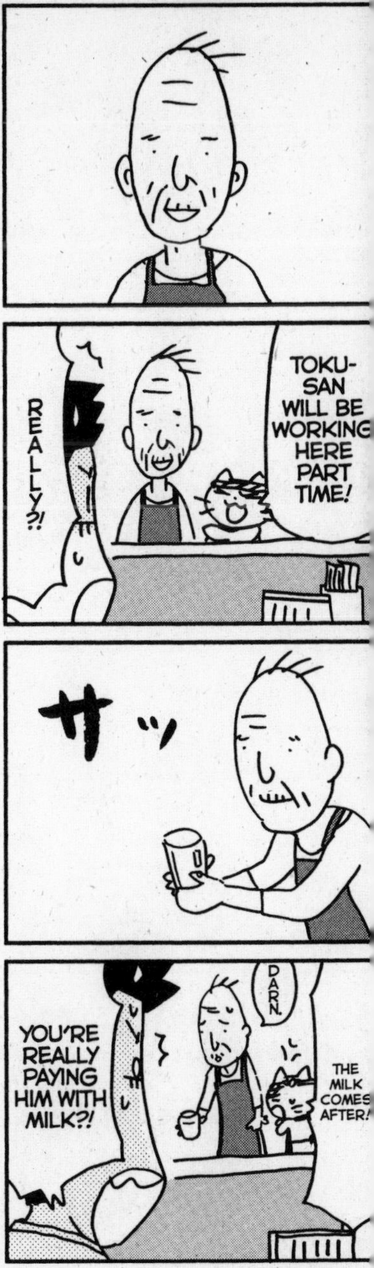
TOKU-SAN WILL BE WORKING HERE PART TIME!
REALLY?!
サッ
YOU'RE REALLY PAYING HIM WITH MILK?!
THE MILK COMES AFTER!
DARN.

Hourly Wage

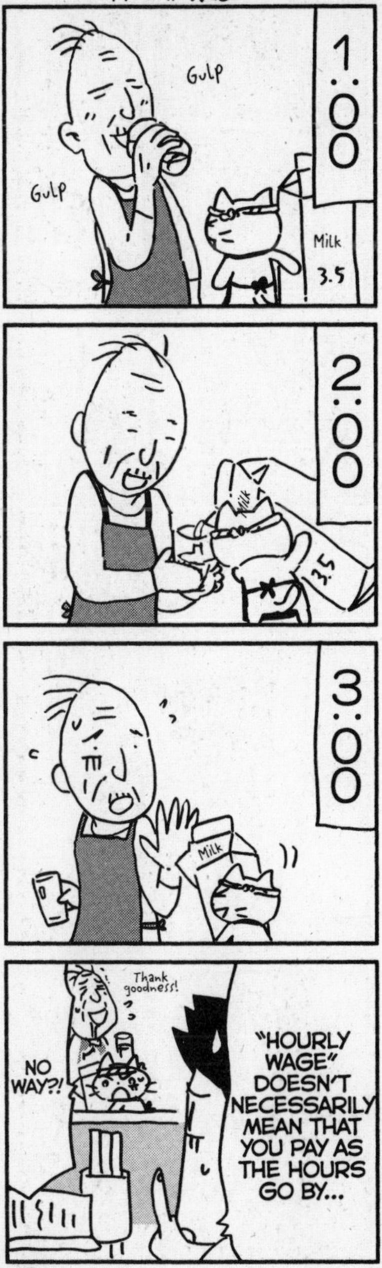
1:00
Gulp
Gulp
Milk
3.5
2:00
Milk
3.5
3:00
Milk
"HOURLY WAGE" DOESN'T NECESSARILY MEAN THAT YOU PAY AS THE HOURS GO BY...
NO WAY?!
Thank goodness!

Advisors

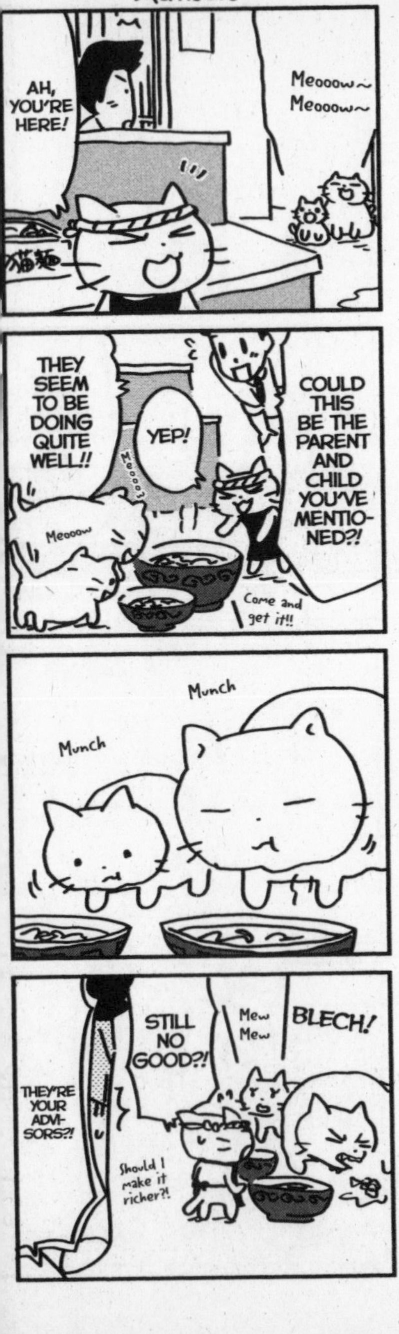
AH, YOU'RE HERE!
Meooow~
Meooow~
猫麺
THEY SEEM TO BE DOING QUITE WELL!!
YEP!
COULD THIS BE THE PARENT AND CHILD YOU'VE MENTIONED?!
Meooow
Come and get it!!
Munch
Munch
STILL NO GOOD?!
Mew
Mew
BLECH!
THEY'RE YOUR ADVISORS?!
Should I make it richer?!

Time Perception

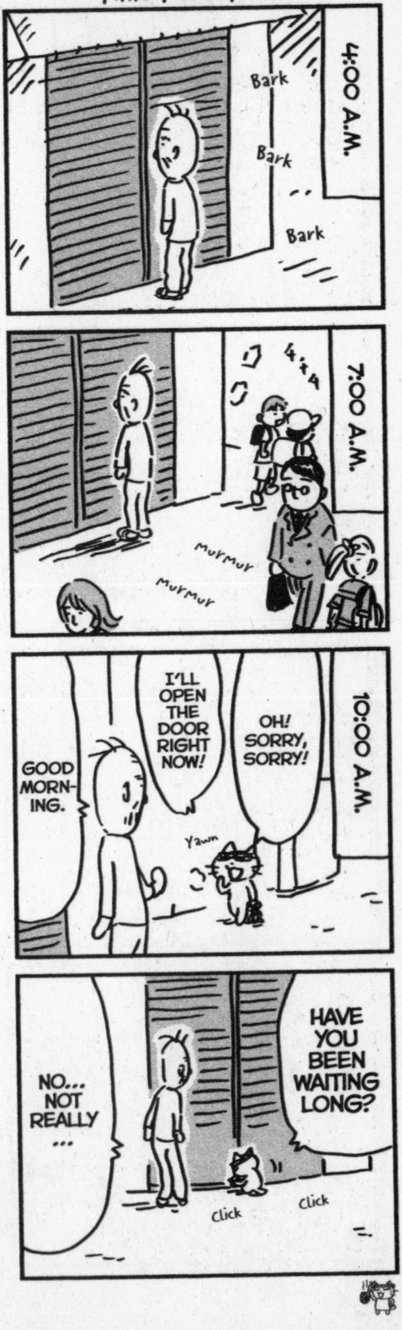
4:00 A.M.
Bark
Bark
Bark
7:00 A.M.
Murmur
Murmur
10:00 A.M.
GOOD MORNING.
I'LL OPEN THE DOOR RIGHT NOW!
OH! SORRY, SORRY!
Yawn
HAVE YOU BEEN WAITING LONG?
NO... NOT REALLY...
Click
Click

Yo! Toku-san!

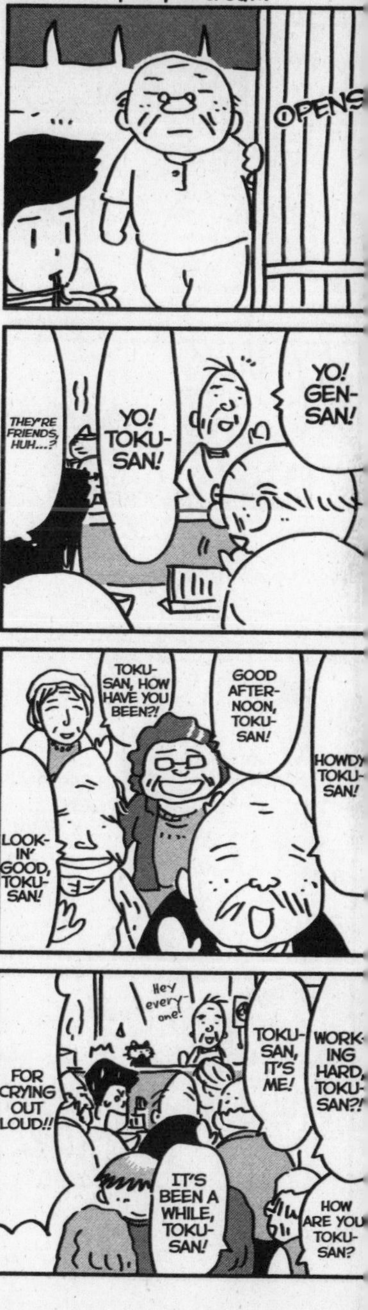
OPENS
...
YO! GEN-SAN!
YO! TOKU-SAN!
THEY'RE FRIENDS, HUH...?
HOWDY TOKU-SAN!
GOOD AFTERNOON, TOKU-SAN!
TOKU-SAN, HOW HAVE YOU BEEN?!
LOOKIN' GOOD, TOKU-SAN!
WORKING HARD, TOKU-SAN?!
TOKU-SAN, IT'S ME!
Hey everyone!
HOW ARE YOU TOKU-SAN?
IT'S BEEN A WHILE, TOKU-SAN!
FOR CRYING OUT LOUD!!

Senior Center

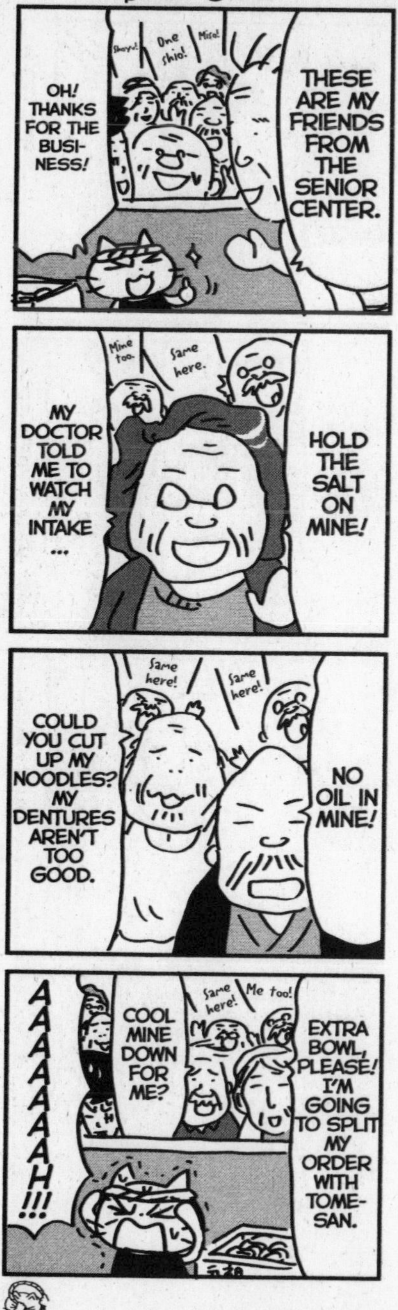
THESE ARE MY FRIENDS FROM THE SENIOR CENTER.
Miso!
One shio!
Shoyu!
OH! THANKS FOR THE BUSINESS!
HOLD THE SALT ON MINE!
Same here.
Mine too.
MY DOCTOR TOLD ME TO WATCH MY INTAKE...
NO OIL IN MINE!
Same here!
Same here!
COULD YOU CUT UP MY NOODLES? MY DENTURES AREN'T TOO GOOD.
EXTRA BOWL, PLEASE! I'M GOING TO SPLIT MY ORDER WITH TOME-SAN.
Me too!
Same here!
COOL MINE DOWN FOR ME?
AAAAAAAAAH!!!

A Surprise

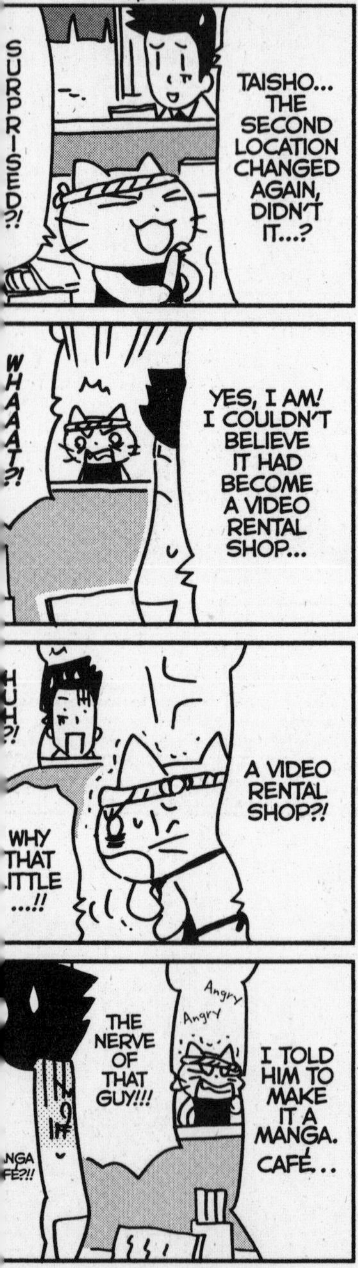
TAISHO... THE SECOND LOCATION CHANGED AGAIN, DIDN'T IT...?
SURPRISED?!
YES, I AM! I COULDN'T BELIEVE IT HAD BECOME A VIDEO RENTAL SHOP...
WHAAAT?!
A VIDEO RENTAL SHOP?!
HUH?!
WHY THAT ITTLE ...!!
I TOLD HIM TO MAKE IT A MANGA CAFÉ...
Angry
Angry
THE NERVE OF THAT GUY!!!
NGA FE?!!

The Second Location

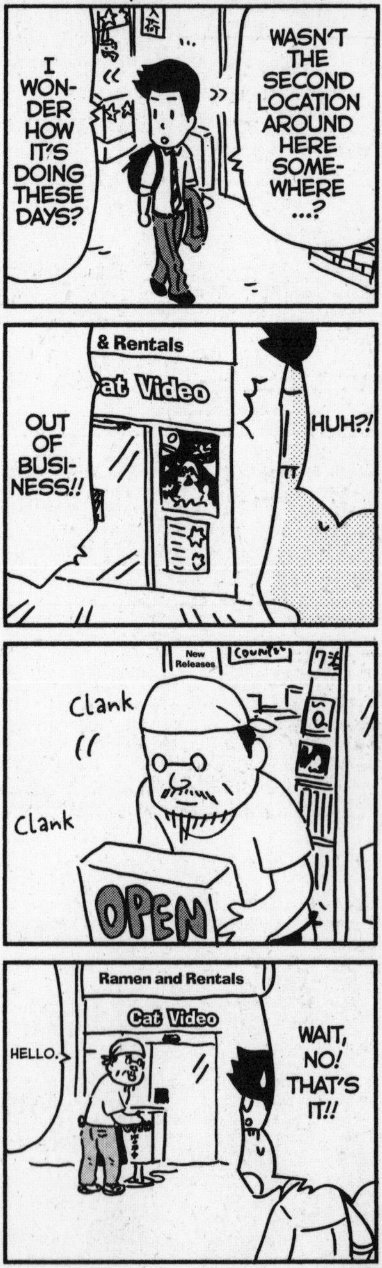
WASN'T THE SECOND LOCATION AROUND HERE SOMEWHERE...?
I WONDER HOW IT'S DOING THESE DAYS?
HUH?!
& Rentals
at Video
OUT OF BUSINESS!!
New Releases
Clank
Clank
OPEN
Ramen and Rentals
Cat Video
WAIT, NO! THAT'S IT!!
HELLO.

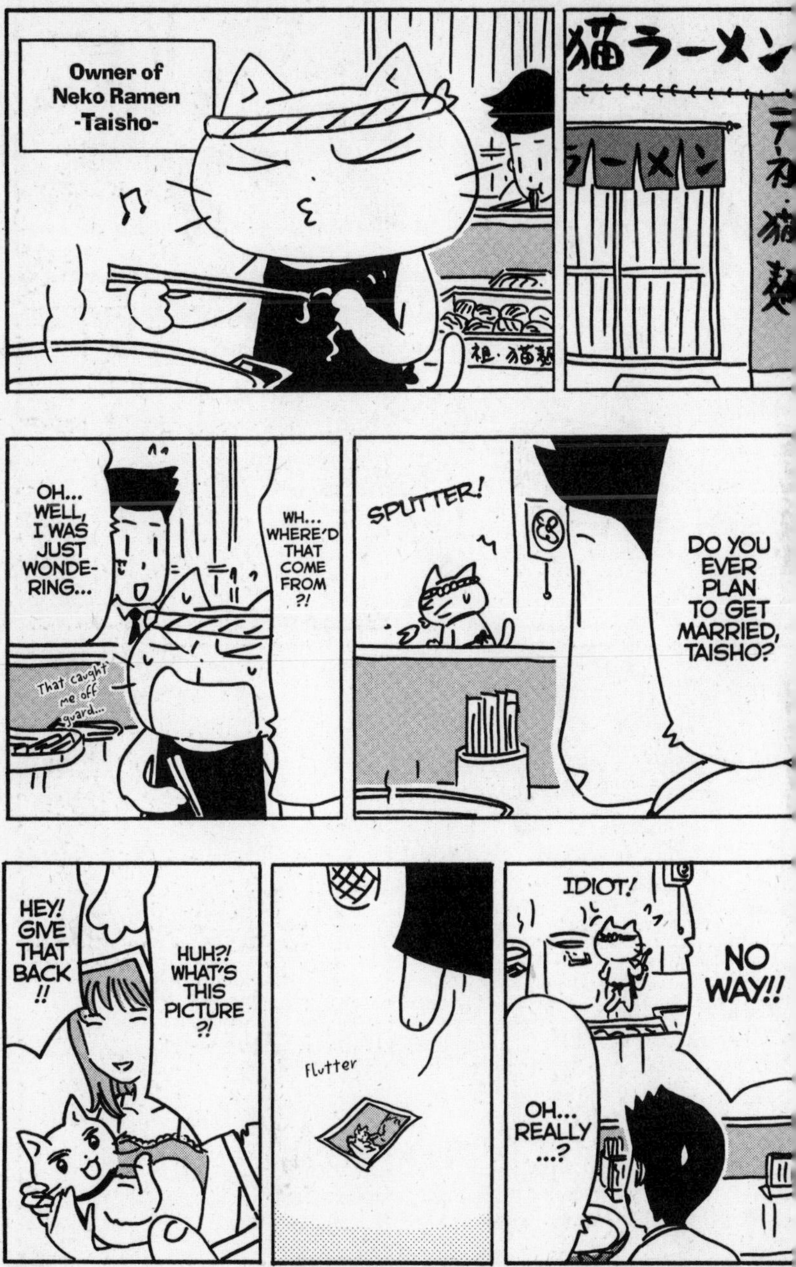
猫ラーメン
ラーメン
Owner of Neko Ramen -Taisho-
DO YOU EVER PLAN TO GET MARRIED, TAISHO?
SPUTTER!
WH... WHERE'D THAT COME FROM?!
OH... WELL, I WAS JUST WONDERING...
That caught me off guard...
NO WAY!!
IDIOT!
OH... REALLY...?
Flutter
HUH?! WHAT'S THIS PICTURE?!
HEY! GIVE THAT BACK!!

猫ラーメン

Short Comic Special

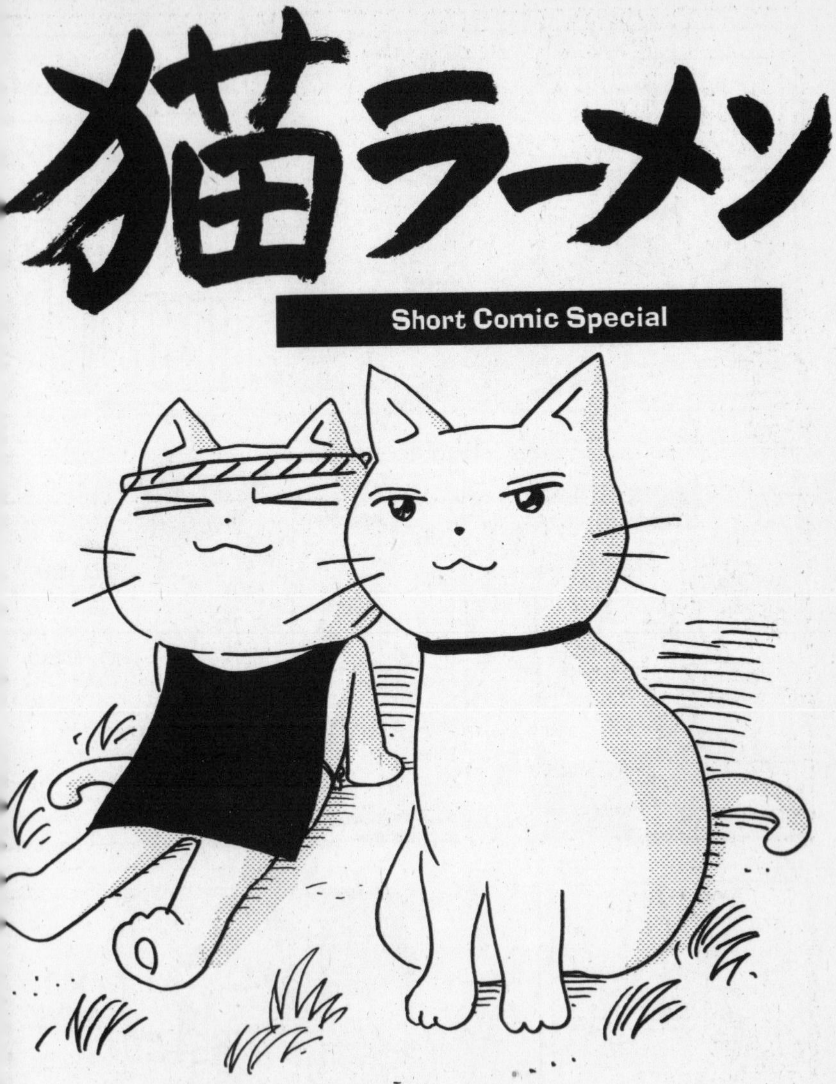

Taisho's Love

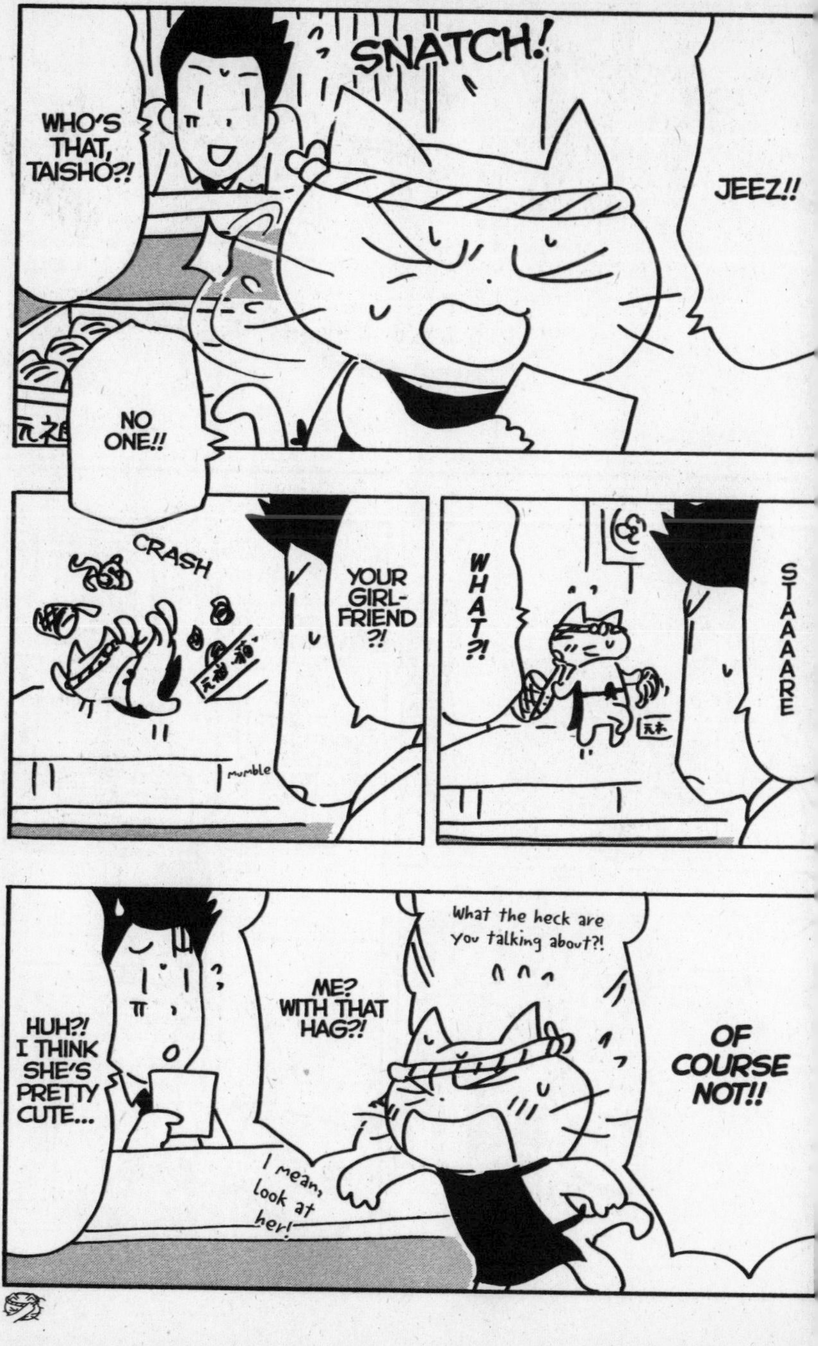

JEEZ!!
SNATCH!
WHO'S THAT, TAISHO?!
NO ONE!!
STAAAAARE
WHAT?!
YOUR GIRL-FRIEND?!
CRASH
mumble
OF COURSE NOT!!
What the heck are you talking about?!
I mean, look at her!
ME? WITH THAT HAG?!
HUH?! I THINK SHE'S PRETTY CUTE...

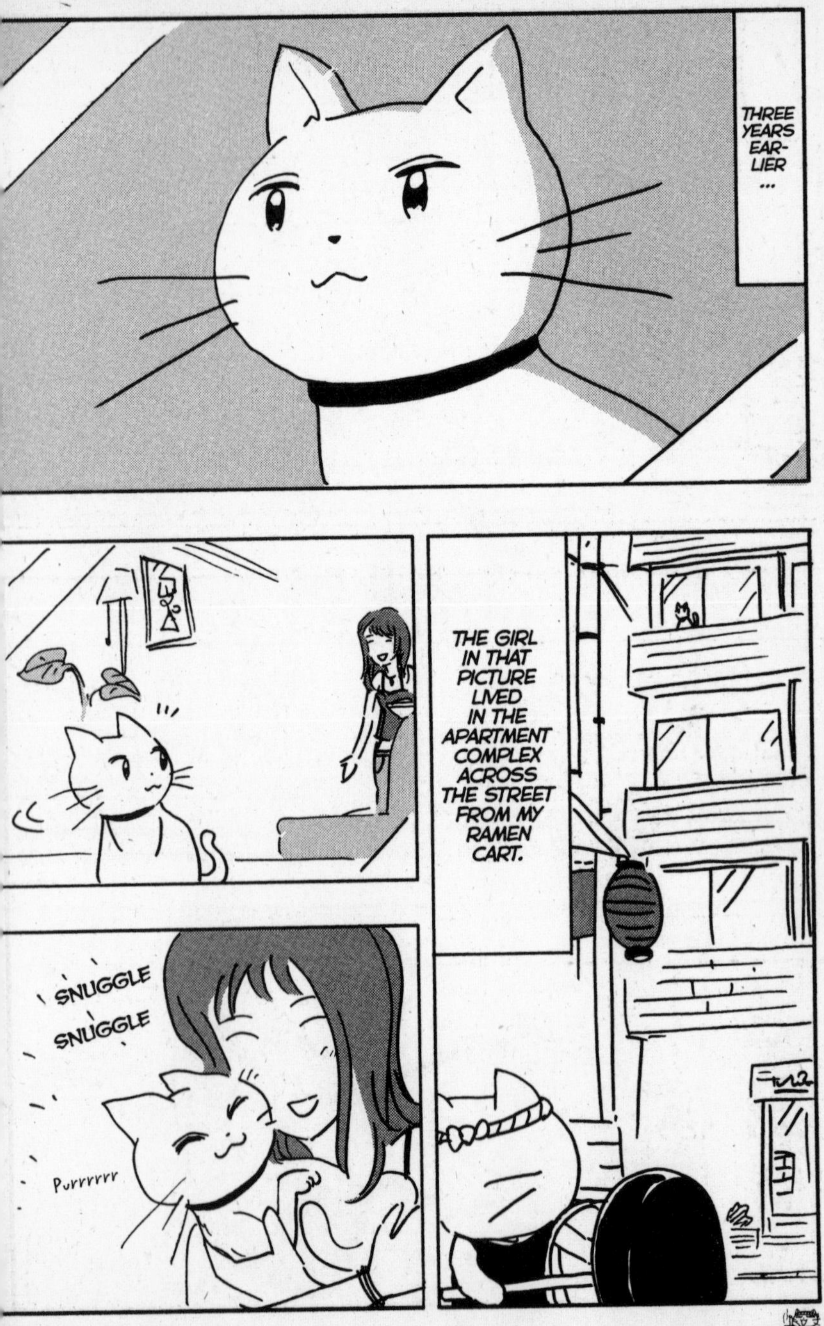
THREE YEARS EAR-LIER ...
THE GIRL IN THAT PICTURE LIVED IN THE APARTMENT COMPLEX ACROSS THE STREET FROM MY RAMEN CART.
SNUGGLE SNUGGLE
Purrrrrr

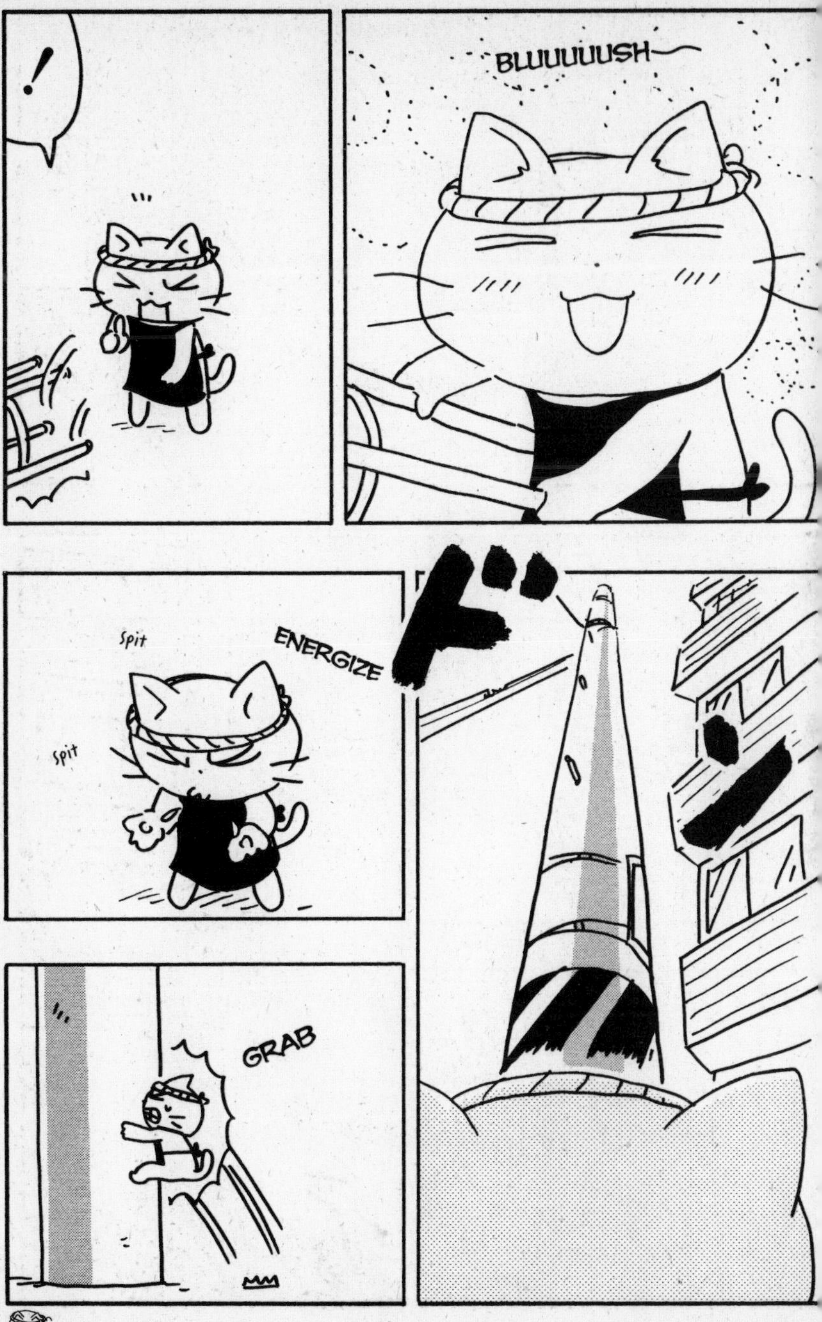
BLUUUUUSH
!
ENERGIZE
Spit
Spit
GRAB

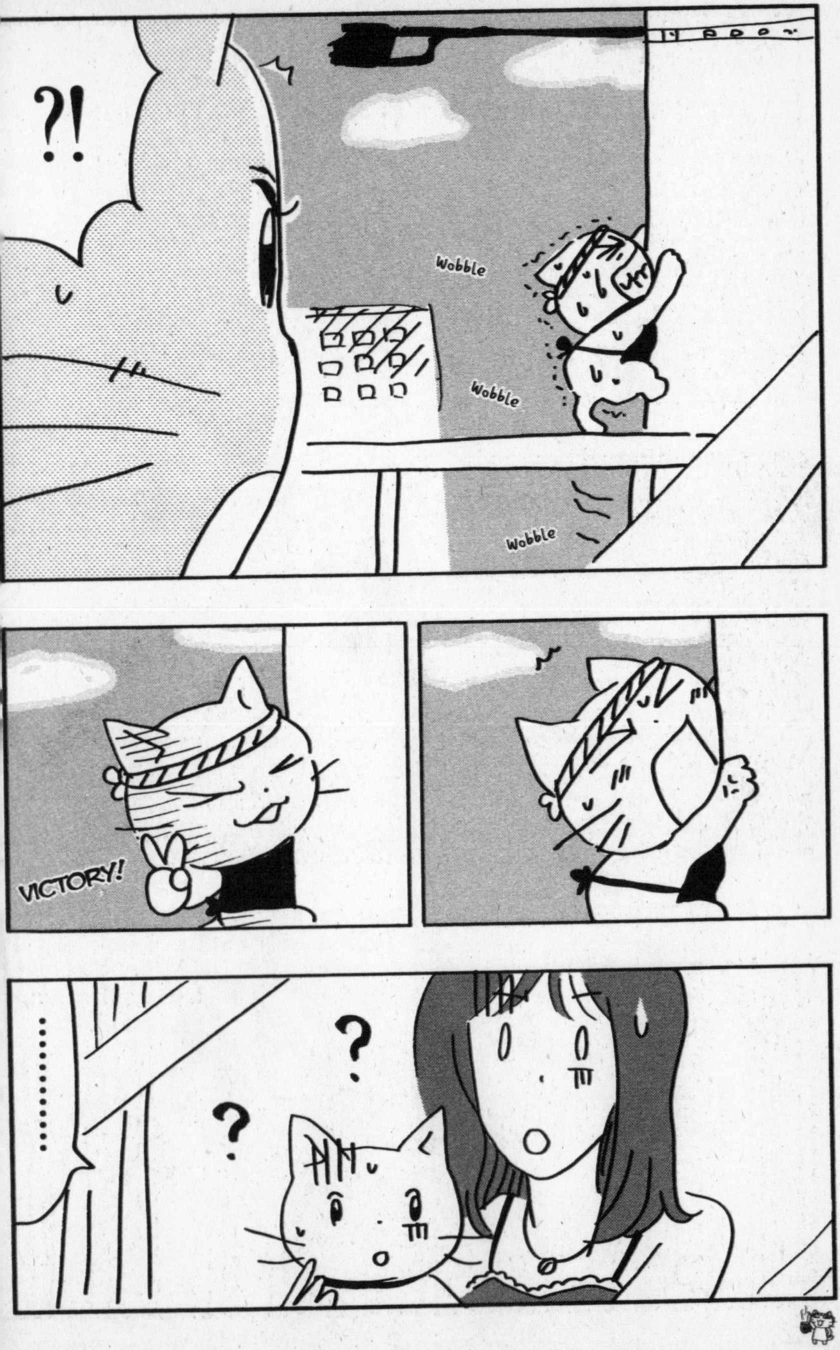
?!
Wobble
Wobble
Wobble
VICTORY!
?
?
......

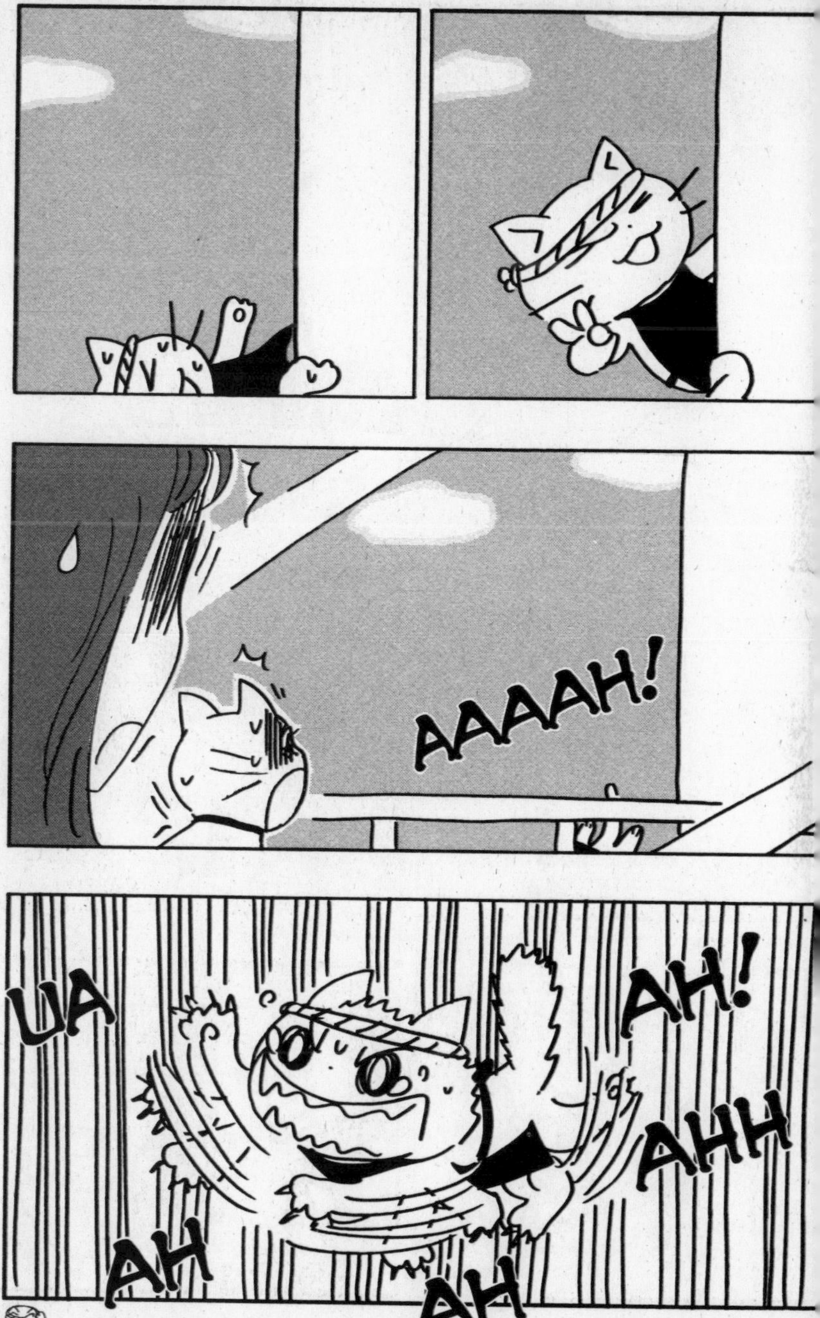
AAAAH!
AH!
AHH
UA
AH
AH

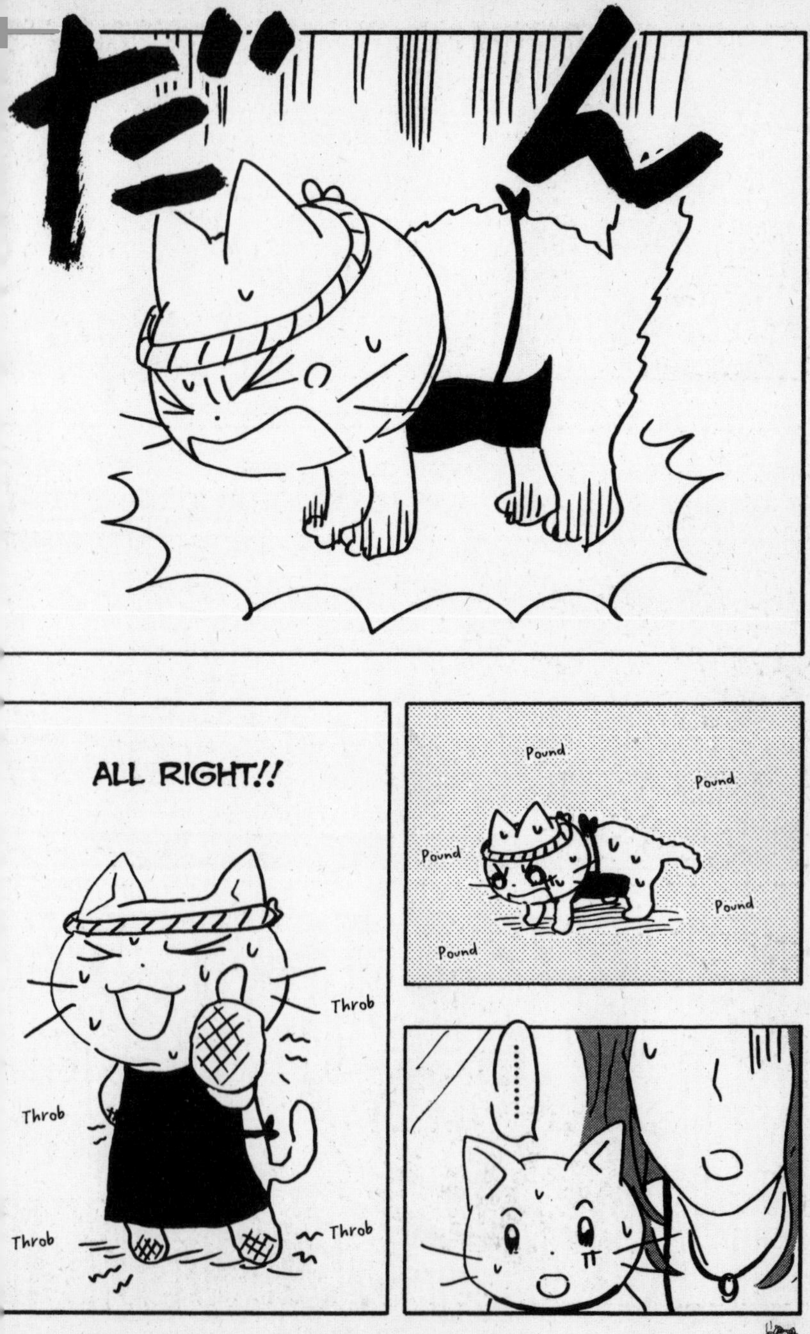

だん
Pound
Pound
Pound
Pound
Pound
......
ALL RIGHT!!
Throb
Throb
Throb
Throb

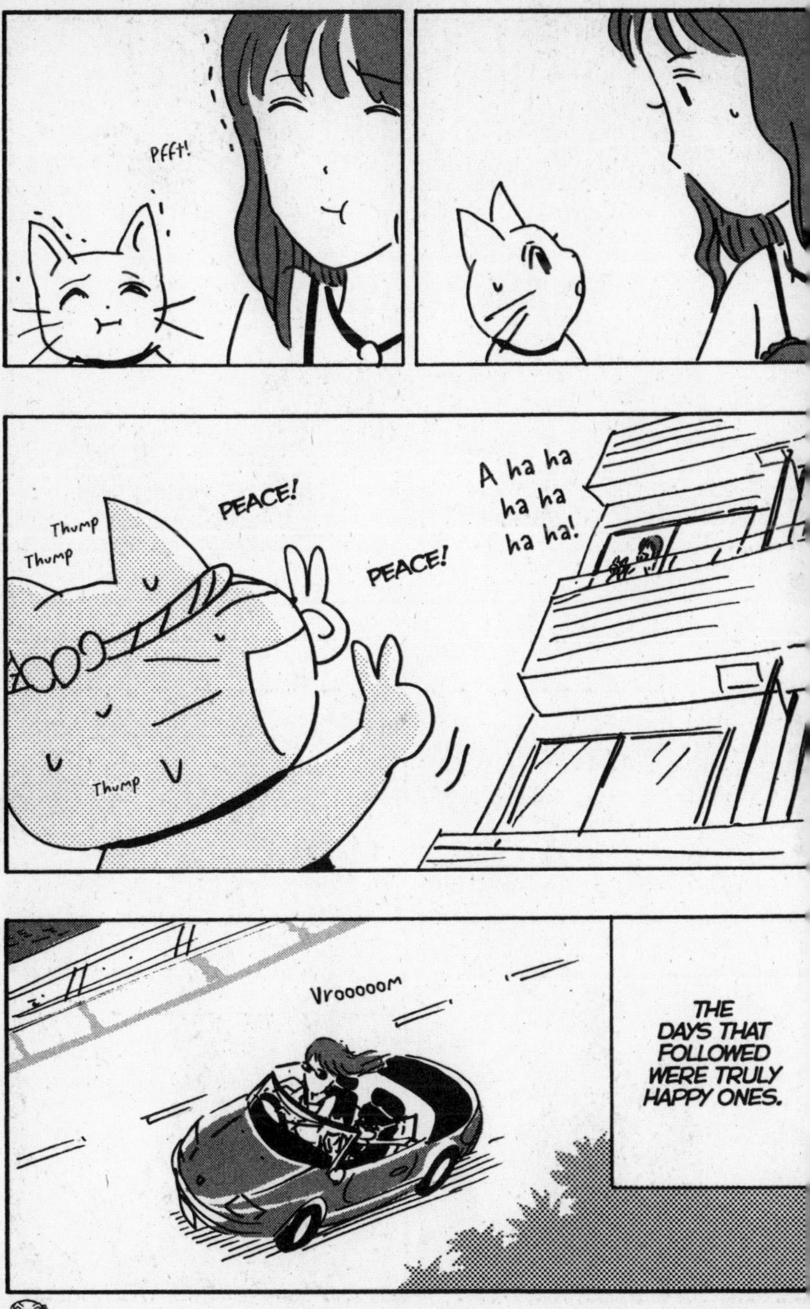
Pfft!
Thump
Thump
PEACE!
PEACE!
A ha ha
ha ha
ha ha!
Thump
Vroooooom
THE DAYS THAT FOLLOWED WERE TRULY HAPPY ONES.

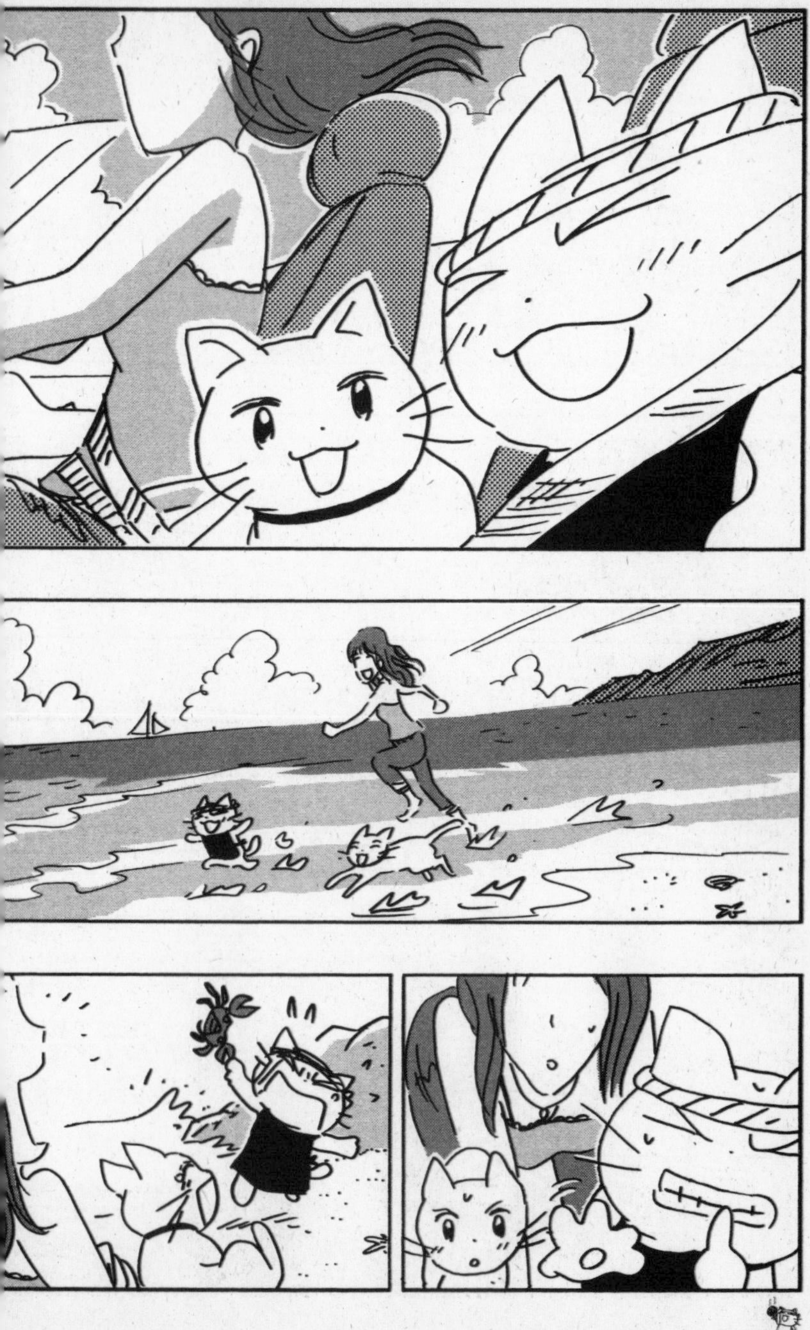

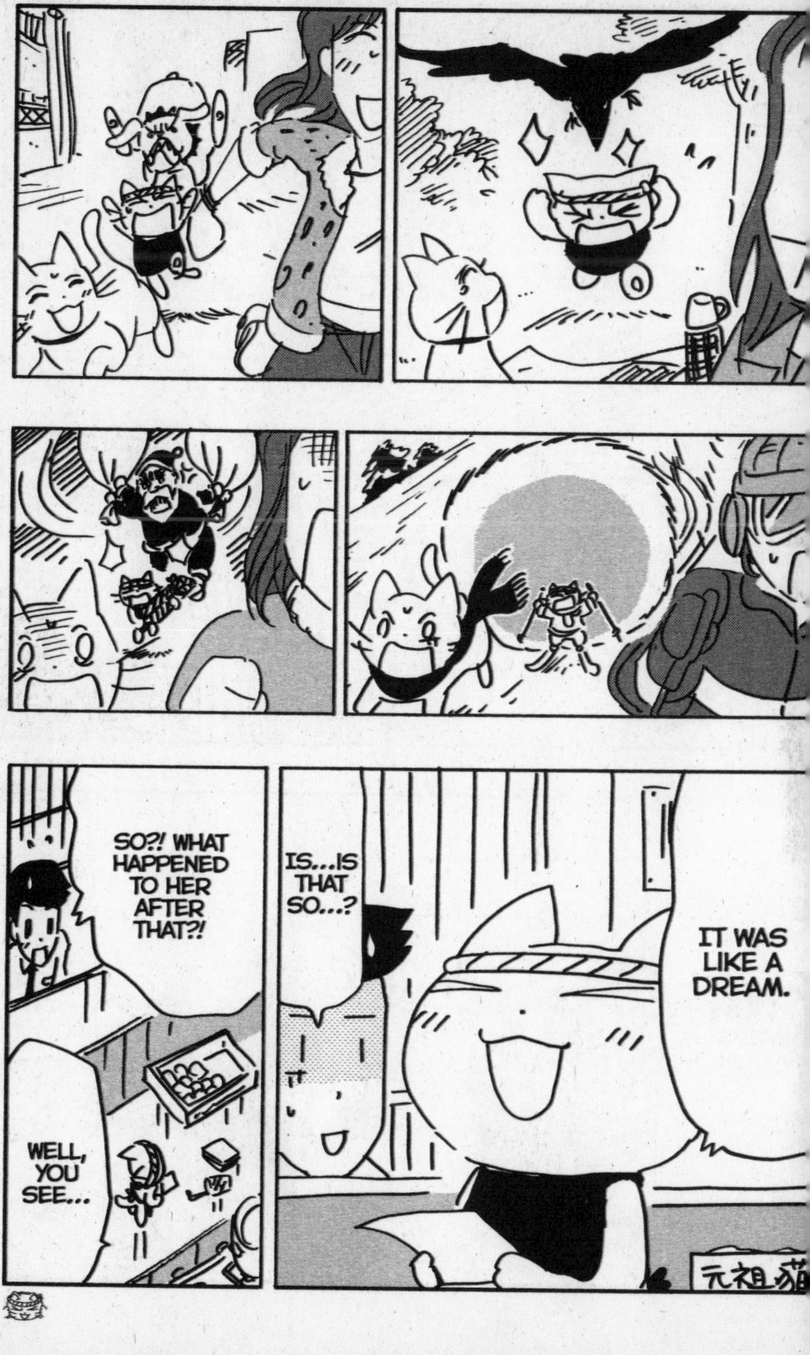
SO?! WHAT HAPPENED TO HER AFTER THAT?!
WELL, YOU SEE...
IS...IS THAT SO...?
IT WAS LIKE A DREAM.

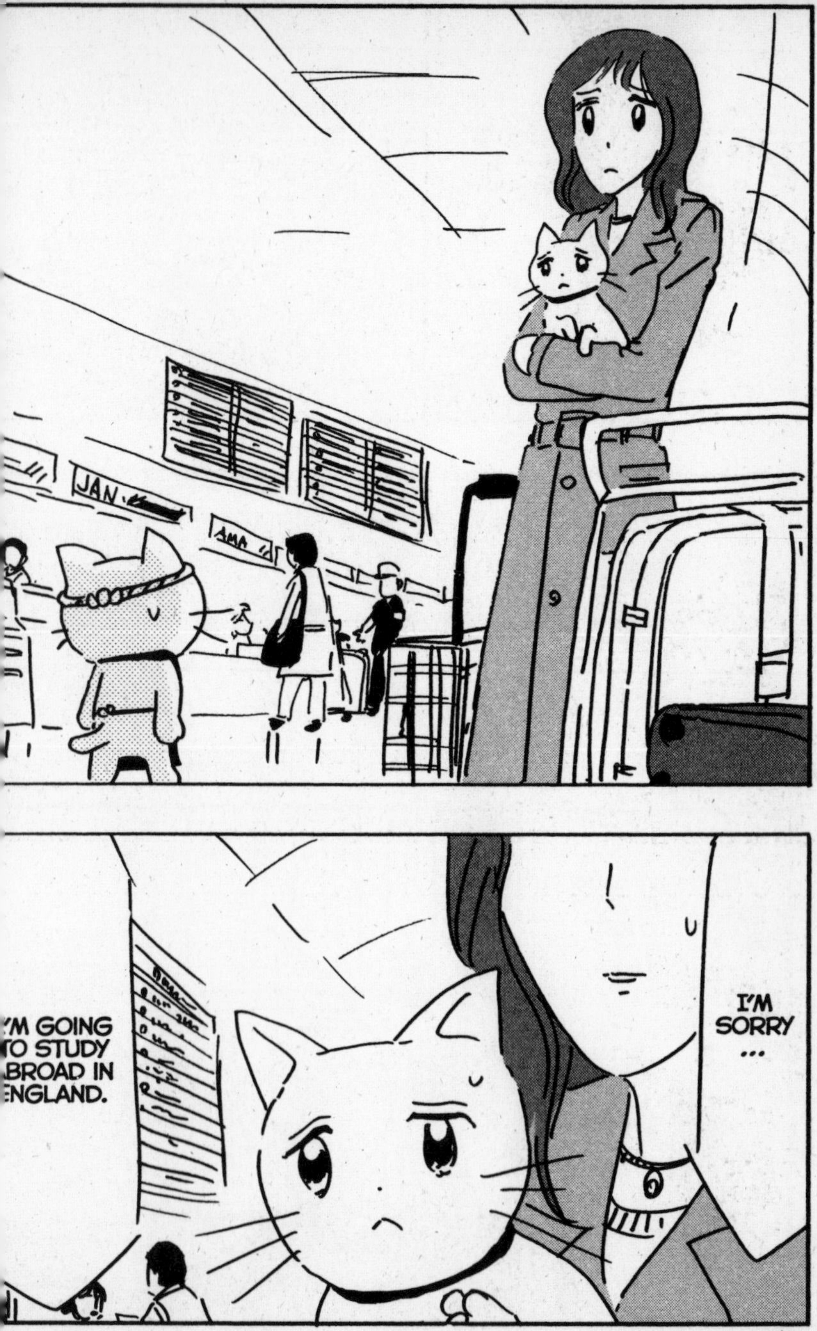
JAN
AMA
I'M SORRY ...
'M GOING O STUDY BROAD IN NGLAND.

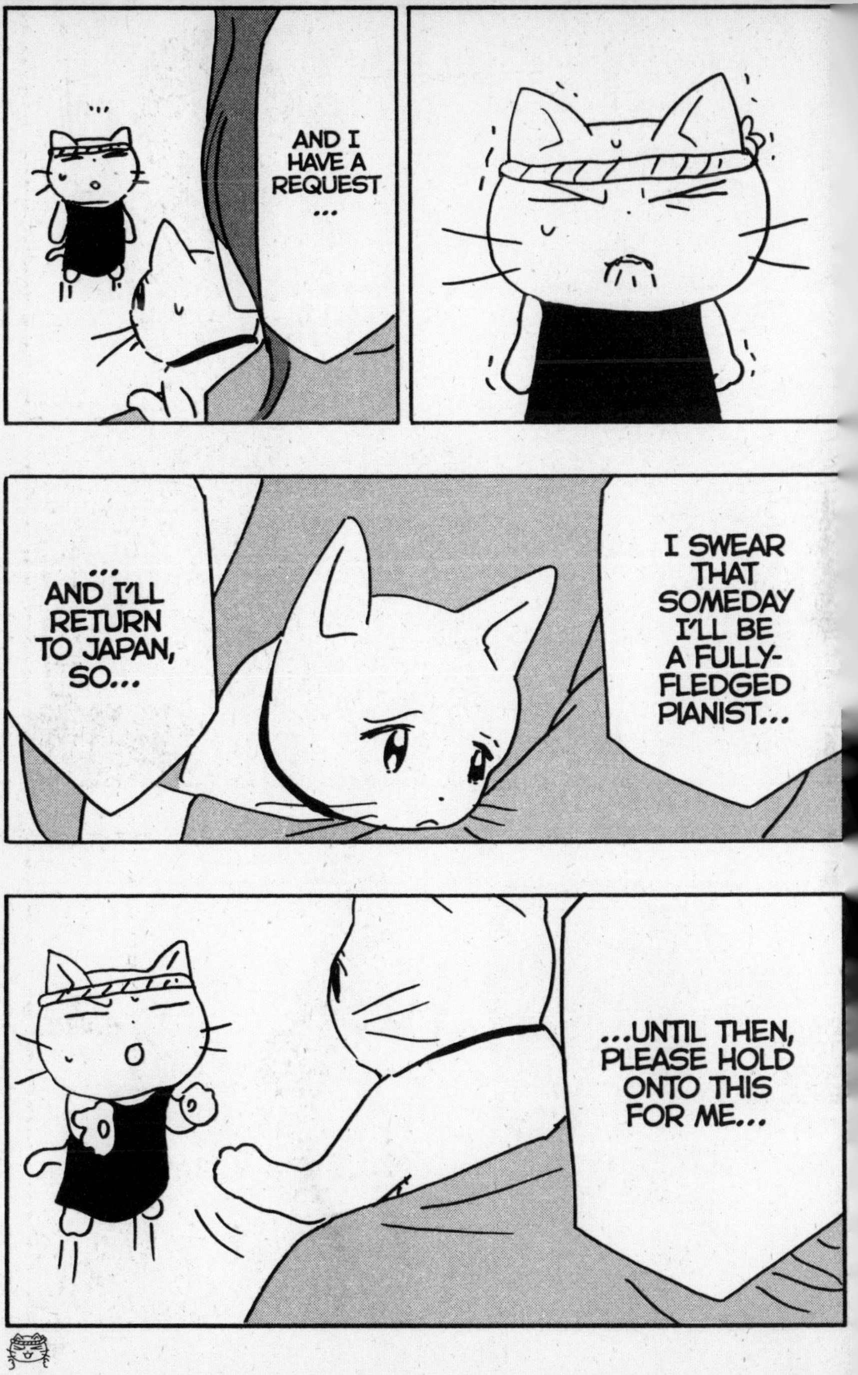
AND I HAVE A REQUEST...
...
I SWEAR THAT SOMEDAY I'LL BE A FULLY-FLEDGED PIANIST...
...AND I'LL RETURN TO JAPAN, SO...
...UNTIL THEN, PLEASE HOLD ONTO THIS FOR ME...

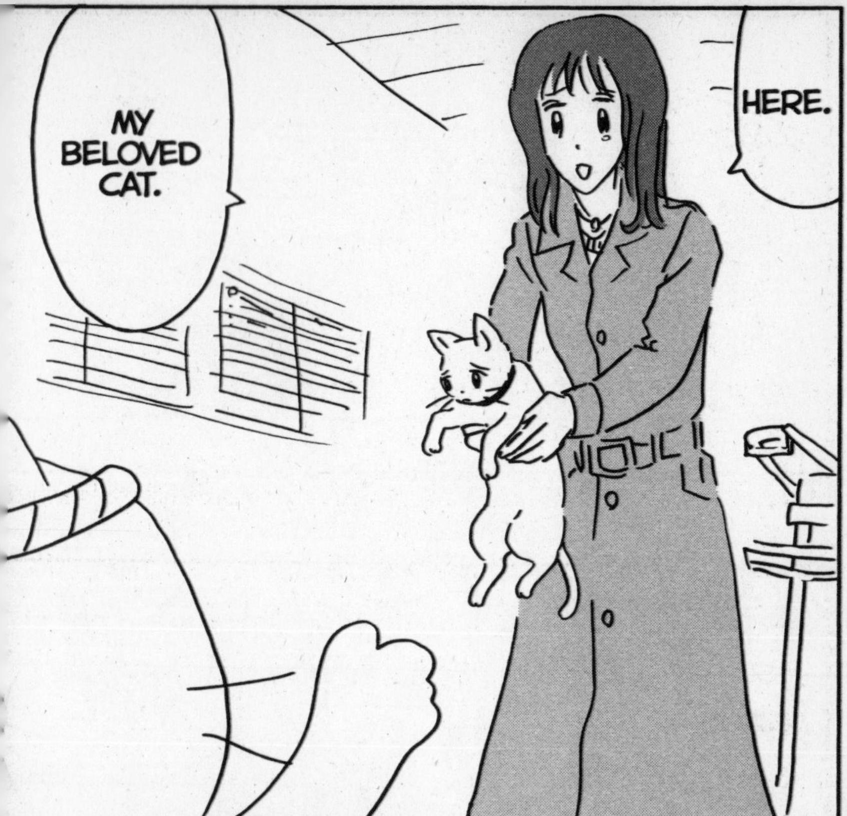
HERE.
MY BELOVED CAT.

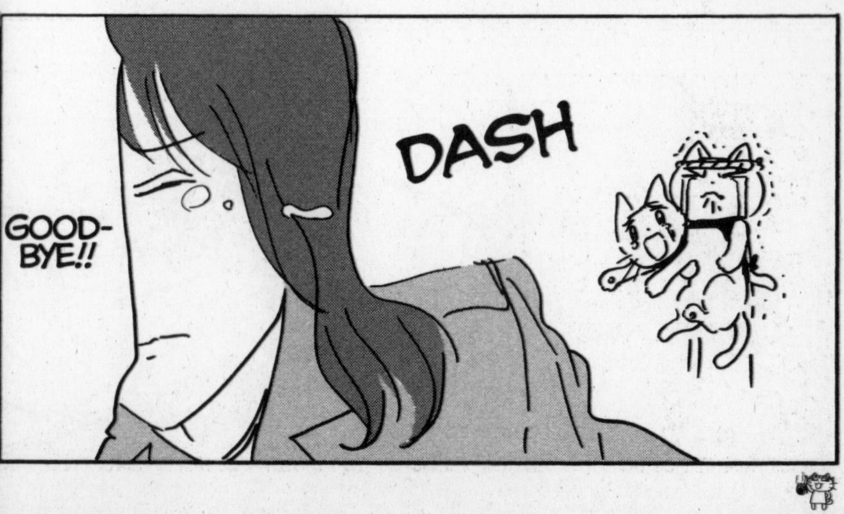
DASH
GOOD-BYE!!

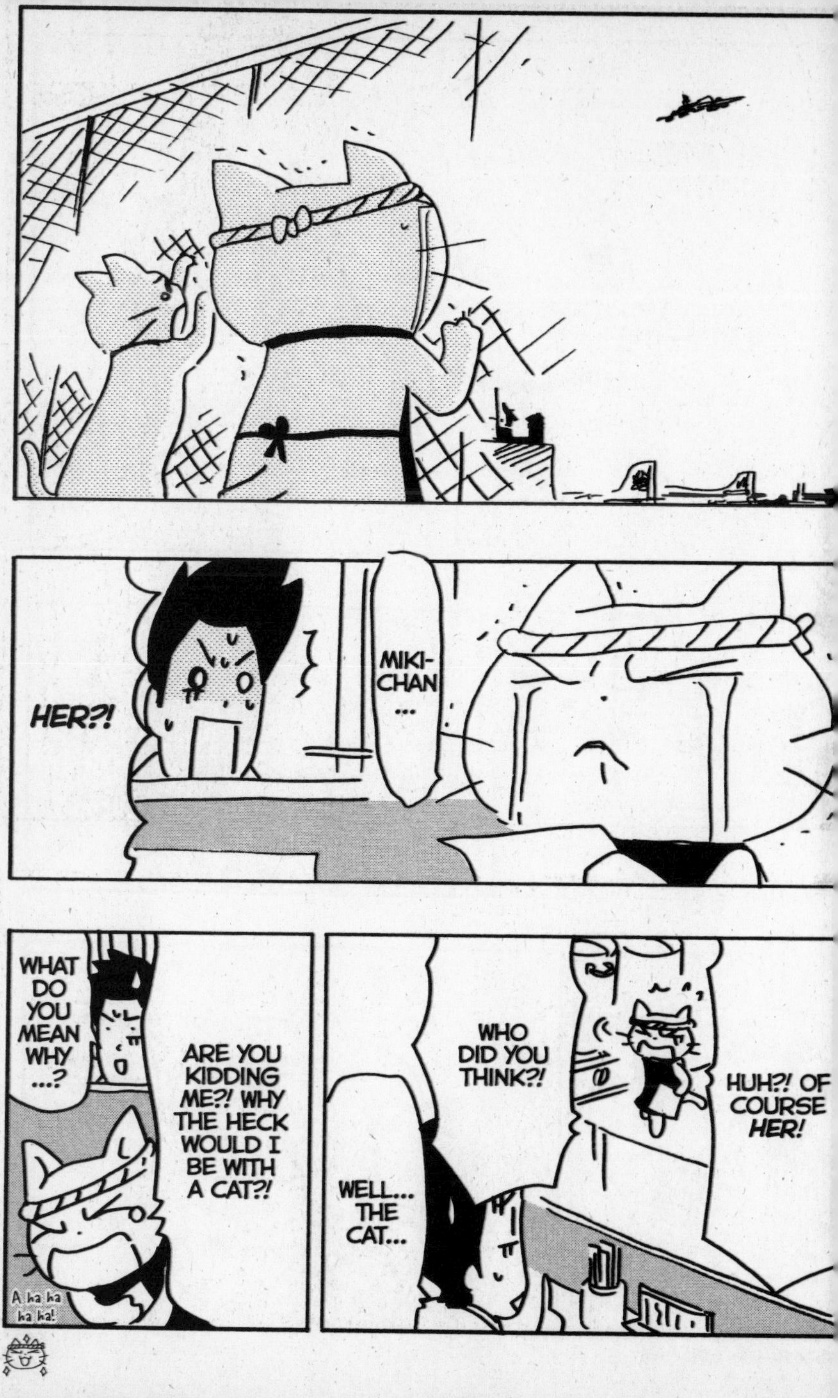

MIKI-CHAN...
HER?!
HUH?! OF COURSE HER!
WHO DID YOU THINK?!
WELL... THE CAT...
ARE YOU KIDDING ME?! WHY THE HECK WOULD I BE WITH A CAT?!
WHAT DO YOU MEAN WHY...?
A ha ha ha ha!

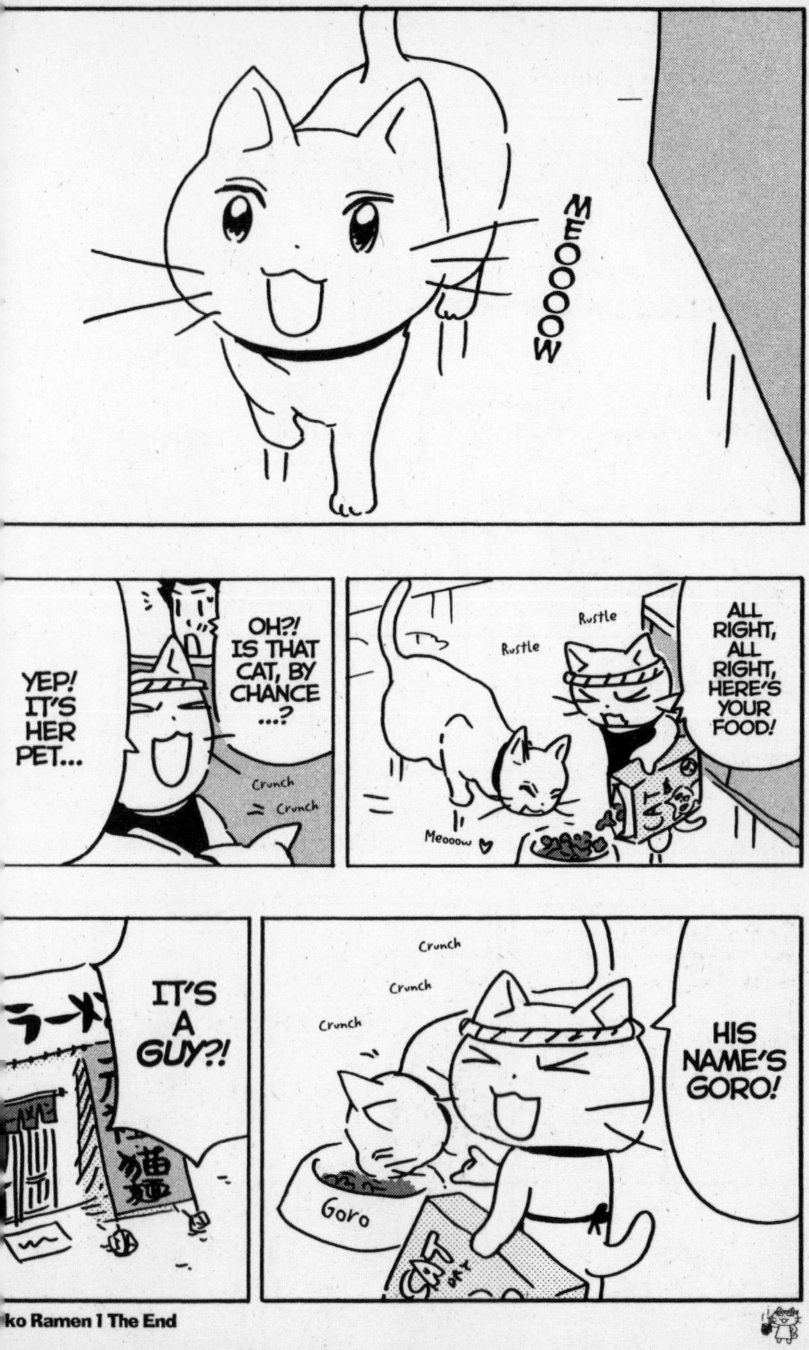
MEOOOOW
Rustle
Rustle
ALL RIGHT, ALL RIGHT, HERE'S YOUR FOOD!
Meooow
OH?! IS THAT CAT, BY CHANCE ...?
YEP! IT'S HER PET...
Crunch
Crunch
Crunch
Crunch
Crunch
HIS NAME'S GORO!
Goro
IT'S A GUY?!
猫麺

ko Ramen 1 The End

Special Supplement

THIS IS TAISHO!!

- Real Name: William Thomas Jefferson III
- Commonly Known As: Taisho
- Breed: American Shorthair
- Blood Type: A?
- Birthday: February 22nd
- Birthplace: Downtown Tokyo
- Hobbies: Shopping online, television shopping
- Residence: Lives alone in an apartment in the park a couple minutes walk from the shop. Currently looking into purchasing a high-rise condo in the near future.

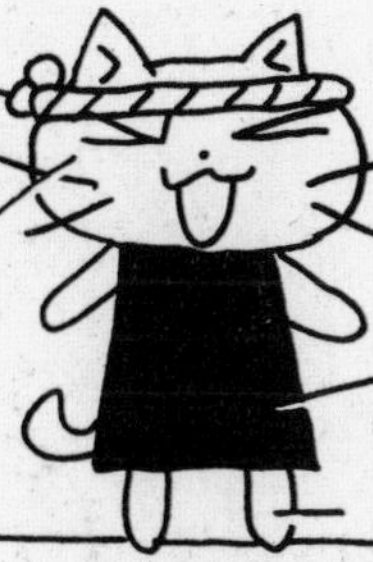

A memorable headband given to him by his mentor. (Has two others.)
Soft contact lenses. (Custom made)
Height: About 2'
Weight: About 13 lbs
Carefully selected Kurashiki-navy apron (purchased online)
Shoe Size: About 1"

And...

THIS IS TANAKA-SAN!!

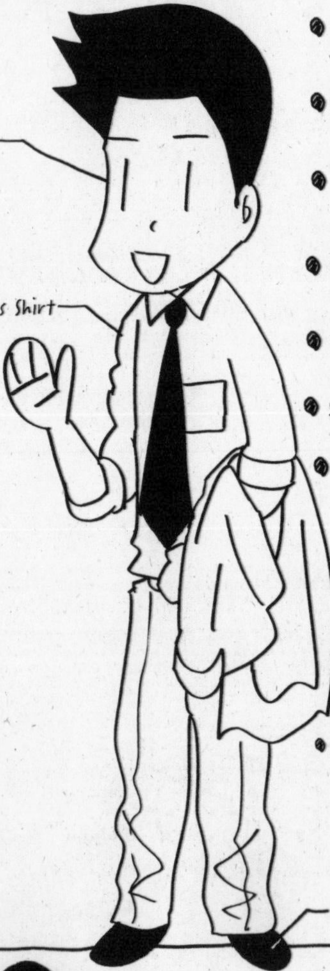

- Real Name: Koichi Tanaka
- Age: 25
- Blood type: A
- Height: 5'9"
- Weight: 132 lbs
- Birthday: April 15th
- Sign: Aries
- Birthplace: Kanagawa Prefecture
- Job: Sales rep for a major telephone manufacturing company (Entry level position)
- Residence: Lives alone in a studio apartment he rents in the city.
- Shoe Size: Size 8½
- Eyesight: Right: 1.2, Left: 1.2
- Permanent Press Dress Shirt
- Hobbies: Music appreciation (always looking for popular songs for karaoke)
- Favorite Sport: Tennis (A member of a tennis club in his college days.)

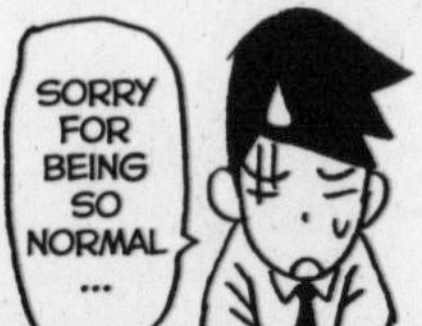

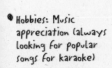

SORRY FOR BEING SO NORMAL ...

IN THE NEXT VOLUME OF...

Kenji Sonishi's

Neko Ramen

猫ラーメン

LOOK OUT FOR MORE OUTRAGEOUS RAMEN RECIPES AS TAISHO TRIES EVERY GIMMICK IN THE BOOK IN ORDER TO MAKE HIS RESTAURANT THE MOST SUCCESSFUL CAT-RUN BUSINESS EVER! NOT ONLY ARE THEIR FRENCH CHEFS, CURRY, FORTUNE-TELLERS AND COOKING COMPETITIONS, BUT TAISHO'S MOTHER COMES TO VISIT AND EXPOSES TAISHO'S MOST EMBARRASSING SECRET! WHAT OTHER CRAZY SCHEME WILL TAISHO COOK UP NEXT?

Interview with Kenji Sonishi

With great luck, we were able to snag a phone interview with Neko Ramen creator, Kenji Sonishi Sensei! He was a very easy going guy with lots of fun and interesting things to say about the manga, cats, ramen and more!

About Neko Ramen

Cindy Suzuki: How did you come up with the idea for Taisho?

Kenji Sonishi: I was eating at a local ramen shop that I frequent and came up with the idea. I've always thought the guys working at these ramen places were funny and interesting. They are so particular about the taste and basically put their all into its creation, and I wanted to write something based on this observation. I was actually first thinking of making Taisho a real person and not a cat.

CS: Why did you choose a cat as your main character?

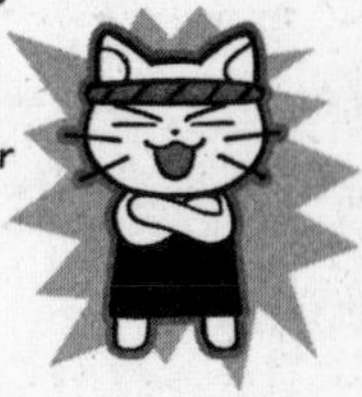

KS: In a short story I've done in the past called Wan-Nyan Friends, there is a cat that looks very similar to Taisho. It's a story where the dog gets bullied. I picked up Taisho's character from that story. It worked better with a cat than it did with a real person.

CS: What do you like most about Taisho?

KS: I love how he never gives up and easily bounces back. He just keeps moving forward, and although he feels down sometimes, he never stays upset for too long.

CS: Why does Tanaka-san keep coming back for the bad ramen?

KS: Tanaka-san is genuinely concerned about Taisho and can't leave him alone. He's a good person and wonders if Taisho's doing all right.

CS: Are you like that as well?

KS: You know, I think I am.

CS: Would you say that Tanaka-san is a reflection of yourself?

KS: In a sense, yes. I was once a "salary-man" when I was about his age. I did it for 10 years, and I have to admit there are some resemblances.

Note: Salary-man = Japanese business man.

CS: Who is a better worker, Shige-chan or Mii-chan?

KS: (Laughs) Mii-chan's a better worker for sure. There are customers who come to Neko Ramen just to see her. Shige-chan--not so much. People won't come by just to see him. Plus, he steals stuff.

CS: Will Taisho ever go back to modeling?

KS: Most likely not.

CS: Not even as a ramen model?

KS: He's pretty traumatized by the whole experience.

CS: But he wants to make his own line of cup ramen. Doesn't he want to put his face on it?

KS: Taisho doesn't really understand himself. If he gets his own line of cup ramen, he'll think that since it's Neko Ramen, he'll have to go out and hire a cat model. He doesn't realize to use himself.

CS: Do you think he'll hire his dad?

KS: No way, his dad will charge too much.

CS: Speaking of which, how much does Taisho's dad make?

KS: As much as a successful Hollywood actor. He's a very active model.

CS: How about Taisho?

KS: (Laughs) I honestly have no idea. I don't even know where he's getting money and where exactly the money is going.

CS: He's doing a lot though, opening up a second store and all.

KS: Taisho's a pretty ambitious guy. He might be borrowing money to keep his business going, but I'm not sure where he's borrowing from. It's very suspicious.

CS: Will Taisho ever go outside Japan in the manga?

KS: There may definitely be a day when Taisho goes overseas. He is thinking about it...and will probably end up causing a ruckus.

About Kenji Sonishi

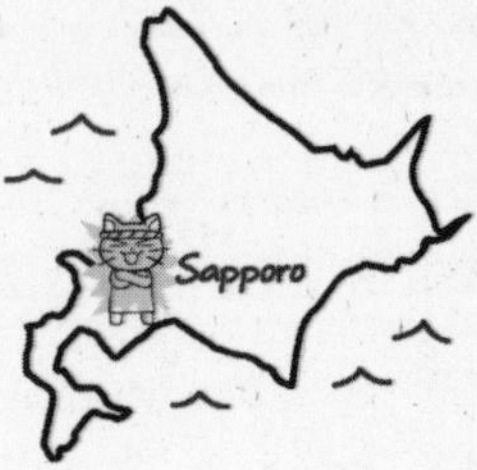
Sapporo

CS: Where are you from?

KS: I was born in Sapporo, Hokkaido, and I live here now as well. When I was about four years old, I lived in the U.S. (New Jersey) and stayed there for six years.

CS: What is your favorite ramen flavor? Favorite topping?

KS: Salt flavor with butter and corn.

CS: Do you make ramen at home?

KS: Yes, I do.

CS: Any tips to make delicious ramen at home?

KS: I find that it's really difficult to mess up ramen if it's instant.

CS: What do you think ramen means to the people of Japan?

KS: It's our soul food.

CS: What do you think of people who use forks to eat ramen?

KS: It's not so bad although it's much more authentic and more enjoyable with hashi (chopsticks) because it brings out the "I'm eating ramen!" feeling.

CS: Do you prefer Ramen or Curry?

KS: (Laughs) Unfortunately, I like curry. Taisho also enjoys curry more. If you ask most Japanese people, they can't eat three straight meals of ramen but three meals of curry is definitely possible.

CS: How do you like your curry?

KS: Medium-spicy. I really enjoy Katsu Curry.

Note: Katsu = Pork Cutlet

CS: Do you have a pet? In particular, a cat?

KS: Yes, I have a cat. There was never really a time period I didn't have one. I had a cat when I lived in the States as well.

CS: What did you do with your cat when you returned to Japan?

KS: Up until now, I've always had male cats. Every male cat I've had eventually wanders out on its own and never comes back. They're independent creatures, only coming home for food. In the end, they just take off. Maybe one of them started a ramen shop somewhere.

CS: What's the name of your current cat?

KS: Her name is Keshi-chan.

CS: What do you like most about your job?

KS: I love seeing people laughing and enjoying my manga. It makes me very happy.

CS: Least favorite part of the job? Would it be deadlines?

KS: I never miss a deadline. But my job gets difficult when I start running out of time. I submit over 80 pages a month, eight of those being Neko Ramen. I'm not complaining though.

CS: Is it hard thinking of new material for **Neko Ramen**?

KS: **Neko Ramen** is fun. I enjoy thinking of silly menus and new characters. Anything goes with this manga.

CS: What is your favorite manga or anime?

KS: I really enjoy Dilbert. They don't have Dilbert in Japan so the only book I have is one that I bought overseas when I went on vacation. I also enjoy the style of work done by Hisaichi Ishii Sensei, especially the yon-koma manga.

CS: Any last comments to your fans?

KS: Taisho is always trying his best with whatever he does, and I hope you'll continue to support him. Also, if you come to Japan, please stop by the local ramen shops. You'll see the many unique and interesting ramen workers with the same type of passion as Taisho.

A very special thank you to Kenji Sonishi Sensei! What a fun interview!

For more information on Neko Ramen, visit www.neko-ramen.com.

Neko Ramen 猫ラーメン Website!

If you haven't already, be sure to check out our awesome Neko Ramen website. It's a cute, funny interactive site where you can experience ordering ramen from Taisho himself! There are also a lot of random surprises and quirks so get ready to click your way into the virtual world of Taisho, Tanaka-san, Mii-chan and more!

Kenji Sonishi's
Neko Ramen
猫ラーメン
TOKYOPOP
Manga Preview
Weekly Comic
About
Buy Manga
TASTY OPTIONS
Creator Interview
Contests
Watch Manga Trailer
Neko Ramen Anime Other Video
左をみる
右をみる
© KENJI SONISHI/ MAG Garden

www.neko-ramen.com

Look right! 右をみる

左をみる Look left!

Explore Taisho's Ramen Shop!

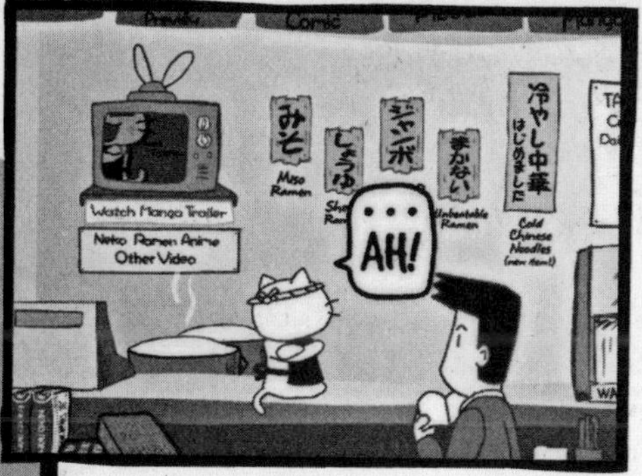

Comic
みそ
Miso Ramen
ジャンボ
しょうゆ
まかない
冷やし中華
はじめました
Cold Chinese Noodles
Watch Manga Trailer
Neko Ramen Anime
Other Video
AH!

Watch Taisho interact with customers!

Don't forget to ask for a glass of water...

Discover tasty ramen recipes...

and some of Taisho's secret toppings, too!

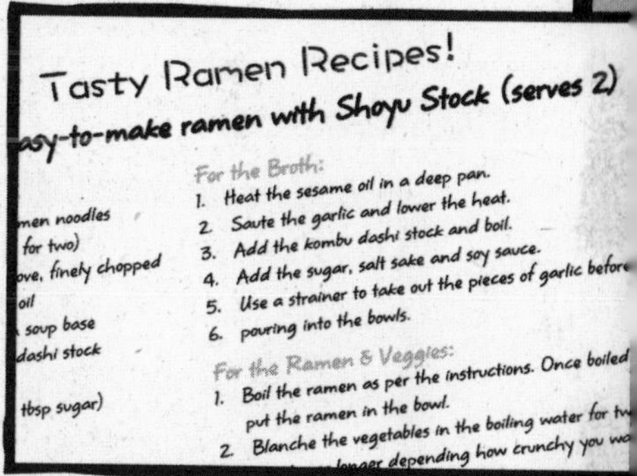

Tasty Ramen Recipes!
asy-to-make ramen with Shoyu Stock (serves 2)
men noodles
for two)
ove, finely chopped
oil
soup base
dashi stock
tbsp sugar)
For the Broth:
1. Heat the sesame oil in a deep pan.
2. Saute the garlic and lower the heat.
3. Add the kombu dashi stock and boil.
4. Add the sugar, salt sake and soy sauce.
5. Use a strainer to take out the pieces of garlic before
6. pouring into the bowls.
For the Ramen & Veggies:
1. Boil the ramen as per the instructions. Once boiled
put the ramen in the bowl.
2. Blanche the vegetables in the boiling water for tw
longer depending how crunchy you wa

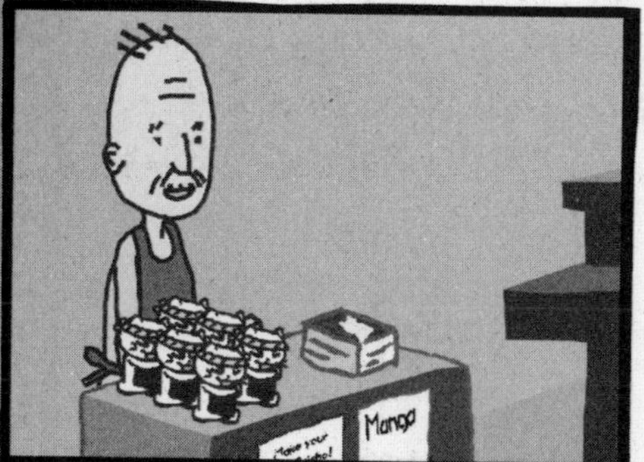

Manga

What's in the Neko Ramen Good's Shop?

Look for a Taisho papercraft pattern!

Keep checking back at neko-ramen.com for updated comic strips, contests, videos and more.

www.neko-ramen.com

Random Ramen (and Cat) Sightings
The Teaser Campaign

If you subscribe to our weekly newsletter, you might have noticed the splashes of random ramen and cat moments. We just wanted to have some fun but didn't really know how it would be received.

Turns out, you all LOVE ramen and cats! We'd like to take this time to thank you for enthusiastically participating in our cat polls and ramen contests! It was great to see all of you rush to comment on your favorite cat and vote on whether or not you would use the ramen spork. We hope you enjoyed it as well. And for those that don't subscribe, here's what you may have missed.

Stupid Cat!

www.Neko-Ramen.com

ramen hair guard!

Let your hair down!

Ramen with a FORK & KNIFE?!

Poll: Ramen with a FORK & KNIFE?!
Do you eat Ramen with CHOPSTICKS or a FORK ar

- ◯ Chopsticks (おはし)
- ◯ Fork & Knife (フォーク&ナイフ)
- ◯ Other (その他)

Only registered members can vote

Poll: Attention Cat Lovers!
Would you rather eat turkey or ramen this Th

- ◯ Turkey (ターキー)
- ◯ Ramen (ラーメン)
- ◯ Other (その他)

Only registered members can vote

ramen spork?!

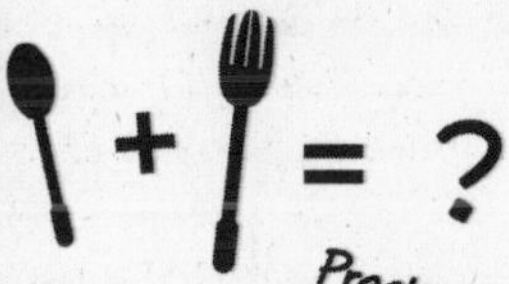

Practical thinking

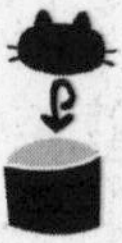

cats on sushi?

Cute! Delicious!

Poll: Meow Meow~
Your favorite cat is...??

- ◯ Hello Kitty
- ◯ Kyo (Fruits Basket)
- ◯ Garfield
- ◯ Luna (Sailor Moon)
- ◯ Cheshire Cat
- ◯ Doraemon
- ◯ Keyboard Cat (the YouTube Phenom)
- ◯ Kuroneko-sama
- ◯ Senryo-kun (Zone-00)

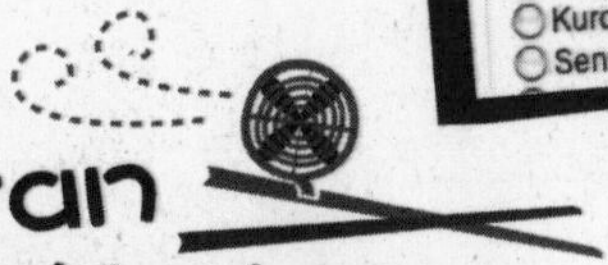

fan attachment for chopsticks???

For "chilled" noodles!

See more at:

www.neko-ramen.com

and click on "About"!

A Note From The Adapters

Hi Neko Ramen Fans!

This is Emily Gordon and Kumail Nanjiani, and we did the English adaptation for Neko Ramen, Order Up! We're married and worked on this project together. Emily is a therapist-turned-writer who writes for the website Lemondrop, her own blog Gynomite! and has also written for Jane and Bust magazines. Kumail is a comedian who writes and performs on Comedy Central's Michael and Michael Have Issues and just recently appeared on The Late Show with David Letterman. Both of us had fun adjusting to the humor of manga, which relies much more on people's reactions and visual humor than American comedy does.

We are fascinated with manga, enjoy eating ramen and are obsessed with our own cat Bagel, so working on this project seemed like a perfect fit. We were totally sucked in to Neko Ramen's world and can't wait to find out more about Taisho's adorable father, his long-lost girlfriend and all of his ridiculous ideas to improve business. We're definitely hoping he moves into the world of social networking sites for the next volume. We would eat at his ramen stand anytime, but we'd probably end up telling him how cute he is which would really irritate him. That's the best thing about Neko Ramen--his complete ignorance of the fact that he's a cat. We like thinking about Bagel like that too, that she constantly wonders why people are cooing over her when she plays with a toy or falls asleep with all four feet in the air. She's just doing her job, you know?

~Emily Gordon and Kumail Nanjiani